Photographs

A Collector's Guide

Richard Blodgett has written widely on art, photography, and investment. He is author of THE NEW YORK TIMES BOOK OF MONEY. Formerly a *Wall Street Journal* staff reporter and an editor at *Business Week,* Mr. Blodgett has also contributed to *The New York Times, ARTNews, Smithsonian,* and other periodicals. He lives in New York City.

Photographs: A Collector's Guide

by Richard Blodgett

BALLANTINE BOOKS • NEW YORK

To Aunt Ruth and Aunt Ethel, the grand ladies of Bristol

A Note of Appreciation

I am deeply indebted to a number of individuals who gave graciously of their time and ideas in helping me with this book: Harry H. Lunn, Jr. and Maurizia Grossman, Lunn Gallery/Graphics International Ltd., Washington, D.C.; Susan Harder, New York; Victor Schrager, Light Gallery, New York; Lee D. Witkin, Witkin Gallery, New York; Anne Horton, Sotheby Parke Bernet, New York; George Rinhart, New York; Janet Lehr, Janet Lehr Inc., New York; Marcuse Pfeifer, Marcuse Pfeifer Gallery, New York; Robert Schoelkopf, Robert Schoelkopf Gallery, New York; Margaret Weston, Weston Gallery, Carmel, California; Scott Elliott, Helios, New York; Marvin Heiferman, Castelli Graphics, New York; Gerard Levy, Galerie Gerard Levy, Paris; Russ Anderson, London; Stuart Bennett, Christie's South Kensington, London; Philippe Garner, Sotheby's Belgravia, London; Sean Thackrey, Thackrey & Robertson, San Francisco; G. Ray Hawkins, G. Ray Hawkins Gallery, Los Angeles; Robert Feldman, Parasol Press, New York; Howard Ricketts, Howard Ricketts, Ltd., London; Tom Burnside, Daguerreian Era, Pawlet, Vermont; Sue Davies, The Photographers' Gallery, London; and John M. Buck, Photographic Collections Limited, London. I also wish to thank Al Hart and Lynne Bair for their enthusiasm and encouragement.

All rights reserved under International and Pan-American Copyright Conventions. Published in the United States by Ballantine Books, a division of Random House, Inc., New York, and simultaneously in Canada by Ballantine Books of Canada, Ltd., Toronto, Canada.

Library of Congress Cataloging in Publication Data:
Blodgett, Richard E.
 Photographs, a collector's guide.

 Bibliography: p.
 Includes index.
 1. Photographs—Collectors and collecting.
I. Title.
TR6.5.B46 770'.75 78-10236
ISBN 0-345-28272-8
ISBN 0-345-27710-4 (ppbk)

This edition published simultaneously in hardcover and trade paperback.

Manufactured in the United States of America
First Edition: April 1979

1 2 3 4 5 6 7 8 9 10

Contents

List of Photographs

Chapter 1

Collecting Photographs

The invention of photography dates back some 140 years. From the very beginnings, the medium captured the public fancy, was widely discussed, and was viewed as one of the great wonders of scientific achievement.

Yet, until the early 1970s, the collecting of photographs—seemingly so natural for a medium of such importance and allure—was a cultural backwater. Certainly there have been photography collectors since the earliest days in 1839. But their numbers have traditionally been very small, and until recently there simply was not any sort of dealer or auction structure to support their activity.

Photography occupies a strange position in the world of art. On the one hand, it is partially mechanical in nature. On the other, there is no getting away from the fact that some photographs are exceptionally beautiful, powerful, and penetrating—in every way equal to the finest paintings.

It is this seeming contradiction, between the mechanical nature of the process and the aesthetic nature of the results, that, perhaps more than any other factor, has held back photography as a collectible.

Additionally, many would-be collectors appear to have been troubled by the ease of duplication of the photographic print. Unlike a painting, any specific photograph can be reproduced ad infinitum. But while it is a problem on a theoretical level, collectors are now learning that, in the real world, this concern is not so grave after all. Many of the photographs being collected today actually are great rarities—in some cases one-of-a-kind items, and in this sense even more scarce than a Rembrandt etching or Rodin bronze. While the issue of rarity remains a central one in photography, it is by no means a dominant problem. Most older photographs, for the very reason that people were wary about collecting photographs in the past, were never printed in substantial numbers (since there were so few buyers). And among living photographers there tends to be little interest in the idea of spending long hours in the darkroom knocking out prints to flood the market. (More on rarity in Chapter 4.)

The more germane issues facing the photography collector, then, are:

1. How to learn.
2. What to buy.
3. Where to buy.
4. How much to pay.

1

There are no magic answers to any of these questions. Buying photographs, like any other field of collecting, requires work and desire. But this work, rather than being at all dreary, tends to be of a most broadening, stimulating, and personally rewarding nature—for the random buyer of an occasional photograph, for the individual who spends a few hundred dollars a year on photographs, for the collector who spends a few thousand dollars a year, or for the substantial collector who spends much more.

Photography collecting is now accessible to practically anybody with an underlying interest in photography as art or as historical documentation. Many of the greatest photographic images, dating back to the 1840s, remain available to collectors. And while some knowledge of the photography market is essential if you are to buy wisely, this knowledge generally can be developed fairly quickly.

How to learn. The first step is to read, look, and ask questions—in other words, to immerse yourself in the market. In nearly every large U.S. city and many small ones there now are at least two or three dealers specializing in photographs (see list beginning on page 223). You might begin by visiting a few of these dealers—to see what types of pictures each is offering, to discuss these works, to ask about prices, and to develop a sense of what makes one photographic print more interesting and perhaps more valuable than another. Similarly, you might visit photographic exhibits at local museums—again, to sharpen your "eye" for photographs and get a better idea of the kinds of works being presented. The reading of books and periodicals also is important, both to learn more about photographic history and to stay abreast of current trends and critical opinions. A list of reading materials can be found on page 220. Highly recommended for the beginning collector are Beaumont Newhall's *The History of Photography* and John Szarkowski's *Looking at Photographs*.

What to buy. The answer is to buy whatever you like and can afford. An initial objective might simply be to begin zeroing in on an aspect of photography that is most personally appealing and where you can develop reasonable expertise fairly quickly. Examples include contemporary photography, nineteenth-century daguerreotypes, photographs from the Photo-Secessionist movement in the early twentieth century, and pictures from the early exploration of the American West, among many other possibilities.

Specialization can be looked at from a variety of viewpoints: time period, country, subject matter, school of photography, type of photographic print. An area of specialization can be very broad, or very narrow. I know of one individual whose entire collection consists of eighty photographs of Shaker scenes and interiors. This individual also collects Shaker furniture, so the photographs complement that much larger collection and reinforce the collector's understanding of Shaker culture. I know other collectors who buy nothing but nineteenth-century stereographs or photographs by Ansel Adams, the outstanding American nature photographer.

Philippe Garner, photography expert at the Sotheby's Belgravia auction house in London, collects in two areas: photographs of Brighton, England, his hometown, and twentieth-century fashion photographs. His photographs of Brighton span a time period of more than 130 years, from the 1840s to the present. As an offshoot of this collection, he currently is researching the history of photography in Brighton.

On the other hand, many collectors define their areas of interest in much more open-ended ways, such as photographs from the nineteenth century.

Of course, it's possible not to specialize at all—to buy whatever you like regardless of period, photographer, or subject matter. The risks are that you will never be able to develop in-depth expertise or to assemble a truly unified collection of the finest works.

Where to buy. This question goes hand in hand with what to buy, for each dealer tends to espouse a specific point of view and to steer customers in a direction befitting that view. For instance, a dealer specializing in contemporary photographers is not likely to recommend the purchase of nineteenth-century stereographs or of contemporary works by photographers represented by other galleries. While it is possible to take a more independent course, buy at auction and pay a little less in the process, beginning collectors are almost always better off purchasing from a good dealer who will offer advice. But picking a dealer tends to be a highly subjective process, like choosing a dentist or an attorney. The recommendations of other collectors, the professionalism of the dealer, and the dealer's quoted prices (versus prices listed by other dealers for similar items) should all have a bearing on your choice. Ultimately, though, the most basic points are whether you get along with the dealer, can establish a good working relationship, and feel that the dealer offers quality pictures of the sort you most like. A word of caution: Don't spend a lot of money with a single dealer until you are absolutely sure of the dealer's integrity. And always try to stay in touch with one or two other dealers in order to maintain a broader view of the market and have a sense of prevailing price levels.

How much to pay. For the most part in photography, there is no single, specific price that any given picture is worth. Values are determined by the interplay of supply and demand, and determining precise value is extremely difficult, perhaps impossible. However, any collector can develop a general sense of values and minimize the risks of overpaying by assembling a price reference library (see Chapter 3) and by keeping track of auction and dealer prices so as to have a gut instinct for prevailing levels. No one should be too concerned about overpaying a bit on occasion. It is the gross price gouging—$10,000 for an item that sold two months earlier at auction for $500—which is unforgivable, in terms of both the dealer who attempts to get away with it and the collector who is sucker enough to bite.

As indicated earlier, photography collecting was a relatively small and totally unpublicized marketplace for decades, then burst forward in the early 1970s. While to outsiders the surge of the seventies may seem farfetched, even manipulated, there are genuine reasons behind this surge and there are growing numbers of knowledgeable, serious collectors who are interested in photography as a full-fledged art form. Photography collecting is for real.

Some collectors trace the beginnings of the boom to the opening in 1969 of the Witkin Gallery, the first New York gallery to deal exclusively in photography and make money at it. But Lee Witkin, founder and owner, sees his role as being less pivotal: "It wasn't as if I or anybody else created this whole world of photography. It existed in every way except a dealership. And I tapped that."

Witkin did, however, have a very good sense of timing. Three factors appear to have led to his enormous success. First, prices for other art media—paintings, sculpture, drawings, prints—had been driven to great heights in the boom years of the sixties, and many collectors were beginning to look for new, less expensive art forms. Second, the public was becoming accustomed to photographlike imagery (particularly television) as the visual expression of our times; in line with this point, millions of Americans were themselves taking photographs and tens of thousands were studying photographic history on college campuses. Third, photography prices, having risen slowly but steadily for more than twenty years, had finally arrived at a point where dealers could make a profit selling photographic prints. At earlier prices of, say, $25 a picture there simply was no room for significant profits. At $100 and rising, the profit potential suddenly began to make sense.

Since Lee Witkin opened his gallery in 1969, many other dealers—certainly more than 200 in the United States alone—have jumped into the market, bidding against each other for available merchandise, in that way driving prices still higher and all the while using their marketing skills to nurture collector interest. The recent rise in prices is a reflection of these changed market conditions.

Today, while works are available at a price of anywhere from $1 to $10,000 or more, the greatest market activity is in the $100 to $800 range.

Photography collecting remains very much on the outermost frontier of the art market, with all the resulting excitement, challenge, opportunities, and risks.

Advantages. Unlike any other field of collecting, historically important photographs still come onto the market in considerable quantity and at affordable prices. As a result, photography is the one major art medium where it is still possible to assemble a significant collection of top-grade works. This possibility is almost totally precluded in any other major type of art. The only sector of photography which has dried up in the flurry of buying activity is very early daguerreotypes—those from approximately 1839 to 1842. These early gems are now owned almost entirely by museums and major private collectors and probably will never again be available for purchase. Other specific areas of photography which are beginning to head in the same direction, though not yet there, include original Lewis Carroll prints, original Alfred Stieglitz prints, original Paul Strand prints, original Thomas Eakins prints, and original László Moholy-Nagy prints.

Besides continued availability of significant amounts of prime material, relatively low prices are a second major advantage in collecting photographs. Although prices have risen sharply since 1970, they remain well below those for comparable works in other media.

A third basic appeal of collecting photographs—the most important of all—is the objects themselves, their aesthetic qualities and historic importance.

Disadvantages. As is true of almost any field which remains so wide open and vaguely defined, photography collecting also has its drawbacks.

Since the field is essentially very new, clear standards of what constitutes an "original" photographic print have yet to be developed. Questions arise, for instance, with posthumous prints made from a photographer's negatives. Are these works "originals"? A clear answer is not to be found, and buyers are left to decide on their own.

Also due in large part to the relative newness of the field, great gaps remain in our knowledge about the work of many important photographers of the nineteenth and early twentieth centuries. Numbers of prints made, dates of prints, identities of some photographers—the blank spots, in many cases, have yet to be filled in. While this can add greatly to the fun and challenge, it also means that a collector must sometimes decide to purchase a work more on the basis of instinct than on concrete facts.

Photographs are among the most fragile art forms, and attention must be paid to proper handling, framing, and storage. (For more information about the proper physical care of photographs, see Chapter 18.)

There is a fairly substantial number of misinformed, get-rich-quick dealers, drawn by the lure of potentially high profits in a new marketplace with great glamour and rising prices. This final problem, of second-rate dealers, is the most troublesome. Art is, in general, a "buyer beware" type of marketplace. There is little governmental regulation. Anybody who wants to become a dealer can set up shop regardless of qualifications. And different dealers are free to charge vastly different prices for similar items, so long as buyers are foolish or ignorant enough to let them get away with it.

An excellent dealer—and there are plenty of them also—can be enormously helpful to a collector. Yet, rip-offs in the photography market are widespread enough that some dealers and collectors are outspokenly concerned. One prominent dealer tells of the time several years ago when, as a novice collector, he agreed to pay $18,000 for an item on the assumption that the seller was honest and was charging a reasonable price. However, before actually handing over the cash, the dealer discovered that the seller, himself now a prominent New York dealer, had recently acquired the same item at a London auction for less than $200. The buyer immediately canceled the transaction, on the basis that such a mark-up was unconscionable, and vows never again to do business with the seller.

With prices rising so rapidly, some less-than-competent dealers have been able to survive, and even prosper, despite the natural long-term tendency of any marketplace to reward the strong and punish the weak. A dealer shakeout probably will occur in the photography market, but may still be several years away. So caution and knowledge are essential before you spend large sums of money for photographic prints.

Chapter 2

_____

Surveying the Market: From Daguerreotypes to Contemporary Photography

The photography market can be roughly divided into four broad segments, each with its own rules as to which kinds of pictures are valuable and which are not:

- Early one-of-a-kind photographs on copper, glass, and tin (from 1839 to approximately 1860).
- Nineteenth-century paper-print photographs (1839 to 1900).
- Works by the master photographers of the twentieth century (1900 to present).
- Contemporary photography (approximately 1960 to present).

Chapters 5 through 14 discuss each of these areas in detail, telling, for instance, how to distinguish a daguerreotype from an ambrotype and what a *Camera Work* gravure really is and whether it is worth buying. The purpose of this chapter, on the other hand, is to provide a basic description of the types of pictures available in each of the four major categories and to discuss typical prices in each of the four areas, with the goal of helping a collector begin to develop a personal focus.

Early photographs on copper, glass, and tin, principally daguerreotypes, ambrotypes, and tintypes. What distinguishes these photographs from photographs on paper is that there is no negative from which the picture is printed. In paper-print photography, a negative is created inside the camera, and this negative is then developed and used to print as many positives as desired (as in the case of most of today's photographic systems). For daguerreotypes, ambrotypes, and tintypes, by contrast, the photograph itself is the physical item that was placed inside the camera, and so each picture is a one-of-a-kind image that stands as the finished product, rather than an intermediary mechanism from which positives are created. (Note the difference this means in terms of reversal of image. Camera lenses, like mirrors, turn images backwards. In paper-print photography, the reversal is corrected when positives are printed from the negative—a double reversal, from true image to negative and from negative to positive, that sets matters straight. For daguerreotypes, the images remain reversed because the process lacks a second stage to correct the initial reversal; left becomes right and vice versa.)

Photography was incredibly popular right from the start, and so there still exists an abundance of these early one-of-a-kind works, available in flea markets, at auctions, at antique shops, and at many photography galleries. Mostly they are portraits of now-anonymous shopkeepers, lawyers, housewives, soldiers, babies, physicians, and other individuals representing a broad cross section of the middle-class populace of the 1840s and 1850s. Run-of-the-mill portraits typically sell for between $10 and $50. (Daguerreotypes, as the finest and earliest process, tend to be the most expensive, while tintypes, as the cheapest and final process, tend to be very inexpensive. Ambrotypes are in between.) Outstanding portraits can go well up into the thousands of dollars, particularly when the subject was a head of state, famous writer, or other individual of great historic importance.

There also is an active market for landscapes, still lifes, and interior views—rarer and therefore generally more expensive than the typical portrait. Niagara Falls was a popular subject for the more accomplished American daguerreotypists, and a large daguerreotype or ambrotype picture of the falls might go for $500 to $1,000 or more.

An example of an even greater rarity: Parisian dealer Gerard Levy owns an early daguerreotype of a Frenchman standing in front of a stone country home. The picture also contains a horse and two dogs. Considering that the exposure time for such a picture was at least thirty seconds—perhaps much longer—and further considering that the animals could reasonably be expected to stand up or sit down or scratch themselves or swat at a fly or turn their heads during that period, few such daguerreotypes were attempted and even fewer came out crisp and blur-free, as is the work owned by Levy.

The identity of the photographer who took the picture owned by Levy is unknown. Sometimes, however, we do know the identity, and this, like rarity, can add to market value, especially if the photographer is considered to be historically important. Among the prominent early daguerreotypists whose work is available to collectors today are Antoine Claudet, a Frenchman who introduced the daguerreotype process to England in 1841; T.R. Williams, a leading London portrait photographer of the 1850s; Mathew B. Brady, the renowned Civil War photographer; and John Edwin Mayall, an American who moved to London in 1846 and achieved great success as one of the most fashionable of all portrait photographers.

Perhaps more than any other area of photography, daguerreotypes tend to achieve high market value primarily on the basis of historic importance. An aesthetically superb daguerreotype will bring a good price, but a historically significant daguerreotype generally will bring even more.

Dealer George Rinhart, for one, has built his career almost entirely around historically important photographs from the nineteenth century. Rinhart once discovered a daguerreotype portrait of President Franklin Pierce and was able to acquire it for $1.50 simply because nobody else realized it was Pierce. "That's a thrill of a lifetime, to discover a presidential daguerreotype," he says. Another of Rinhart's many discoveries was an 1846 daguerreotype, taken in a Massachusetts hospital, depicting a reenactment of the first ether-anesthesia operation performed in the United States. The photograph was known to exist and occupies an important position in both photographic history and the history of medicine, but it had been missing for more than fifty years when Rinhart came across the work in an antique shop. He acquired it for $500, an extremely low sum for such a landmark work.

Paper-print photographs from the nineteenth century. These works include salt prints, albumen prints, platinum prints, and prints based on the use of other sensitizing materials.

Two rival processes were announced to an astonished world in 1839: daguerreotypes, introduced on January 7 by Daguerre in Paris, and salt prints on paper, introduced just eighteen days later by William Henry Fox Talbot in London. For more than a decade these two rival processes engaged in a heated race for supremacy, with paper prints eventually winning out.

There is great variety here, in terms of prices, subject matter, and type of print. A collector can buy portraits, landscapes, photogenic drawings (milky-toned pictures made by placing leaves, butterflies, and other objects directly on a piece of photosensitive paper and exposing the paper to light), travel pictures, still lifes, strips of sequential pictures showing animals in motion. He can acquire copies of the first pictures taken atop Mont Blanc, pioneering photographs of the American west, portraits of Abraham Lincoln or Queen Victoria, architectural studies of French cathedrals, and much more.

In almost all the better pictures, what comes through so strongly is the awe of the photographers themselves as they explored the world around them through the lens of a camera. Unlike daguerreotypists, who were pretty much confined to their studios by the nature of the daguerreotype process, paper-print photographers were able to travel about and portray whatever they wanted, from the Grand Canyon to the jungles of Ceylon.

At the upper end of the price scale stand works by the masters of nineteenth-century photography, including Julia Margaret Cameron. Mrs. Cameron, who was Virginia Woolf's great-aunt, took up photography in 1863 at age forty-eight after receiving a camera as a gift. She is most noted for her portraits of the great writers and artists of Victorian England; her portraits of Tennyson are among her best. She developed a soft-focus technique which, combined with unusual poses, gave her subjects a dreamy quality so loved by the English romantics. A rare and truly outstanding Cameron portrait might sell for as much as $4,000, while her more familiar works typically bring between $300 and $1,800.

That is the upper end of the market. At the bottom stand cartes de visite (literally, "visiting card" pictures), available for anywhere from a few cents to a few hundred dollars each. These were mass-produced photographs, much like baseball cards today, distributed widely to the public. The typical carte de visite is $3\frac{1}{2}$ by $2\frac{1}{4}$ inches in size and is mounted on a card 4 by $2\frac{1}{2}$ inches. Many of these cards show full-length or head-and-shoulders portraits, of both the famous and the unknown. There also are city scenes, pictures of important historic events, animal pictures, and group pictures of Western Indians. Although originally produced in large quantities, many cartes de visite have become rare through loss and destruction over the years. The best of these cards are highly prized today, by wealthy as well as less affluent collectors. (See Chapter 8.)

Nineteenth-century stereographs—double-picture photographs which give an illusion of depth when viewed through a stereoscope—are another potentially interesting area for the low-budget collector, with many superb works available for $20 or less. (See Chapter 7.)

Besides Julia Margaret Cameron, the big, higher-priced names in nineteenth-century paper-print photography include the team of David Octavius Hill and Robert Adamson, Scotsmen who worked between 1843 and 1847 and were perhaps the finest of the very early portrait photographers; Mathew Brady, Alexander Gardner, Timothy O'Sullivan, and George N. Barnard, who broke new ground in documenting the agony and destruction of the American Civil War; Roger Fenton, who photographed the Crimean War and later produced large-scale, extraordinary flower still lifes; Louis-Auguste and Auguste-Rosalie Bisson, best known for their early views of Alpine peaks; Nadar, the greatest of all French portrait photographers; John Thomson, known for his photographic books on China, Cambodia, and the working-class poor of London; Eadweard Muybridge, an American who was a pioneer in stop-action techniques for depicting animals in motion; and Peter Henry Emerson, the leading British "naturalist" photographer and one of the earliest champions of photography as a full-fledged art form. As we shall see in Chapter 6, this list is only the beginning, for there are literally several dozen important nineteenth-century photographers whose work regularly comes onto the market. Even pioneering works by Fox Talbot, the inventor of paper-print photography, remain available to collectors, at prices from approximately $250 to $2,500 each.

In sum, no other sector of the photography market offers the variety and opportunities of nineteenth-century paper-print photography, and in such a wide price range. A collector can still find interesting items for a few dollars, or spend several thousand dollars, each. There is a great deal of quality work from which to choose. On the other hand, there also is an abundance of boring and undistinguished pictures—all those dreary photographs of volunteer fire departments and British landscapes. Discrimination and taste are called for. Rarity and old age will not make a picture valuable; aesthetic quality counts a great deal in this section of the market. Probably more "sorting out," by both dealers and collectors, goes on here than in any other period of photography. As an example, Francis Frith, one of the leading documentary photographers of the nineteenth century, took more than 60,000 pictures of Egypt, the Middle East, continental Europe, and rural England. His best work is very good and brings prices of up to $1,000 per print. But most of his photographs have very little to offer and would not likely fetch more than $10 or $15 at auction.

Another problem: We still have much to learn about the pioneers of paper-print photography and, in particular, the degree of rarity of their major works. (By contrast, this is not an issue in daguerreotypes, since each picture is unique.) In the face of these problems, to buy wisely in nineteenth-century paper-print photography requires a good eye, the energy to go out and look and study and do some digging, and a willingness to take occasional risks (since documentation is so sparse).

Works by the master photographers of the twentieth century. By 1900, the battle over the status of photography as art was in full fury. No individual spoke a more powerful voice in this battle than Alfred Stieglitz, photographer, editor, and director of the avant-garde New York art gallery named for its street number, "291." The photographs of Stieglitz and his great protégé, Edward Steichen, are among the finest (and most expensive) in the marketplace. Stieglitz's masterpiece, *The Steerage*— glowingly praised by Picasso—is perhaps the most famous and widely reproduced photograph in history (see reproduction on page 179).

Besides Stieglitz, the two giants of twentieth-century photography are Paul Strand and Edward Weston. The work of Strand is noted for its straightforward, highly realistic, almost brutal treatment of subject matter, whether a picket fence, blind beggarwoman, or nude torso. Weston's work, on the other hand, tends to be more sensual and classical than that of Strand—a close-up, highly erotic, semiabstract view of a halved artichoke heart, for instance, or a photograph of white California sand dunes forming layer upon layer of textured horizontal bands stretching off into the distance. Both Weston, who died in 1958, and Strand, who died in 1976, would spend hours in the darkroom working on a single print and making sure it met the very highest technical standards. Strand, in fact, would devote as many as three days to a print. The resulting richness and subtlety of tone have been equaled by few other photographers and surpassed by none. Fine early prints of Strand and Weston photographs are rare and expensive—up to approximately $10,000 each for Strand's work. Later prints, on the other hand, are readily available and not nearly so costly—as little as $200 for posthumous prints of Weston's work made from the original negatives by his son Cole.

Besides Stieglitz, Strand, Weston, and Steichen, important twentieth-century photographers include Eugène Atget, Baron Adolph De Meyer, Alvin Langdon Coburn, Lewis Hine, Charles Sheeler, Man Ray, László Moholy-Nagy, Walker Evans, Ansel Adams, Henri Cartier-Bresson, André Kertész, and August Sander. Again, this list is only a beginning. Prices are typically in the $200 to $5,000 range.

More than any other sector of the photography market, this is where the big investment money is being channeled—particularly into rare works from the early part of the century. There is a blue-chip quality here that is matched only by a few of the very top names in nineteenth-century photography, most notably Cameron, Nadar, and Emerson. Prices are relatively high, but the very best pictures are rare and important and can form the nucleus of a truly superb photography collection. They are every bit the equal of, say, a fine early Picasso etching.

Contemporary photography. The term "contemporary" refers to the more advanced work of the past fifteen or twenty years, particularly by younger photographers—as opposed to an Ansel Adams, who is still alive and working but is doing so in a more traditional style and whose reputation is fully established. Adams is what might be called a "master" photographer, while the younger generation of less established, more iconoclastic photographers makes up the contemporary market.

Prices are relatively low here—a general range of approximately $100 to $1,000 per picture, with a great deal of very good material available in the $200 to $300 area.

At the same time, this is the most tumultuous and challenging section of the marketplace, simply because so many different photographers are currently pushing contemporary photography in so many different directions. Three examples:

Duane Michals (see page 211) tells fantastic stories through sequences of made-up pictures. In one seven-picture sequence titled *Alice's Mirror* (apparently a reference to *Alice in Wonderland*), the initial picture shows a huge pair of metal-rimmed eyeglasses, next to an easy chair, leaning against what appears to be a wall.

11

Then frame by frame the camera moves back, showing each scene merely to be part of a much larger scene. The second picture shows that the eyeglasses and chair are actually on top of an old-fashioned kitchen stove, with the glasses leaning against the upright back of the stove. The stove, in turn, becomes a reflection in a round mirror. In picture four, that round mirror becomes an image in a large rectangular photograph held by a man on his lap. The rectangular photograph then becomes a reflection in an even bigger square mirror; by now the eyeglasses and chair are so tiny they can barely be seen. Finally, the square mirror is revealed to be held by a large, ominous hand which, true to the bizarre nature that runs through much of Michals's work, crushes the mirror and, by implication, all that went before. *Alice's Mirror* was produced in an edition of twenty-five copies. Approximate retail price per copy is $1,000.

While Michals's sequences are dreamlike and fantastic, often with strong cosmic overtones, the work of Lewis Baltz is rooted in the everyday world around us. Perhaps his best-known series of photographs is titled *The New Industrial Parks near Irvine, California,* showing fifty-one views of industrial parks in various stages of construction. At their worst, these pictures are stark and commercial. But at their best the pictures are bold, even lush. Shapes, patterns, richness of detail—these are the qualities that set Baltz's work apart. *The New Industrial Parks near Irvine, California* was published in 1974 in an edition of twenty-one and has since sold out. Approximate retail price is $3,000 for the entire portfolio, if you can find one, and $250 for individual pictures from the series.

Both Michals and Baltz work in black and white. William Eggleston is one of a small but growing number of contemporary photographers who have turned to color photography. His pictures, of scenes and people in northern Mississippi and southwestern Tennessee, broadly depict an old way of life—southern gentility and grace—under pressure from a newer, more fast-moving world. One untitled photograph shows two faded, rusting trade signs mounted, one on top of the other, along the peak of a corrugated metal roof. The bottom sign, with "PEACHES!" in large, peach-colored letters against an off-white background, is attached directly to the roof; the second, an old Art Deco Coca-Cola sign, is on top of that. The roof itself thrusts toward the viewer at a sharp angle and takes up the entire bottom third of the picture. It is covered with small rocks and is strafed by the orange-red light of a sunset, like an eerie moonscape. Overhead is a pastel sky, moving gradually in color from blue at the very top of the picture to pink where the sky meets the roof. Seven converging telephone or power lines—it is impossible to tell which—burst out of the upper right-hand corner of the picture, moving by the peaches sign into an unknown distance. The shadow of the photographer's head intrudes tentatively into the very bottom of the image. Eggleston's work, like much contemporary photography, is extremely controversial. John Szarkowski, influential director of the department of photography at the Museum of Modern Art in New York, has called Eggleston "one of the most talented and accomplished" members of the new generation of photographers working in color and, in a burst of enthusiasm, has referred to his work as "perfect." To which Hilton Kramer, art critic for *The New York Times,* has replied: "Perfectly banal, perhaps. Perfectly boring, certainly."

One reason for the surge of interest in photography collecting is that photographs are so real, so easy for the average person to relate to, so strong in the personal responses they often evoke. But, as the Michals, Baltz, and Eggleston examples indicate, this is not necessarily true in contemporary photography. Increasingly, contemporary photography appears to be going off in diverse directions that only people actively involved in the photography scene—critics, curators, leading dealers and collectors, and the photographers themselves—can understand. Much of what is being done in contemporary photography relates to the conceptual problems of extending the frontiers of photographic aesthetics, not to any broader issue facing art in general. Self-consciousness pervades much of the work. There is an increasing rejection of the more classical style of Stieglitz, Strand, and particularly Weston.

Thus, to understand contemporary photography and buy wisely, it may be important to have a background in art history or spend a great deal of time looking at photographs. Many of the buyers are young professionals who studied photography in college. The contemporary market combines lower prices with the excitement of participating in what is happening today, rather than being tied to the past.

Edition sizes are something of an issue in contemporary photography. Paul Strand, who died in 1976, made only limited numbers of "vintage" prints of his work and there is a defined ceiling on the availability of these early prints, regardless of any posthumous prints being made today from his negatives. Many buyers worry, however, that there is nothing to stop a young, living photographer from churning out prints by the dozens and flooding the market, to the disadvantage of collectors who already own the photographer's work. This is not really the problem it might seem; no photographer wants to spend his life in a darkroom making prints. But it is nonetheless a point about which to exercise some degree of care, by asking the dealer or the photographer for a general indication of numbers of prints being made. (More on this complex issue in Chapter 4.)

Chapter 3

"What's It Worth?"
How to Determine the
Value of a Photograph

The pricing and valuing of art is, in general, a subjective and fairly complex matter. Nowhere is this true to such a degree as in photography.

Typically, the market value of a painting is determined by the identity of the artist, subject matter, quality, rarity, size, historic importance, the period of the artist's career in which the work was created, the relative certainty or lack of certainty that the piece is indeed a genuine work by the named artist, and the condition of the work.

Because photographs (unlike paintings) are multiply-produced objects, additional variables come into play in determining market value. These include when the photographic print was made and by whom (by the photographer himself or by someone else after the photographer's death), the type of process used to make the print (for instance, a platinum print, being of higher quality, generally is more expensive than a silver print of the same photograph), and whether or not the work is signed by the photographer.

For the collector, an understanding of values is important to avoid overpaying. One of the first questions the beginning collector often asks is, How can I possibly know what a photograph is worth? And while pricing can indeed seem treacherous at first, in most cases the collector will develop an instinct for prices in a matter of months—by asking, reading, and looking.

In general, the identity of the photographer is the most important determinant of market value. Even lesser pictures by a big-name photographer will usually cost more than superb pictures by an unknown—unless the pictures by the unknown are of exceptional historic importance. There is something of a hierarchy in the marketplace, with each photographer fitting into his or her own particular price niche for reasons that may or may not be rational. Among late-nineteenth-century naturalist photographers, for instance, works by Peter Henry Emerson tend to bring high prices (approximately $300 to $2,500), while those of Frank Meadow Sutcliffe usually bring much less (approximately $50 to $850). Approximate price range for many important nineteenth- and twentieth-century photographers is discussed, photographer by photographer, in Chapters 5 through 14. Check the index in the back of the book to find the appropriate reference to a specific photographer. These prices are, of course, broad ranges rather than precise numbers to be followed blindly, and they reflect the prevailing price levels of early 1979, when this book went to press.

But even within a single photographer's body of work, prices can vary widely according to a number of factors. For instance, it is essential in photography to attempt to learn when and by whom the particular print was made. The general rule is this: The earlier the print and the closer to the photographer's own hand, the more valuable it will be. A print made by the photographer himself in the year the picture was taken generally commands the highest price, while one made after his death by a technician who did not work directly with the photographer usually goes for the least.

There are some fairly specific standards for determining how the date and maker of the print will affect value. Dealer Harry H. Lunn, Jr. suggests the following descending scale of values for works by major twentieth-century photographers:

At the top of the list is a "vintage" print—one made at the same time as the negative or within the next year or so—printed and hand signed by the photographer. On a scale of 100, this type of work would command 100. Any special dedication or annotation might add value above 100.

The next-most valuable is a print made by the photographer a number of years after the picture was taken and negative developed, such as a 1970 print from a 1935 negative. The approximate value would be 80.

Next in value would be a print made by an assistant to the photographer, but under his supervision. The value would be about 40.

A posthumous print made by one of the photographer's assistants trained in printing his work is somewhat less valuable. Such a print would rate about 20.

At the bottom of the list is a posthumous print made by a technician who never worked with the photographer. The value would be about 5.

Edward Weston is a specific case in point. Margaret Weston of the Weston Gallery in Carmel, California, notes that there are five basic categories of Edward's pictures:

The most expensive are vintage prints made by Weston in the 1920s, 1930s, and early 1940s. The approximate price range is $1,800 to $8,000.

Then come prints that were included in the *Fiftieth Anniversary Portfolio*, published by Weston in 1955 in an edition of 100 with the help of his son Brett. These go for approximately $1,500 each.

Next are "project prints" made by Brett in 1955–1956. Stricken with Parkinson's disease, Weston was no longer able to make prints himself. Instead, with the financial support of friends, he chose some 800 negatives from over the years which he considered his best and supervised Brett in making eight prints from each. The approximate price range is $400 to $700 per print.

Least expensive are posthumous prints made by another of Edward's sons, Cole. Edward Weston died in 1958, and he asked in his will that Cole be the only person allowed to print from his negatives. Edward had worked with Cole, himself a photographer, for a number of years to make sure that the latter understood just how Edward wanted each negative printed. These prints retail for $200 each.

The fifth category is a special edition of small-size palladium prints made by photographer George Tice in 1977. This edition consists of six different nude studies of another Weston son, Neil. Edward took these photographs in 1925, when Neil was a child, and later gave the negatives to Neil. The 1977 prints from these negatives, published in an edition of twenty-five plus five proofs, carry a retail price of about $250 each.

It is very easy to tell one type of Weston print from another, if you simply know to look. The portfolio prints, project prints, Cole Weston posthumous prints, and George Tice posthumous prints all are identified as such on the back.

However, in the case of Edward Weston's own vintage prints, there are more subtle variations that can affect value. There is the basic distinction, for instance, between a platinum and a silver print. The platinum prints, which are more expensive because of their superior quality and greater rarity, were made primarily in the 1920s; after 1937 no more were produced at all, since platinum printing paper was taken off the market that year due to declining demand. Margaret Weston says that a platinum print of *Hands, Mexico,* 1924, would go for about $7,500, while a silver print of the same picture would bring about $3,500.

There also are price variations within Weston's work according to subject matter. At a recent exhibition of signed vintage Weston prints at the Lunn Gallery in Washington, D.C., the price range was $1,500 to $3,500. The low price was for a 1940 portrait of photography historian Beaumont Newhall, while the high was for a 1923 nude portrait of Tina Modotti, the Italian-born actress and photographer who lived and studied with Weston in Mexico. Compared with the Newhall portrait, the Modotti portrait is simply a better, earlier, and more significant work—enough so to dictate a $2,000 price difference.

Another example, cited by Harry Lunn, Jr. involves the work of the early photographic team of David Octavius Hill (1802–1870) and Robert Adamson (1821–1848). Lunn notes that prints continued to be made from the Hill and Adamson negatives even after Adamson's death, and that various levels of types of prints have resulted:

Most expensive are calotype prints made between 1843 and 1847 by Adamson. A fine print of an interesting subject might be worth about $1,800 to $2,000 today.

Calotype prints made after Adamson's death by other assistants of Hill come next. The price here would be about $900.

In the late 1890s, a Scottish photographer named J. Craig Annan rephotographed the Hill and Adamson calotypes and made photogravure prints of them from etched copper plates (rather than from the original negatives). Some of these gravures were subsequently published in *Camera Work* magazine after the turn of the century. A fine example would go for about $200. (More on the pricing of photogravures later in this chapter.)

In 1915, another Scottish photographer, Jessie Bertram, obtained the original negatives and used them to make a new series of carbon prints, in editions of fifty prints per picture. Lunn says that while these prints do not have the look and feel of the original calotypes of seven decades earlier, their color is nonetheless closer to the originals than is the color of the Annan gravures. The market value, at about $300, thus is somewhat higher than that for the gravures.

Still another example of variations in pricing: Imogen Cunningham, who died in 1976 at age ninety-three, made her own prints until she was in her early nineties. These prints bring an average retail price of about $750 to $1,000 each. In 1974 she founded a trust to reproduce and preserve her work. Concurrently, she turned over all print-making to a laboratory, while continuing to approve and sign these "trust" prints. Signed trust prints bring about $500 each. There are also trust prints which were made in the laboratory under her supervision but were awaiting her signature at the time of her death. These go for about $250 each. Finally, trust prints made after her death are about $150 each.

The Weston, Hill and Adamson, and Cunningham examples are the oft-cited, classic cases of variations in types (and hence in values) of prints available to collectors. But they are by no means the only examples. Other important photographers for whose work similar variations come into play include the following:

Henry Peach Robinson: There are both original prints from the nineteenth century and 1976 reprints of four works from the original negatives by Photographic Collections Ltd.

Lewis Carroll: There are original prints, from approximately 1855 to 1880, and 1976 reprints of eighteen works from the original negatives by Graphics International Ltd.

Nadar (real name Gaspard-Félix Tournachon): There are original albumen prints, from approximately 1853 to 1886. There are carbon prints and Woodburytypes made from 1876 to 1885 for publication in *Galerie Contemporaine* magazine. And there are 1977 reprints of twelve of Nadar's most famous images, issued in France.

Mathew Brady: There are original prints, from approximately 1845 to 1865; ongoing reprints of Brady's Civil War images from the negatives on file in the Library of Congress; and recent "limited edition" reprints (5,000 copies) published by Time-Life Books. The Library of Congress reprints can be ordered (from the Library of Congress, Photoduplication Service, 10 E. First St., S.E., Washington, D.C. 20540) for $3.50 on up, depending on size and print quality. The Time-Life reprints are $75 each. Original Bradys, on the other hand, sell for at least several hundred dollars each.

Peter Henry Emerson: There are platinum prints from *Life and Landscape on the Norfolk Broads,* published in 1886, and photogravures from other works, published between 1887 and 1895.

Frank Meadow Sutcliffe: There are original nineteenth-century prints and twentieth-century reprints made from the original glass negatives by W. Eglon Shaw.

Thomas Eakins: There are original prints from the late nineteenth century and enlarged 1975 "copy prints" (photographs of Eakins photographs, rather than prints made from the original negatives) published in limited editions of twenty-five by art historian Gordon Hendricks. I would advise collectors to avoid all copy prints, since they are furthest removed from the photographer's hand and have nothing to do with original photographic prints.

Frederick Evans: There are original platinum prints, from the early 1880s until about 1914, and *Camera Work* photogravures published in 1903.

Alphonse Marie Mucha: There are original prints, from the late nineteenth and early twentieth centuries, and 1975 reprints of ten photographs published in an edition of 150 by Academy Editions and Graphics International Ltd.

Eugène Atget: There are original gold chloride prints by Atget, from approximately 1898 to 1927, and reprints, less gold in tone, made after his death from the original negatives by Berenice Abbott.

Alfred Stieglitz, Edward Steichen, Gertrude Käsebier, and other members of the Photo-Secessionist movement: There are original platinum and silver prints, primarily from the early twentieth century, and photogravures published in *Camera Work* magazine from 1903 to 1917.

Paul Strand: There are original prints made by Strand from approximately 1915 through the 1960s, prints made by Richard Benson under Strand's supervision, prints made by Benson after Strand's death in 1976, *Camera Work* gravures published in 1917, and gravures from Strand's *Mexican Portfolio,* published in 1940.

Jacques Henri Lartigue: There are vintage prints made by Lartigue shortly after the turn of the century and prints made by Lartigue in the 1960s and 1970s, in response to belated collector discovery of his work.

Edward S. Curtis: There are original sepia-toned "orotypes," platinum prints, silver prints, and photogravures, all from approximately 1896 through the 1930s.

August Sander: There are vintage prints made by Sander, primarily before World War II, and posthumous prints by his son Gunther after 1964.

Walker Evans: There are vintage prints by Evans, primarily from the 1930s and 1940s, prints by others for the 1971 Ives-Sillman portfolio, prints from a 1974 portfolio of fifteen works published by Double Elephant Press Ltd., and posthumous prints from the 1977 Portfolio I.

Brassaï: There are vintage prints from the 1930s and later prints primarily from the 1970s.

Diane Arbus: There are vintage prints made by Arbus prior to her death in 1971 and posthumous prints by Neil Selkirk. The Selkirk prints fall, in turn, into two categories: those from a ten-print portfolio selected by Arbus and subsequently printed in a limited edition of 50 by Selkirk (more expensive) and those from a broader selection of her work printed in varying editions from 25 to 100 by Selkirk (less expensive).

Ansel Adams: There are original prints by Adams (hand signed on the mount with his full name), from approximately 1930 to present, and prints made by Adams's students under his supervision (initialed on the mount).

In each of these cases, it is crucial to find out just what you are buying, since vintage prints carry much higher market values than nonvintage prints, posthumous prints, or gravures. To cite another example of the huge price differentials that sometimes are involved, a fine original Arbus might go as high as $2,000 to $2,500, while a Selkirk portfolio print would bring $400 to $500 and other Selkirk prints only $200.

To avoid becoming a victim of misrepresentation, it is important to buy only from reputable dealers and auction houses (unless, of course, you are experienced enough to spot variations in a particular photographer's work on your own); ask with great specificity just what it is you are buying; brush up on the variations in the photographer's output, by looking at catalogs, auction records, magazine articles, and other background materials; examine the item carefully for any clues as to just what it is (most posthumous prints are identified as such on the back); and insist that the bill of sale specify whether the work is a vintage print, a nonvintage print made by the photographer, a posthumous print, a gravure, or whatever. By having the nature of the item spelled out on the invoice, you will protect yourself in case the work turns out to be not what it is claimed.

Even with all these precautions, there may be times when it will simply be impossible to know with certainty when and by whom the print was made, and you will be forced to reach a purchase decision on the basis of subjective judgment rather than hard facts.

Perhaps surprisingly, rarity seems, in the emerging standards of the photography market, to have relatively little to do with photography prices—except in the case of very rare early photographs, where it can be extremely important. The demand side of the equation, rather than supply, tends to have the greater influence on prices. Popular, high-quality, important images generally bring high prices regardless of the quantity available in the market. Pictures from the 1886 Peter Henry Emerson illustrated book *Life and Landscape on the Norfolk Broads,* produced in an edition of 200 copies and therefore not unusually rare, sometimes command prices above $2,000 each; they happen to be very good and very important pictures which many collectors want to own.

There are exceptions to this broad rule—in other words, cases where a paucity of original prints has helped drive prices higher. Examples include the works of Thomas Eakins (1844–1916), Man Ray (1890–1976), Charles Sheeler (1883–1965), and László Moholy-Nagy (1895–1946). Incidentally, it is worth noting that each of these four artists is probably best known for work in a visual medium other than photography. Any photograph by a painter or sculptor of great historic importance will almost always bring a high price. Often, these photographs are exceedingly rare—such as a Degas, Brancusi, or Morton Schamberg. A Brancusi flower still life, circa 1930, sold recently at auction for $1,900.

But back to our main point—that demand, rather than supply, is more often the dominant force in determining market value. To cite two examples:

Ansel Adams's most famous and popular photograph is, without doubt, *Moonrise, Hernandez, New Mexico,* 1944. In fact, it has been estimated that this picture is so popular that Adams has sold close to 1,000 prints over the years. This is one of the most printed photographs in history, and one might easily conclude that the price would be low because the supply is so exceptionally large. But that conclusion would be wrong. Indeed, the opposite is true. *Moonrise* has become the most expensive Adams photograph of all. Until the end of 1975, Adams charged the same price for all of his works. That across-the-board price had risen steadily since the late sixties and was $800 at the end of 1975. Then Adams stopped taking further print orders and, in effect, threw the pricing for his existing prints onto the open market, allowing each work to find its own free-market level. *Moonrise* quickly jumped to $1,500, a level exceeded by no other Adams photograph and equaled by few. The reason: It is a very big favorite among collectors. Many people want to buy a copy, and so dealers are in the position of being able to charge more than for most other Adams pictures. Subsequently, as collectors bought all the available copies, *Moonrise* became almost impossible to obtain and rose to an estimated retail value in excess of $6,000.

The second example involves the work of William Eggleston, whose color photographs are discussed briefly in the previous chapter. All his pictures except one are limited to a total edition of twenty each, and they sell at retail for $600. The one major exception is his most popular picture, of a red ceiling. No limit has been set on the number of prints which can be made, and yet this picture goes for a higher price, $900.

Collectors, then, are less concerned with quantity than with quality—which is as it should be, short of the point where the market is being absolutely flooded with a particular work. Of course, rarity rightly becomes more of an issue for higher-priced works. Nobody wants to spend $4,000 or $5,000 for a photograph which is not rare.

The Adams and Eggleston prices cited above are retail prices, charged to collectors by dealers. There also is a wholesale price level, charged by one dealer to another or by a distributor to a dealer—generally 20 percent to 40 percent below retail. And there are auction prices, which tend toward the wholesale level. Auction prices are not always lower than retail prices; sometimes, for a particular type of photograph, the relationship between the two will temporarily reverse, with auction prices surpassing dealer prices, as has happened at times with Ansel Adams prints. But that is the exception rather than the rule.

In general, photography pricing is more troublesome for older pictures and less so in the contemporary market. These two broad market segments are quite distinct in their pricing structures.

Typically, for work by a living (contemporary) photographer, the photographer's primary dealer establishes a single worldwide price, and that is the price you must be prepared to pay (as was the case for Ansel Adams's work before he stopped taking further orders at the end of 1975). There is very little give-and-take between dealer and collector, except that some dealers may offer a 10-percent price discount to favored buyers. And there usually is little or no auction activity, so that auctions do not undercut dealer retail prices. For instance, prices for photographs by Judy Dater are $250 each, with the single exception that a print of her best-known image, *Imogen and Twinka,* costs $300. You can simply call the Witkin Gallery in New York, her primary dealer, and find out Dater's prices, or you can look up the information in Witkin's catalog. No matter where you buy, you must be prepared to pay that amount, and you will know exactly what the standard retail price is.

For older photographs, on the other hand, there is no established, across-the-board price structure which will enable you to know with assurance what you should pay. Values in older photographs can seldom be determined precisely. They are instead an approximation based on a number of subjective factors. Each dealer charges whatever he or she feels should be the going market rate, and prices can vary significantly from one gallery to the next—sometimes by as much as 50 or 100 percent.

Fortunately, dealer prices are very much out in the open, perhaps more so than in any other sector of the art market. Many dealers publish annual catalogs listing prices for works in their inventory, and these catalogs become a valuable reference source for any buyer who wants to comparison shop before agreeing to a price on a work being acquired. In fact, any collector who does not subscribe to at least three or four catalogs is taking great risk of being overcharged.

In addition to dealer catalogs, at least eight auction houses in the English-speaking world hold regular photography auctions, and in at least four cases their auction catalogs and post-sale price lists (showing the price paid for each item in the sale) are available by annual subscription. Any active collector will want to assemble a basic price-reference library consisting of both dealer and auction catalogs. (See catalog listing on page 217.)

For about $100 annually, a collector could subscribe to the following catalogs: auction catalogs from Sotheby Parke Bernet and Argus Ltd. in New York and from Sotheby's Belgravia and Christie's South Kensington in London, plus dealer catalogs from the Light, Witkin, and Lehr galleries in New York, Lunn Gallery in Washington, Graphics Antiquity in Illinois, Daguerreian Era in Vermont, Charles Wood in Connecticut, and Stephen White's Photo Album Gallery in Los Angeles. This combination of catalogs from four leading auction houses and eight leading dealers — in the East, Midwest, and West, as well as in London, and covering all basic periods of photographic history — would enable the collector to establish, within a few years, a price-reference library just about as good as any in the world.

By leafing through each catalog after it arrives in the mail, you will be able to keep abreast of current market levels. And when a question arises about a price for a specific item you are interested in buying or selling, you will be able to refer to these catalogs to see whether the price is in line with going market rates.

You also should feel free, when visiting dealers, to ask about the works being offered for sale — what type of print each work is, who printed it, when, where the dealer acquired the work, etc. — and the price differentials from item to item. On higher-priced items — say, over $500 — deduct 10 percent or more from the stated price to get a more accurate idea of the actual retail value. Many dealers overstate prices, particularly for rare items, to allow room for bargaining. Good dealers can be most helpful in explaining price variations to a collector. If, in fact, a dealer shies away from discussing prices, it may be a sign to buy elsewhere.

Sometimes, in checking catalogs, you will be able to make direct comparison with a published price for the exact same work you are considering buying. For instance, the Peter Henry Emerson picture *The Gladdon-Cutter's Return* recently was listed in very fine condition in a dealer catalog at $1,800 and was sold in somewhat lesser condition at auction for $625. (The dealer, whom I know, probably could have been bargained down to about $1,400.) So those two prices give a range within which you should expect to pay.

At other times, direct comparisons of this sort are not possible because another print of the same picture has not come up for sale in recent years or because the print in question is unique, with no other copy in existence. In this case you must try to assess how the picture fits within the photographer's overall body of work and, from there, estimate its value based on the established values for comparable pictures. For instance, you might be interested in buying a portrait by Julia Margaret Cameron but cannot find the same picture in any of the catalogs in your reference library. In that case you could check through the catalogs and find that the broad price range for all Cameron portraits is approximately $300 to $4,000, and from there you would try to narrow in on the prices for pictures of similar importance, subject matter, quality, rarity, size, and condition.

Photogravures present their own pricing considerations. Many of the "photographs" being offered for sale today — particularly works by Alfred Stieglitz, Alvin Langdon Coburn, Clarence H. White, Baron Adolph De Meyer, Edward Steichen, Frank Eugene, J. Craig Annan, and a number of other leading photographers from around the turn of the century — are not actually original photographic prints but high-quality reproductions. Usually they are labeled by the dealer or auction house as photogravures, but sometimes, unfortunately, they are not. Photogravures (or simply gravures) are not printed from the negative, but instead are created through a superfine printing process using a metal plate and printer's ink. They were an especially popular means for reproducing photographs in limited editions in the late nineteenth and early twentieth centuries, and today they trade actively in the market right alongside photographs themselves.

Occasionally, direct price comparisons are possible between a photogravure and a photographic print of the same picture. Such was the case in 1976, when a platinum print and a gravure of the 1894 Alfred Stieglitz work *The Letter Box* came up for sale at auction within six months of each other. The platinum print brought a price of $3,250 and the gravure, $230, which works out in this case to a price ratio of approximately 14 to 1. Overall, a ratio of anywhere between 4 and 15 to 1, for a photograph versus a gravure, would seem to be reasonable.

Chapter 4

Problem Areas:
Authentication,
Rarity, Modern Prints
from Old Negatives

Photography collecting, as indicated in the first three chapters, probably is more of a no-man's-land than any other segment of the art market. Collectors must concern themselves with:

- Concepts of rarity, including the pros and cons of limited editions of photographs.

- Whether to stick with vintage prints or buy later prints (which are less expensive) as well, and whether posthumous prints have any merit at all. Standards of "originality" are becoming increasingly difficult to define, as rising prices have prompted dealers, museums, and publishers to begin reprinting old negatives from as far back as the 1850s.

- Problems of authentication. Particularly for some older pictures, it often is hard to determine with any degree of certainty the identity of the photographer and/or the period when the print was made. Serious research into the work of many nineteenth-century photographers may take decades to complete. However, this seeming drawback also can be an advantage to the collector who has done a lot of personal research—by talking with dealers and collectors, looking at a great many nineteenth-century photographs, and doing a lot of reading—and who knows how to spot bargains.

- Outright fakes—reproductions created with the specific intent of deceiving buyers. While the market has so far remained almost entirely free of

fakes, there is some concern that rising prices
will began to attract a criminal element.

These problems are not at all insurmountable. But they do add to the complexity of the buying process, and they reinforce the point that anybody who isn't willing to take occasional risks probably should not go into photography collecting in the first place—or should at least stick to more recent works where there is a reasonable amount of documentation. Ultimately, many photography collectors end up buying a great deal on faith.

As mentioned previously, some novice and would-be collectors worry that (1) since any photographic negative can be printed time and again without limit, photographs can hardly be rare; and (2) since the photographic process allows any competent technician to reproduce an existing photograph with considerable fidelity, fakes must be a terrible problem.

Certainly it is *possible* for photographers to churn out prints by the hundreds or thousands, and certainly it is *possible* for someone to make copies of high-priced photographs and attempt to pawn them off as originals. In practice, however, these are relatively minor problems and need not be of too great concern to the collector.

Regarding the "problem" of limitless printings, the reality is that few photographers want to spend their time printing existing negatives. Making prints is both expensive and time-consuming. Most of the better photographers, seriously devoted to their work and producing original and outstanding images, simply do not have the time or inclination to go into the darkroom for extended periods. Sometimes several months will go by before a photographer can be coaxed into the darkroom at all to fill collector orders. Over the years, photographers have typically made prints only in direct response to demand, and for that reason vintage prints of most photographers' work are scarce. This is one of the great ironies of the photography market: that a process which is theoretically limitless actually has resulted in works of considerable rarity.

As mentioned earlier, many photographic prints are unique; only one print of the work is known to exist. Edward Weston's best-selling image in his lifetime was *Pepper No. 30.* He sold twelve prints. In an interview in the July-August 1973 issue of *The Print Collector's Newsletter,* Aaron Siskind estimated that he had seldom sold more than ten prints of any single picture. Thomas F. Barrow, one of the finer contemporary photographers, typically makes two prints of a work initially and makes more only after those are sold; seldom does he go beyond a total of six prints per picture.

Of course, there is always the possibility that a specific photographer will flood the market to make a killing and that unknowing buyers will suffer. But that is simply a risk of the marketplace—not a great risk, but one that certainly is there and which a collector must learn to accept, or not buy photographs at all.

Perhaps more to the point, many collectors would at least like to know, before buying, how many prints of the work have actually been made—regardless of whether this number is large or small. They would like to be confident that their money is being well spent. And they would like some assurance that dozens of additional prints will not be made after they buy.

However, for most older photographs it is just not possible to find out how many prints were made; records seldom were kept, and if they were they probably have been destroyed. Instead, an experienced dealer or collector will develop a general sense of whether the work in question is rare or common. For instance, prints of certain older works keep coming onto the market, and we know from this fact alone that they cannot be especially rare. Julia Margaret Cameron's portrait of Tennyson, titled *The Dirty Monk,* is an example. Other works, such as almost all vintage prints by Thomas Eakins, appear with great infrequency and so are presumed to be exceedingly rare.

In contemporary photography, some photographers will say how many images of a picture they have printed, while others don't keep records or won't say. Light Gallery in New York has done some of the best work in publicly documenting the output of the approximately forty photographers it represents. A brief discussion of approximate output for each of the forty is presented in Light's annual catalog. Hopefully, more dealers will follow this example and even go beyond the effort made by Light.

Limited editions represent an increasingly popular response by photographers and dealers to the desire of collectors to know how many prints of a particular picture have been made. While the limited-edition concept has great appeal in theory, I feel it has little to offer in reality.

Limited editions in photography are similar to the common practice in graphics. Only so many prints of a particular work are made—twenty-five in the case of photographer Duane Michals's work—and each picture from the series generally is numbered. The number on a picture might, for instance, be "4/25," indicating that this is the fourth print from a total series of twenty-five of this picture.

But this is not a cure-all. There are some very real problems in the limiting of editions. For one, while the theoretical objective is to hold down the output of a picture and protect the buyer, in reality limited editions tend to expand output. Typically, in an edition of twenty-five, all twenty-five prints are made, whereas if the photographer had followed the traditional practice of printing to order, maybe only two or three prints would ever be made. In other words, limited editions often do the opposite of what they are supposed to do: They tend to increase rather than reduce supply.

Second, the limit may apply only to that particular printing, and the photographer may feel free to continue making additional prints outside the numbered edition. There is no consistency whatsoever in the practices being followed. Some photographers continue to print to order, either without limit or establishing in their own minds a general but flexible maximum. Others print only in editions and stick to those edition sizes. Others turn their negatives over to publishers or print technicians and let them make all prints, either in editions or not. Others print to order and, after a number of individual prints have been made, create an edition and then destroy the negative. Still others print their works in editions but do not destroy the negative and feel free to continue making individual prints beyond the edition. Sometimes photographs are printed in limited editions only in the marketing of a portfolio of work—ten pictures in an edition of fifty each, for instance. The ten pictures would be sold as a unit, but individual prints of the same images might be sold without limit. (See Chapter 15 for a further discussion of portfolios.) While the prints from a limited edition generally are numbered on the prints themselves, sometimes they are not. There also are wide variations in whether the prints are hand signed by the photographer—on the front, on the back, on the mounting, or not at all.

Whatever specific approach is being used, limited editions seldom offer any real legal protection to the buyer. Richard Avedon remains one of the few photographers who has given buyers a signed guarantee that he will produce no more than a specified number of prints per picture—fifty in Avedon's case. Most others are free to print at will beyond the specified edition, unless the negative has been defaced or destroyed (something that most photographers are understandably reluctant to do, since the negative generally has a very deep personal meaning for the photographer).

The essential point to keep in mind is that editions have nothing to do with photographic artistry and are instead primarily a marketing concept, designed to offer some assurance of rarity—or perhaps merely an appearance of rarity—to nervous buyers. It therefore is very important to buy what is good, regardless of whether the edition is "limited" or not.

By all means, ask the dealer or photographer about the number of prints being made and about editions and about concepts of rarity. But don't get hung up on limited editions as the way to buy photographs.

Fakes are another area which seems to trouble many would-be buyers. But while they represent a major theoretical problem, they have so far avoided becoming a significant practical one. That may change, if photography prices climb high enough to attract swindlers.

However, even if some fakes do begin to appear on the market, the problem is not likely to become an overwhelming one. An experienced collector or dealer can discern most fakes fairly easily—by the tone of the paper, the quality of the printing, the way in which the photograph has been framed or mounted, etc. Direct comparison with a known original is the ultimate test.

It would seem that photographs, as the end product of a series of mechanical and chemical processes, are more susceptible to precise copying than any other art form. But the opposite actually tends to be true, particularly for older photographs, since it is almost impossible to duplicate the effects of aging and to recreate the exact chemical processes used in the past.

As an example, the British firm of Photographic Collections Limited has spent tens of thousands of dollars reproducing four works by Henry Peach Robinson, one of the earliest and most influential "art" photographers. Robinson's works are technically complex, highly sentimental pictures that were extremely popular with the Victorians. They often tell stories or create tableaux, such as *Fading Away,* showing a young woman in her dying moments. In constructing these pictures, Robinson would make a pencil sketch and then, using this sketch as a guide, photograph the picture section by section in his studio. As many as nine different negatives, each depicting a specific fragment of the overall picture, would be taken and then printed one by one to form the finished "composite" print.

Few original Robinson prints survive today, and they are very valuable. So Photographic Collections decided to make reprints of four works from the original negatives, which are owned by the Royal Photographic Society in London. But this proved to be a very difficult and lengthy process, even using Robinson's own negatives and his detailed written printing instructions, and the reprints have a very different look and feel than Robinson originals. For instance, the tone of the new prints is crisper, less aged, and more golden-hued.

The point is that faking an old photograph (which was by no means the intent in the case of the Robinson prints) can be a formidable task. The complexity of photography, which sometimes confuses collectors, protects them as well by making it difficult for modern copyists to reproduce old works in a form close to the originals. In many cases, the materials used a century ago are no longer even available. Robinson, for instance, used an albumen-based "printing out" paper (a type of paper on which the image appears during the exposure and which does not require any chemical developer) for the originals. But this type of paper is no longer produced, so Photographic Collections was forced to employ different materials which create different effects.

As in any area of art collecting, an active photography collector might end up buying two or three fakes over the course of the years. But you can protect yourself by (1) buying only from competent, reputable dealers who are careful about what they sell and will not knowingly palm off a fake as the real thing; (2) comparing the work in question with a known original of the same piece (if one can be found) or, short of that, with another work by the same photographer; (3) looking at each work carefully; and (4) being especially wary in higher-priced purchases where the financial stakes are greater.

For major twentieth-century works, it may also be possible to ask the seller for a provenance—a list of previous owners back to the photographer. Many important twentieth-century photographic prints are now coming into dealer hands from the photographers' personal collections, from their estates, and from their families. And although few dealers like to disclose their sources of inventory, a provenance, if you can convince the dealer to give you one, provides additional assurance of the genuineness of the work.

"Problem" pictures actually represent a much bigger everyday concern than outright fakes. These photographs are ones which may have been innocently misattributed to the wrong photographer or were altered years ago without intent to defraud or raise questions in other ways. Often, the origin or genuineness of a problem picture will never be resolved.

In one case I remember vividly, even two of the world's most renowned dealers disagreed on whether an item was all that it seemed to be. The item in question was a French stereoscopic daguerreotype of a nude young woman provocatively posed in front of a couch. The work was described in the auction catalog as taken in the 1850s. The label of the nineteenth-century French daguerreotypist Jules Duboscq was affixed to the back.

There was no question about the work being an original nineteenth-century daguerreotype. The only issue was whether Duboscq had actually taken the picture or whether someone had doctored the work by adding his label. An original Duboscq daguerreotype generally brings much more than an anonymous daguerreotype, so a few hundred dollars in market value was riding on this question.

I was talking with a leading European photography dealer the day before the auction, and he scoffed at this particular work, contending—accurately, I think—that a "respectable" nineteenth-century French daguerreotypist like Duboscq never would have attached his label to a nude. He suggested that the label must have been added, perhaps even in Duboscq's own time, by someone seeking to boost the value of the work.

However, a leading American dealer said he once had owned this particular work and was convinced the labeling was genuine. He also told me he had bought it from a rival of the European dealer, and he charged that this was the only reason the European dealer was casting aspersions on the work.

All of which goes to show that (1) there is a lot of backbiting in the world of photography and (2) some pictures are under a cloud that may never lift.

Another photograph which raised questions in the minds of some collectors was a Charles Sheeler view of the Ford Motor Company plant at River Rouge, Michigan. Sheeler photographs are rare and expensive. This particular print was auctioned in 1976. As noted in the auction catalog, the print is "scaled in pencil on the reverse." This would seem to indicate that Sheeler made this print for a book or magazine for use in reproduction rather than necessarily intending it to be a finished print for display. Scaling on the back of a photographic print generally is used by a printer to reduce or enlarge the picture so it fits the format of the book or magazine in which it is being reproduced.

Was the Sheeler worth buying? There was widespread disagreement among many of the people at the auction. Nonetheless, the work ended up bringing a very handsome price of $3,100, well above the presale estimate made by the auction firm. So somebody, obviously, was not at all put off by the implication that the work was not intended to be a finished print for display.

A Mathew Brady portrait of Abraham Lincoln was offered at the same auction. The auction catalog stated that the picture was taken on February 23, 1861, and described the work briefly, without raising any questions as to its originality. However, at the sale itself, the auctioneer announced that the picture was a silver print—a very common type of photographic print in which a silver salt is the chemical used to create the photographic image. The auction catalog had not said anything about the process used to make this print, but almost all original Brady paper-print photographs are albumen prints. After announcing that the work was a silver print, the auctioneer said that prospective bidders should make of that information whatever they saw fit. There was an immediate murmur throughout the crowd. A gentleman to my left, whom I did not know, turned to me and whispered that the work was obviously a copy of a Brady, probably made in the late nineteenth century, rather than an original from the 1860s. At least a few other collectors apparently did not agree—or, if they did agree, didn't care that much. The work sold for $275, only slightly less than had been anticipated before the auctioneer made his announcement.

Then there is the problem that certain major twentieth-century photographers—including André Kertész, Henri Cartier-Bresson, and Duane Michals—seldom make their own prints. Almost all the prints that can be purchased today have been made by a laboratory or technician working on behalf of the photographer—a point that, to some collectors, detracts greatly from the allure of the prints. Certainly we cannot dismiss a photographer of Kertész's, Cartier-Bresson's, or Michals's standing simply because he chooses a printing arrangement we do not like. But then again, all too often a laboratory-made print simply does not achieve the same subtleties and high quality as a print labored over by the photographer. This "problem" also demonstrates that some photographers can take great pictures but are not especially interested in working in the darkroom.

Ultimately, though, no single issue hangs over the market to anywhere near the degree as the controversy over vintage versus nonvintage prints. A "vintage" print generally is considered to be one which has been made within a few months or perhaps a few years of the taking of the image—say, a 1935 or 1936 print from a 1935 negative. This contrasts with a "serial" print, which is made several or more years later—such as a 1960 print from a 1935 negative. However, there is no precise dividing line, no specific point in time at which all further prints become serial prints. The concept is much more subjective in nature. Going back to our example of a 1935 negative, a 1938 print would almost certainly be considered a vintage print, but a 1948 print probably would not. In addition to vintage and serial prints, there are posthumous prints made by a relative, photographer, technician, or publisher.

Chicago attorney Arnold Crane, owner of one of the world's largest photography collections, has stated flatly that he would not buy anything but a vintage print and has suggested that there is "an ethereal presence in vintage material that many of the new photographic people do not understand." He has offered this advice to other collectors: "Run, don't walk, from anything but a vintage work," and has termed posthumous prints "useful only as classroom reference materials—or for fireplace tinder." Crane's views have been endorsed by some dealers and collectors, and vigorously disputed by others.

Parisian dealer Gerard Levy sees vintage prints as the central issue of photography collecting and says, like Crane, that he would never buy anything except a vintage work.

On the other hand, Lee Witkin, the well-known New York dealer, says people like Crane are essentially trying to protect their own heavy investments in vintage prints by dismissing serial and posthumous prints out of hand.

Certainly the reprinting of old negatives is not, in and of itself, a rip-off. Even in the case of posthumous prints, the merits of the prints vary with the motives of the people who make them and the care and skill with which the printing has been done. For instance, reprints of works by Hippolyte Bayard (1801–1887) have recently been made under the sponsorship of the Société Française de Photographie, which owns the negatives. Bayard was one of the inventors of photography. Little of his work remains on the market, and the reprints can be viewed as a justifiable attempt to broaden public awareness of Bayard and his pioneering efforts.

Yet, Crane's advice to stick with vintage material cannot be totally pushed aside. Vintage prints generally do have a richness, vitality, and historic significance not matched by nonvintage prints. The problem becomes financial. Many collectors simply cannot afford a vintage work by an important photographer like Lewis Carroll, Eugène Atget, August Sander, Edward Weston, Walker Evans, or Diane Arbus. On the other hand, nonvintage prints are available in each of these cases, and in quite a few others, at prices within reach of the average buyer.

The ultimate choice, then, is purely personal. What is your objective in collecting photographs? If you want to assemble a truly fine collection of outstanding works, you probably would do well to stick with vintage prints and pay more. Alternatively, you could turn to a lower-priced sector of the market, like contemporary photography or nineteenth-century stereographs, where premier works remain available at prices well below those for vintage prints by the great masters.

However, if your primary goal is to own some outstanding images by master photographers and you don't have a lot of money to spend—or if you aren't really concerned about owning the best, earliest prints—then by all means buy nonvintage works. But in this latter case you probably would be wise to check the quality of any nonvintage print by comparing it with a vintage work by the same photographer — before you buy.

Chapter 5

Collecting Daguerreotypes and Other One-of-a-Kind Photographs from the Nineteenth Century

Throughout the history of photography, there have been two broad types of photographic processes: (1) those where each work is unique and the image is produced directly on a metallic or glass surface and (2) those where the image is produced initially in negative form and can then be printed multiply, generally on paper. This chapter reviews the first of these two broad categories.

Three major types of one-of-a-kind photographs have been passed on to us from the nineteenth century: daguerreotypes, ambrotypes, and tintypes.

Daguerreotypes are the earliest of the three, as well as the finest in quality. Daguerreotypes are shiny, very precise photographs produced on silver-coated copper plates which have been sensitized with iodine and then developed by exposure to mercury vapor.

Daguerreotypes are often housed in miniature cases or frames, sometimes with a glass sheet covering the daguerreotype to protect its delicate surface. The case can, by itself, be quite valuable, selling for anywhere from $1 to $100 or higher. In the early part of this century, daguerreotypes were so common that buyers would sometimes melt down the plates for their metal content and sell the cases as cigarette boxes.

Daguerreotypes can be distinguished from other one-of-a-kind photographs by their mirrorlike reflection (caused by the silver coating) when viewed head-on. To see the image, you must turn the work to a slight angle, away from bright light. The basic tones of a daguerreotype are silver and black, although some daguerreotypes—particularly portraits—were hand tinted. A careful and subtle job of tinting generally adds value to the work, while poorly applied tinting will not increase the value and may even reduce it. Also, some daguerreotypes were toned with gold in order to protect the silvery image, create a rich brown cast, and make the naturally cool grays seem warmer.

Daguerreotypes were enormously popular, from the announcement of their invention by Louis Jacques Mandé Daguerre in 1839 through the late 1850s—more specifically, from 1843 to 1855. Thousands of daguerreotype portrait studios were opened in Europe and the United States, and members of the middle and upper classes flocked to these studios to have their pictures taken, at prices of about $2 to $3 per pose. Overall, it has been estimated that more than 30 million daguerreotypes were taken in America between 1840 and 1860, plus tens of millions more throughout the rest of the world.

At the height of activity, daguerreotypes were produced on assembly-line principles, with duties divided between the polisher of the copper plate, the sensitizer, the camera operator, the gilder, and the tinter. But the daguerreotype process eventually proved to be a dead end in the development of photography and fell by the wayside in the late 1850s and early 1860s.

Very few daguerreotypes have survived in perfect condition. Minor deterioration is almost inevitable. Furthermore, many daguerreotypes on the market today are in very poor condition. Years of neglect and overexposure to light have caused the image to become dark, obscure, spotted and/or tarnished, and these works have little market value unless of unusual historic importance. In addition, many daguerreotypes are marred by small patches where the image has been scratched away, indicating that somebody once made the mistake of trying to clean the work with a cloth.

Daguerreotypes should never be cleaned with a cloth or silver polish. The preferred method for cleaning a daguerreotype is to remove it from its case, rinse both sides in cold running water, gently rock the image for up to thirty seconds in a mild solution of instant silver dip, rerinse, and immediately blow dry the image. (For a more thorough discussion on how to clean and restore daguerreotypes and other old photographs, see *Caring for Photographs,* from the Life Library of Photography, published in 1972 by Time-Life Books.)

Ambrotypes, invented in the early 1850s, were a less expensive substitute for daguerreotypes. Often, like daguerreotypes, they were put in ornate cases. Again, portraits predominate.

Ambrotypes are sometimes referred to as "daguerreotypes on glass," but are actually products of a much different process. An ambrotype image has been developed in negative on the back of a small glass plate (rather than on the silver-coated front of a piece of copper, as with a daguerreotype). The work is backed with a thin coat of black varnish, and this makes the negative image appear in positive. Ambrotypes can be distinguished from daguerreotypes in that their surface is not nearly as reflective.

Ambrotypes are in general sturdier than daguerreotypes. Often, if the back of the image appears to be peeling or flaking, the work can be restored by scraping off the shellac and substituting a piece of black paper.

Ambrotypes began to supplant daguerreotypes in 1855, being less expensive and eliminating troublesome glare. Within a year, ambrotypes were *the* process in vogue, although some of the more established studios clung (hopelessly, it turned out) to daguerreotypes as the superior process. Ambrotypes, in turn, lost out rather quickly to paper-print photographs, which were far more versatile. The great popularity of the ambrotype thus lasted only about three years, until approximately 1858.

Tintypes are the final, and least expensive, of the three processes and are of more limited interest to most collectors. They sometimes are called ferrographs, ferrotypes, or melainotypes and are occasionally referred to as "the poor man's daguerreotype."

Tintypes were invented in 1856 by an Ohio chemistry professor named Hamilton Smith and remained popular well beyond the turn of the century. However, the process was considered distinctly inferior and, while used widely for inexpensive portrait photography in the United States, never really caught on abroad.

As with a daguerreotype, the image was created on a metal plate exposed in the camera, but the metal was iron (not tin as the name suggests) instead of copper and the coating was a black japan varnish. Thus, a tintype can be distinguished by its darker surface tones and the thin iron plate on which the image has been developed.

Until about 1865, tintypes were placed in cases like daguerreotypes, then in cardboard holders, and finally in nothing at all. Early tintypes were black and white in tone, but after 1870 they often were brown-toned. To have any value today, a tintype should be smooth and unbent, with a clear image. If the surface is very dark, stained, badly cracked, or faded, the work generally is not worth buying.

Daguerreotypes, ambrotypes, and tintypes were made in many sizes, but the standard sizes referred to by collectors are (in terms of approximate plate size, not case size) as follows:

Whole plate	$6\frac{1}{2}$ by $8\frac{1}{2}$ inches
Half plate	$4\frac{1}{2}$ by $5\frac{1}{2}$ inches
Quarter plate	$3\frac{1}{2}$ by $4\frac{1}{2}$ inches
Sixth plate	$2\frac{3}{4}$ by $3\frac{1}{4}$ inches
Ninth plate	2 by $2\frac{1}{2}$ inches
Sixteenth plate	$1\frac{5}{8}$ by $2\frac{1}{8}$ inches

(In describing works of art, height generally is listed before width; thus, the above table describes horizontal pictures. The dimensions would be reversed for vertical works.)

In general, a good daguerreotype is worth somewhat more than a good ambrotype, and a good ambrotype is worth much more than a good tintype. But there are wide price variations even within each category.

Subject matter, aesthetic quality, historic importance, size, physical condition, and identity of the photographer can all influence market value. The date the picture was taken, if known, also can be important. The earliest daguerreotypes, from approximately 1839 to 1842, are very rare and therefore quite expensive. Works from approximately 1843 to 1849 are somewhat less rare. And works from the great commercial boom period of daguerreotype photography, in the 1850s, are still widely available, although a fine daguerreotype from this decade will nonetheless command a premium price.

Another important consideration in determining market value is whether the work remains in its original case. Casing adds value for two reasons: (1) the preference of collectors for works as close as possible to their original state and (2) the fact that the design of the case often provides the best clues to the date of the photograph.

American Daguerreotypes

Albert Sands Southworth (1811–1894) and Josiah Johnson Hawes (1808–1901), Boston daguerreotypists who worked together from 1844 to 1861, often are regarded as the premier American daguerreotypists, and their work is among the rarest and most expensive. Unlike almost all other American daguerreotypists, Southworth and Hawes considered themselves artists first and commercial photographers second. They consistently sought to capture each sitter's personality and character, and they refused to settle for the bland, mundane portraits that were being churned out by thousands of other daguerreotype galleries across the United States. It is said that when Chief Justice Lemuel Shaw of the Massachusetts Supreme Court came to their studio, one of the partners met him at the entrance beneath a skylight. So striking was the light which strafed across Shaw's deep-gouged face that Southworth and Hawes chose to picture him right where he stood. That famous daguerreotype, a superb example of daguerreotype portraiture at its best, is now owned by the Metropolitan Museum of Art in New York.

Besides producing thousands of portraits, Southworth and Hawes depicted an exceptional range of other subject matter, including Boston edifices, building interiors, ships in dry dock and in harbor, a reenactment of the first ether-anesthesia operation in the United States, and even a ship at sea.

In addition, Southworth and Hawes were the only important daguerreotypists in America to set aside a large body of their work. Most daguerreotypists sold whatever pictures they made. Southworth and Hawes, on the other hand, retained many of their pictures—either the originals or duplicates shot directly from the originals (in other words, daguerreotypes of daguerreotypes). This rich and historically important collection, maintained intact for nearly eighty years, was offered for sale at auction in 1934 by Dr. Edward S. Hawes, Josiah Hawes's son. The bulk was acquired by three museums: the Metropolitan in New York, the Boston Museum of Fine Arts, and the George Eastman House in Rochester. Few Southworth and Hawes daguerreotypes remain available, therefore, to private collectors. In one recent case where examples did come onto the market, the International Museum of Photography at George Eastman House offered two portraits of Daniel Webster—both Southworth and Hawes copy daguerreotypes of original daguerreotype portraits—at public auction. Minimum asking price was $2,500 on one and $3,500, on the other, but neither price was achieved. Occasionally, Southworth and Hawes paper-print photographs also come up for sale, generally at prices well below those for the daguerreotypes. In October 1977, two Southworth and Hawes paper-print portraits of orator Rufus Choate—one an original portrait, the other a paper-print photograph of a daguerreotype—sold together for a combined price of $600.

In addition to Southworth and Hawes, other leading American daguerreotypists include Mathew B. Brady (1823–1896), Jeremiah Gurney (active 1840–c. 1865), M. M. Lawrence (active 1842–?), Edward Anthony (1818–1888), and Charles R. Meade (d. 1858) of New York; William (1807–1874) and Frederick (1809–1879) Langenheim of Philadelphia; and Robert H. Vance (d. 1876) of San Francisco.

Brady, the most fashionable and commercially successful of all American portrait daguerreotypists, entered the daguerreotype business in 1844, at age twenty-one. Implementing an idea advocated by others, he rented the top floor of a building at Broadway and Fulton Street in New York and had several large skylights installed for natural illumination. He probably was the first photographer to employ this method, subsequently in wide use.

Particularly in his early years, Brady was a tireless worker and leading experimenter. He was quickly recognized as one of the finest daguerreotype artists in the world, and his works won first prize at the annual fair of the American Institute each year from 1844 to 1846.

In about 1845, Brady conceived the idea of photographing all the notable Americans he could convince to sit before his camera. As an indication of the overwhelming success of this effort, he portrayed every American president from John Quincy Adams, the sixth, through William McKinley, the twenty-fifth—with the single exception of William Henry Harrison, who had died three years before Brady went into business. Of course, in some cases portraits were taken while presidents were not in office. Brady also depicted hundreds of lesser statesmen as well as generals, writers, and foreign dignitaries.

In 1847 Brady opened his second gallery, in Washington. By this time he had essentially withdrawn from being an active photographer. Like most other successful daguerreotypists of the era, he became a manager who employed assistants to handle all day-to-day photography. Nonetheless, all daguerreotype portraits continued to bear the imprint of the Brady gallery. As a result, we will probably never know which specific daguerreotypes are by the master and which by cameramen in his hire. Price range for routine daguerreotypes and ambrotypes from the Brady gallery is about $50 to $800. On the other hand, a portrait of someone who is historically important might bring several thousand dollars.

The careers of photographers like Brady, Gurney, Lawrence, Anthony, Meade, the Langenheim brothers, and Vance are reasonably well documented. Very little is known, however, of the lives of most other pioneering daguerreotypists. Take the case of Rufus Anson, one of whose portraits is reproduced on page 141. Essentially all we know is that Anson had a studio on Broadway in New York and was active from approximately 1850 to 1867, and that his studio turned out quality portraits.

The same obscurity shrouds hundreds of other daguerreotypists whom we know today only through their work and perhaps through their advertisements in old newspapers and listings in old business directories. Examples of obscure photographers whose work is occasionally available in the market include William North of Dayton, S. L. Carleton of Portland, Maine, and McDonnell, Donald & Co. of Buffalo, among many others. The identity of the photographer will, in this case, add little if any market value to the work. The most important factors influencing value become date, subject matter, quality of image, and condition of the work. The general price range for portraits by identified, but obscure, daguerreotypists is approximately $10 to $150—again with the exception that portraits of historically important sitters will almost always go for much more.

Finally, there is a much, much larger body of daguerreotype portraits by photographers whose identity is not known at all. As an example, a recent dealer sales catalog offered seven works by known photographers (most of them obscure) and forty-three by anonymous daguerreotypists. But lack of identity is not really a drawback—if you have an "eye" for photography and a sense of what to look for in a daguerreotype. These anonymous works, like those by identified but obscure photographers, should be judged primarily on the basis of approximate date, subject matter, photographic quality, and physical condition.

Among the rarest and most prized daguerreotypes are presidential portraits; pictures of famous writers, statesmen, and other individuals of historic significance; nudes; still lifes; city buildings and street scenes; ships; interiors; train wrecks and other disasters; and landscapes and other outdoor scenes (including Niagara Falls, perhaps the most photographed natural landmark during the nineteenth century).

Somewhat less rare, but still more prized and expensive than routine portraits, are children's portraits (difficult to take because the sitters had to remain absolutely still for ten to twenty seconds or more); occupational portraits (pictures of firemen, pharmacists, gold miners, blacksmiths, and other workers either in occupational garb or on the job); people with animals; houses; death portraits; side-view portraits; and military personnel.

Some recent dealer and auction offerings will give an indication of the types of daguerreotypes which draw substantial prices:

Dealer Janet Lehr of New York recently offered an unusual sixth-plate view of a wrecked ship, towed into harbor (probably in a Great Lakes port) and being viewed by a crowd on a second ship, for $5,000.

Witkin Gallery, New York, offered two pictures of a wooden house with a white picket fence, for $175 each.

A quarter-plate ambrotype of a horse-drawn bakery wagon in front of a building destroyed by fire, in Richmond, Virginia, circa 1856, sold at auction for $275.

A sixth-plate frontal nude of a young woman carrying an amphora on her shoulder sold at auction for $600.

A sixth-plate still-life study of a skull and hourglass, with an open book, pair of spectacles, and a compass, sold for $220.

Graphic Antiquity, Arlington Heights, Illinois, recently offered a rare half-plate scene of an early California gold mine, with nine miners posed in front, for $2,500. Among other occupational portraits, that same gallery offered a sixth-plate portrait of a cobbler for $150 and a sixth-plate ambrotype portrait of a carpenter for $125. And a sixth-plate portrait of a New York fireman sold at auction for $250 in November 1976.

A whole-plate ambrotype view of Niagara Falls, circa 1855, sold at auction for $720.

In one of the most publicized photography transactions in recent history, a sixth-plate portrait of Edgar Allan Poe sold at auction in 1973 for $9,250 and was resold privately to collector Arnold Crane of Chicago for a rumored $35,000.

In addition to the dealers already mentioned, leading U.S. dealers in daguerreotypes and ambrotypes include Rinhart Galleries, New York; Daguerreian Era, Pawlet, Vermont; America Hurrah, New York; and Jan Maillet, New York. Many other galleries handle more limited quantities of daguerreotypes. While the major U.S. art auction houses tend to shy away from dealing heavily in daguerreotypes, there are occasional exceptions—such as the exceptional offering, by the Los Angeles branch of Sotheby Parke Bernet in February 1978, of fifty-three daguerreotype and ambrotype portraits from the Brady studio. Also, some less well known auction houses, such as Swann Galleries in New York, deal fairly actively in this sector of the photography market. Finally, many antique shops and flea markets sell daguerreotypes, although the quality of these works can be spotty.

British Daguerreotypes

As in the United States, there is an active British market for daguerreotypes and ambrotypes. Both Sotheby's and Christie's, the two great London auction houses, include substantial offerings of daguerreotypes in their regular photography sales, and many dealers carry inventories of these works.

Antoine Claudet (1797–1867) is widely viewed as the most important of the British daguerreotypists. French by birth, Claudet settled in London in 1827 as an importer of glass. Twelve years later, when the invention of the daguerreotype was announced in Paris, Claudet immediately recognized the commercial possibilities of the process, and he went to France to receive instructions from Daguerre himself and to purchase the first license for the taking of daguerreotypes in England. His portraits are renowned for their bold, straightforward style and high technical standards. Almost every major photography auction in London now contains at least one or two Claudet daguerreotypes, which typically bring prices between $50 and $300.

Other leading British daguerreotypists whose work appears regularly in the auction room include T. R. Williams (1825–1871), who worked for several years as Claudet's assistant and then set up his own gallery in about 1850; Edwin Mayall (1810–1901), an American who moved to London in 1847 and became wealthy as one of the most popular portrait daguerreotypists; Richard Beard (1801/1802–1885), whose fortunes reversed those of Mayall, from great success in the early 1840s to bankruptcy by 1850; and William Edward Kilburn (active 1846–1862), perhaps best known for his early ninth-plate "miniature" portraits.

The British market is similar to the American market: Portraits of unidentified sitters predominate, and rarities like outdoor scenes and nudes command premium prices. Very early photographs having to do with the art of photography also tend to draw high prices, because of their great historic interest. In recent years, few of these pictures have come onto the market in the United States. But in March 1977, Christie's in London offered such a work, an unusual gem depicting photographer Jabez Hogg (1817–1899) taking a daguerreotype portrait of a Mr. Johnson in Richard Beard's studio. The picture, dating to August 1843 or earlier, may be the first photograph ever taken of the act of photography. Befitting its historic significance, the work brought $9,900.

Chapter 6

Nineteenth-Century
Paper Prints

Photographs on paper were the dominant photographic medium in the latter part of the nineteenth century and are the method on which all modern photography is based.

This market is quite distinct from that for daguerreotypes: mostly different photographers, a different price structure, and much wider variety from which to choose.

This market also gives collectors the flexibility to play it safe and stick with important, expensive rarities—such as a Lewis Carroll portrait or a Gustave Le Gray seascape—or to chart a more venturesome course and seek to choose wisely from the hundreds of thousands of works of lower price and less clear-cut pedigree.

The nineteenth century was a period of great experimentation in paper-print photography and of far-ranging efforts to record events, landmarks, and peoples throughout the world. Examples include the earliest war photographs, taken in the Crimea in 1855 by British lawyer Roger Fenton; the first photographs of Middle Eastern landmarks and topography, taken from 1849 to 1851 by Maxime Du Camp, a French writer and photographer; the earliest published views of the Yosemite Valley in California, taken prior to 1867 by a San Francisco photographer named Carleton E. Watkins; and the first successful "aerial" photographs, taken in 1858 in a balloon by Nadar, the flamboyant Parisian writer, lithographer, and portrait photographer.

Paper prints also were the primary medium used in nineteenth-century "art" photography—that is, conscious attempts to take photographs in an artistic, painterly way. The ornate and stylized photographs of O. G. Rejlander and Henry Peach Robinson, from the late 1850s and early 1860s, are primary examples.

And paper prints were the medium for a number of important technical achievements, including the stop-action analysis of motion by Eadweard Muybridge and Étienne Jules Marey in the 1870s and 1880s.

Daguerreotypes can generate their own excitement by recapturing people, events, and scenes of the past. But the big drawback of collecting daguerreotypes is that they were used primarily in formal portraiture. And portraits, unless exceedingly well done, can become wearisome—which is one reason why routine daguerreotype portraits are so inexpensive relative to other types of old photographs.

Not all paper-print photographs are gems that command high prices. There is a great deal of inexpensive—and in some cases not especially interesting—material, and it takes a reasonably good eye and the experience of having seen many pictures to cull out the superior works. But the big advantage of collecting in this area is that the variety of quality photographs, for those who do develop the ability to distinguish, is truly substantial and diverse. In addition, many of these pictures have tremendous historic appeal.

Another advantage—or potential drawback to those who don't have the time to do some looking and reading—is that nineteenth-century paper-print photography remains largely uncharted waters. A great deal of research still has to be done into the output of specific photographers and the very existence of others. For the independent-minded collector, this can add to the challenge, opportunities, and excitement.

London dealer Russ Anderson notes that, partly as a result of the lack of information, there still is great diversity of opinion among collectors, dealers, and curators as to which photographers are important and which are not. While Anderson himself is heavily committed, for instance, to the work of Charles Clifford (d. 1863), a leading photographer of Spanish architecture and landscapes, other dealers have their own favorites.

Adding to the turmoil and challenge is the fact that every few months a new photographer seems to surface whose work was hidden away in a descendant's attic or in some venerable library and whose existence comes as a total surprise to even the most ardent students of nineteenth-century photography. There were a number of highly talented amateur photographers whose work is just beginning to gain recognition. An example is John Wheeley Gough Gutch (1809–1862), a prominent British surgeon whose photographs made their market debut in June 1976 at an auction at Sotheby's Belgravia in London. Gutch's name does not appear in any of the photographic history books, nor was it familiar to collectors or dealers before the Sotheby's sale. Not knowing how buyers would react, Sotheby's was rather cautious in its presale estimates, about $40 to $50 per picture. Every one of the five photographs sold for much more, with one going for $250. At its next photography sale, in October 1976, Sotheby's offered eight more lots of Gutch pictures, with the presale estimates approximately doubled. Again the bidding was very strong, and seven of the eight estimates were exceeded. Top price this time was $400 for a photograph of a country house with people and horses in the foreground, circa 1855. Since that second sale, at least two or three Gutch photographs have been offered in nearly every major photography auction in London and New York, and Gutch has begun to win acceptance as an important nineteenth-century photographer.

Rarity is another aspect of nineteenth-century paper-print photography that has so far lacked much attention—and that may defy precise analysis anyway, since records of print editions seldom were kept. Certainly some of the more popular nineteenth-century photographs were produced in considerable quantity, perhaps on the order of several hundred or more copies. On the other hand, dealer Anderson says that about half the works he has ever handled may be unique, or at least he has never seen or heard of another print.

Public announcement of the invention of paper-print photography dates, as with the daguerreotype, to 1839. However, paper prints were slower than daguerreotypes to gain widespread public recognition, and it was not until the mid-1850s that paper-print photography finally came into its own. During the 1840s, in particular, daguerreotypes were king, and paper-print photography was practiced by relatively few amateur and even fewer professional photographers. Daguerreotypes produced crisper, more precise, more permanent images, were easier for a photographer to master, and were unencumbered by licensing problems. Their big drawbacks were surface glare and the inability to create multiple copies of a picture. So while it took paper-print photography more time to develop into a viable medium, when it finally did reach that stage in the mid-1850s, the daguerreotype, with its two big disadvantages, was quickly pushed aside.

The steady development of paper-print photography from 1839 through the end of the century is linked to two separate areas of technical experimentation: a constant series of new ways for making negatives and new ways for making positive prints from these negatives.

Several dozen different paper-print processes were introduced during the nineteenth century. The ones of greatest significance today to photography collectors and historians include calotypes, albumen prints, carbon prints, and collotypes.

In the 1840s, *calotypes* (also called salt prints and Talbotypes) were the dominant form of paper-print photography. Almost all pictures dating from that decade are either daguerreotypes on metal (very popular on the Continent and in the United States, as well as in many other areas of the world) or calotypes on paper (most popular in England, along with daguerreotypes).

The calotype was invented by William Henry Fox Talbot (1800–1877), a British classical and scientific scholar of some renown. A calotype negative could be created from a sheet of writing paper by first soaking the paper in silver nitrate solution and then letting it dry. The paper was then placed in a solution of potassium iodide, washed with water, and again dried. When required for use, the paper was treated, in very subdued light, with a freshly prepared solution of "gallo-nitrate of silver" (a mixture of silver nitrate, gallic acid, and acetic acid). The sheet was now light-sensitive and could be placed inside a camera. Once exposed, the negative was removed from the camera and the image gradually "brought out" by further treatment with gallo-nitrate of silver. After washing, the image was "fixed" (made permanent) with hot "hypo" solution.

This negative could then be used for making positives by the same process or, in some cases, by a somewhat modified version of that process. Each positive was exposed to the negative outdoors in a printing frame.

The calotype was the first practical method for making photographs on paper. It was used for producing negatives from approximately 1841 to 1855 and, after that, remained popular as a method for producing positives from other kinds of negatives until about 1860. Calotype prints generally can be distinguished by their very flat, nonglossy sepia tones and their tendency to fade. Most of these prints, except those which have been stored fairly consistently in darkness over the years, have something of a washed-out look.

The calotype era was dominated by the work of Talbot and of the Scottish photographic team of David Octavius Hill (1802–1870) and Robert Adamson (1821–1848). No other paper-print photographers of the 1840s achieved the same high degree of prominence, and by far the most active collector market in calotypes today is in their work.

The calotype also was used fairly widely in France, where Talbot apparently did not enforce his patent. In 1851 Gustave Le Gray (1820–1882) invented a waxed-negative process that was a derivative of the calotype, and this became a popular medium for landscapes and architectural studies. Le Gray's own work is rare and expensive. His 1852 salt print from a waxed negative of the entrance of Napoleon III into the Tuileries after his coronation was offered recently by a dealer for $4,000.

Other important French photographers of the 1850s, working in either the waxed-negative or calotype process, include Édouard-Denis Baldus (1815–1882), Henri Le Secq (1818–1882), Charles Marville (dates unknown), and Charles Nègre (1820–1880). Their work, like Le Gray's, tends to be rare and costly. The major exception is that Baldus made many prints of his work in the 1860s, and these later prints are regularly available for approximately $50 to $200 apiece.

Each of these photographers is known primarily for a specialty: Le Gray for seascapes; Baldus for architectural studies; Le Secq for still lifes and his studies of the Strasbourg, Rheims, and Chartres cathedrals; Marville for views of Paris; and Nègre for candid portraits of urban "street" people.

Still another important early French photographer is Maxime Du Camp (1822–1894). Du Camp was commissioned by the French Ministry of Education to undertake the first photographic recording of monuments and views in the Near East. These pictures, taken between 1849 and 1851, were published in 1852 in an illustrated book titled *Egypte, Nubie, Palestine et Syrie*. Salt prints from this book are now extremely rare. Two recently were offered by a dealer at $4,250 and $4,500 each.

In the United States, William (1807–1874) and Frederick (1809–1879) Langenheim purchased rights to the calotype from Talbot for $6,000 in 1849 in hopes of licensing the process to other American photographers. But they were totally unsuccessful and ended up in great financial difficulty. So the American calotypes which survive today are those few examples of works by the Langenheim brothers themselves. A pair of Langenheim calotypes sold for $1,900 in September 1975.

As for Talbot, his pictures encompass a variety of subject matter, primarily in and around his home in Lacock Abbey near Bath: his favorite tree, the garden outside his window, a portrait of his gamekeeper, and other views meant to illustrate the versatility of the calotype process. A rare Parisian view is reproduced on page 137. These important early works, so pivotal in the beginning stages of photography, still come up for sale, at prices of approximately $250 to $3,000. For instance, a fine, very early picture of a dormer window on the roof of the old brewery in Lacock Abbey was offered recently by Colnaghi's, the London art dealers, for $2,250.

"Photogenic drawings" represent a second basic category of Talbot calotype. These are marvelously delicate and subtle works which were produced by placing leaves, butterflies, seeds, or other small objects on a piece of photosensitive paper and exposing the paper to sunlight for approximately two hours, reproducing the soft, milky outlines of the objects. The making of photogenic drawings was very popular around 1840, the year after the invention of photography was announced, and these works come up for sale regularly at the two big London auction houses, Sotheby's and Christie's, typically for $10 to $50 per picture. The big problem in buying these works is that it is very hard to know which, if any, photogenic drawings are actually by Talbot and which by other, anonymous photographers (and therefore worth much less money).

One photogenic drawing bearing Talbot's signature came up for sale at a London auction. There was considerable disagreement as to whether the signature was genuine, and the auction house was careful not to make any claim of authenticity. Nonetheless, the possibility that the work was actually by Talbot proved strong enough to drive the price to $370, ten times the presale estimate of the auction firm and six times higher than the price for any other photogenic drawing in that particular sale.

While Talbot invented the calotype, Hill and Adamson raised the process to its highest levels of artistic achievement. Between 1843 and 1847, Hill and Adamson took approximately 1,500 photographs, mostly portraits and architectural pictures as studies for Hill's paintings. Hill became interested in photography when he was commissioned to paint a group portrait of 474 ministers of the newly formed Free Church of Scotland. Realizing the impossibility of painting such a work from life, he turned to Adamson for help in photographing each of the 474 ministers. The project was so successful that Hill and Adamson continued taking pictures together until Adamson became critically ill in the fall of 1847. Hill's paintings are now considered to be overblown and boring. By contrast, the calotype portraits, so full of vitality and insight into character, represent one of the great photographic treasures of the nineteenth century. A reproduction of a Hill and Adamson portrait appears on page 139.

The typical price range for Hill and Adamson calotypes is $300 to $2,000. These works come up for sale in both England and the United States, at both auction houses and dealers' galleries. As with Talbot's work, many of the prints are faded or torn, so condition is vital in determining market value.

In 1851, a British inventor named Frederick Scott Archer devised the *collodion "wet plate" process* for making negatives on glass. Talbot immediately sued for infringement of his own patents, but lost in 1854. Within a year after that, the daguerreotype and calotype were for all practical purposes dead, victims of Archer's invention.

Collodion glass plates could be used to make prints on paper or, when backed with a coating of dark shellac, the plate itself became an ambrotype (see previous chapter). The process was the fastest negative system yet devised, and it produced negatives equal in detail to the results produced by the daguerreotype process. When properly prepared, developed, and dried, a wet-plate negative could be used to make as many prints as desired. Furthermore, Archer, unlike Talbot, did not patent his invention, made no money from it, and offered it freely to all. The process remained in wide use until 1880, when it was replaced by the dry-plate glass negative, the other major variant on the glass negative.

Photography grew enormously after the introduction of the wet-plate negative, which freed the photographer to pursue all sorts of new subject matter difficult to capture with the daguerreotype or calotype. It was the wet-plate process, for instance, which was used to photograph the American Civil War and was employed by Julia Margaret Cameron to create her powerful, dreamy portraits of Victorian notables.

However, preparing a successful wet-plate negative was by no means an easy task, and we can look back with wonder and admiration at the skill of the many photographers who mixed their own chemicals, applied them to a thick glass plate, exposed the plate in the camera, and then developed the plate in a darkroom. Since the plate had to be developed almost immediately, outdoor photographers were forced to take portable darkrooms—usually tents or horse-drawn wagons—with them.

Seven basic steps had to be followed in creating a collodion negative, and from steps two through six the glass plate had to be kept constantly moist and out of the light. The seven steps are as follows:

1. The glass was thoroughly cleaned and polished.

2. A viscous collodion—a mixture of guncotton, alcohol, and ether—was combined with iodide and sometimes bromide and was then flowed over the glass to form a smooth, even coating. Often, however, the emulsion coating was uneven and contained air bubbles, which detracted from the quality of the finished photographic print.

3. The coated plate was made light-sensitive, in the subdued light of the darkroom, by soaking it for several minutes in silver nitrate. Then, while still wet, it was placed in an opaque plate holder and the holder was placed in the camera.

4. The photograph was taken almost immediately, so the plate would not dry.

5. Back in the darkroom, the plate was removed from the holder and doused in a solution of pyrogallic acid and protosulfate of iron. The image quickly began to emerge on the surface of the plate. When it was felt to be fully developed, the plate was rinsed with water.

6. The plate was flushed with "hypo" or with potassium cyanide in solution to dissolve any remaining unreacted silver salts and was once again rinsed well with water.

7. The plate was warmed over a flame until dry and, finally, was varnished while still warm.

Because each collodion plate had to be prepared by hand just before the picture was taken, the quality of collodion negatives varied widely and this, in turn, affected the quality of the finished prints. Yet, many wet-plate photographers overcame the handicaps of this lengthy and difficult series of steps to create some of the outstanding photographs of the nineteenth century.

Most nineteenth-century prints were the same size as their negatives, since equipment for making enlargements was not yet readily available. This is one reason why any large-scale nineteenth-century print of an image taken under at all difficult conditions, such as the William Henry Jackson photograph reproduced on page 167, generally is highly prized by collectors. Collectors appreciate the work that went into successfully making a large negative.

The era of the wet-plate negative largely overlapped the era of the *albumen print* positive. This method was introduced by Louis-Désiré Blanquart-Evrard (1802–1872) in May 1850. It was in almost universal use by the late 1850s and remained the main system for printing positives until about 1890.

Albumen paper, unlike salt prints, was produced commercially, eliminating the need to prepare each print by hand. The major substance used in producing albumen paper is the whites of eggs, containing salt and made photosensitive before use with silver salts. Albumen prints are easy to distinguish by their semiglossy surface (unlike the very flat tone of a calotype) and the sense that the image is on the surface of the paper, rather than embedded in the paper (as with calotypes). Like calotypes, albumen prints are subject to fading. Unlike calotypes, they tend to discolor as well. Often this discoloration is around the outer edges of the work, creating a halolike effect. Some albumen prints also are cracked, the result of an excessive coating of albumen.

The photographic boom of the 1860s created great demand for albumen paper. According to one estimate, 6 million eggs a year were being used in 1866 to provide albumen for photographic prints. (What happened to all the egg yolks? Apparently they were thrown away.) Most albumen paper was made at the time of year when eggs were cheap. At the paper-making companies, there were rows of women who did nothing but break eggs and separate the whites from the yolks. The frothy albumen was then treated with bromide or chloride and poured into shallow trays. Finally, the paper was floated on the surface of the liquid and hung to dry. High-quality albumen prints often were toned with gold chloride; this process imparted a distinctive warm brown color that is an almost certain sign that the work is a nineteenth-century albumen print.

From a collector's viewpoint, one problem with the combined wet-plate/albumen-print process is that an unlimited number of prints could be made from a single negative. Although few exact records exist, some pictures—particularly portraits of notables and photographs of Egypt, Jerusalem, and other Near East lands, which were so popular with the British—may have been run off by the thousands. Commercial publishers, like the British art firms of Agnew's and Colnaghi's, got into the photography business and distributed albumen prints of images by leading photographers. Thus, many of the best-known works are not at all scarce—all to the good if you are looking to acquire one for a reasonable price, but a definite drawback if you are concerned with rarity.

Many important photographers worked in the combined wet-plate/albumen-print process. Roger Fenton, Julia Margaret Cameron, Nadar, and Mathew Brady are among the photographers whose original prints are regularly available to collectors today.

Roger Fenton (1819–1869) is one of the giants of nineteenth-century photography. He was the first war photographer, taking pictures of the Crimean War from March to June 1855, and also produced exceptional flower still lifes. (See example on page 147.) In addition, he is known for his views of Moscow, taken on an 1851 visit; his work in the late 1850s for the British Museum, photographing objects in its collection; and his large-scale views of British cathedrals, abbeys, and landscapes. Fenton probably covered a wider range of subject matter than any other photographer of the

47

1850s and apparently used long exposures, as indicated by the many blurred heads in his pictures. Most of Fenton's early prints are salt prints; most of his later works are albumen prints. Price range is approximately $400 to $3,000, although a large and rare still life, in good condition, might sell for $5,000 or more.

When Fenton returned to England in mid-1855, Agnew's—which published his war pictures—assigned James Robertson (active 1852–1865) and Felice Beato (active c. 1852–1885) to replace him. They stayed about three months and made some sixty negatives. Their Crimean War prints, like Fenton's, trade fairly actively in the market, at prices from about $200 to $600 each.

In addition to his early work in assisting Robertson, Beato became an important photographer in his own right. He was in India from 1858 to 1860, photographed the Opium War in China in 1860, and spent most of the next decade in Japan. His prints generally are available at prices of approximately $50 to $500 or more each.

Other important landscape, architectural, and "travel" photographers from the wet-plate/albumen-print era include the following:

— Louis-Auguste (b. 1814) and Auguste-Rosalie (b. 1826) Bisson, best known for their Alpine views.

— Francis Frith (1822–1898), whose early Near Eastern views won tremendous public acclaim in England.

— Adolphe Braun (1811–1877), known for his "instantaneous" (fast exposure) street views in Paris and his mountain and landscape photographs in Switzerland.

— George Washington Wilson (1823–1893), the earliest "instantaneous" photographer of London street scenes as well as a leading photographer of Scottish landscapes.

— John Thomson (1837–1921), a Scotsman who traveled widely in the Far East in the 1860s and early 1870s.

— Thomas Annan (1829–1887), whose finest documentary photographs are contained in the illustrated book *Old Closes and Streets of Glasgow*.

— Francis Bedford (1816–1894), who specialized primarily in pictures of English landscapes and cathedrals.

— Samuel Bourne (1834–1912), one of the leading landscape photographers in India.

— Robert MacPherson (1811–1872), the leading photographer of Roman architecture.

— Carlo Ponti (active 1858–1875), a prominent

Italian optician and the leading photographer of Venetian scenes.

— Felix Bonfils (1829–1885), who had a studio in Beirut in the 1870s and photographed ancient cities and historic landscapes throughout the Middle East.

— William James Stillman (1828–1901), an American artist, journalist, and photographer, who documented the Acropolis in 1869–1870.

— William Notman (1826–1891), the leading Canadian landscape and portrait photographer of the period.

In general, the work of these photographers sells in a range of approximately $40 to $800 per print. But there are exceptions. Particularly in the case of the Bisson Frères, prices can go quite a bit higher—to $1,500 or more.

The Bisson brothers are among the most important of all nineteenth-century photographers. They are best known for their large-scale Alpine views, taken in the late 1850s and early 1860s. One of these is reproduced on page 149. They obtained the first views from the summit of Mont Blanc; twenty-five porters were required just to carry their wet-plate chemicals and equipment on that historic 1861 journey. In addition, the Bissons were among the most prominent photographers of French cathedrals in the early 1850s.

Thomson also is considered to be especially important. He is best remembered for three photographically illustrated books: *The Antiquities of Cambodia,* 1867; *Illustrations of China and Its People,* 1873–1874; and *Street Life in London,* 1877. More than any other photographer of the period, Thomson depicted peoples and their customs rather than buildings and landscapes. In many ways, his work is a forerunner of the "social documentary" photography of Jacob Riis and Lewis Hine more than two decades later. *Antiquities of Cambodia,* which contains sixteen albumen prints, is extremely rare. Only about four intact copies are known to exist. Recently one was offered by a dealer for $7,000. On the other hand, individual prints removed from *Street Life in London* trade regularly at prices between $150 and $700 each.

Frith is an interesting photographer because dealing with his work illustrates the problems faced by the collector in evaluating many nineteenth-century images. Frith probably ranks as the most prolific British landscape photographer in history. He took more than 60,000 photographs in a career dating from approximately 1856 to 1898. He achieved his initial fame on three expeditions to the Near East, including a voyage deep down the Nile, systematically photographing historic sites and landmarks. He subsequently photographed in Germany, Austria, Switzerland, Spain, and Portugal, as well as producing a large body of English landscapes and architectural studies. In addition, in 1858 he formed the firm of F. Frith & Co., extremely active in publishing photographic prints for illustrating books and for sale in stationers' shops. The Frith archives are, in fact, still in existence. Large blow-ups from Frith negatives currently are being marketed in England as wall decorations. Some obviously superior original Frith prints—particularly his early large-scale Egyptian views—have sold for

$1,200 to $1,300 or more. But the great majority of his original prints bring less than $200 and, in some cases, as little as $10 to $15. Frith's Durham Cathedral is shown on page 169.

Portraits were another major area of photographic activity from 1860 to 1880, and it is here that some of the highest prices in all of photography are being paid. Two photographers stand apart as the most significant of the nineteenth-century portrait artists: Julia Margaret Cameron (1815–1879) in England and Nadar (1820–1910) in France.

Cameron, wife of a distinguished British jurist and great-aunt of Virginia Woolf, took up photography at age forty-eight. She proceeded, with boundless enthusiasm and persistence, to cultivate friendships among the foremost literary, artistic, and scientific personalities of her day. In the course of time, such notables as Lord Tennyson, Charles Darwin, Thomas Carlyle, Holman Hunt, G.F. Watts, and Sir John Herschel succumbed to her charm and sat—sometimes for hours—for photographic portraits at her studio in Freshwater on the Isle of Wight. Besides portraiture, Cameron is known for her elaborate, costumed depictions of scenes from literary works, particularly Tennyson's *Idylls of the King,* and for her pictures of children. One of her prints, *The Turtle Doves,* is shown on page 161.

While an artistic master, Cameron was less than expert in the technical aspects of photography. In particular, she often was careless in the preparation of her wet plates. But to the Victorians, who loved her pictures, the rough-hewn nature of many of her images merely added to the charm. Her work remains highly prized today for its soft focus, rich tones, and romantic manner. Cameron herself fully realized the importance of her photographs. Many of them were published in large editions by Colnaghi's, the London art dealers. And Cameron personally put together a number of albums of her prints which she presented to members of her family and her close friends. One of these albums, presented to Herschel, was purchased at a London auction for $120,000 in 1974 by Samuel Wagstaff, Jr., a leading American collector. However, the album was then ruled a national treasure and denied an export license, pending a fund-raising drive to match Wagstaff's bid and keep the album in England. When the legal deadline elapsed and the fund-raising drive had fallen short, Wagstaff agreed to allow more time. Sufficient funds subsequently were raised, and the album now is owned by the National Portrait Gallery in London.

Dealers love Cameron's work because it brings high prices, is available in considerable quantity, and is of impeccable artistic merit. To many dealers and collectors, Cameron is *the* superstar of photography, from 1839 to present. The overall price range for individual Cameron prints is approximately $300 to $4,000. However, physical condition—and thus market value—can vary greatly from one Cameron print to another. A specific image might sell for $2,000 in excellent condition and for $300 or less in poor condition.

Nadar (professional name of Gaspard-Félix Tournachon) was, like Cameron, strong-willed, energetic, and extremely talented. In addition, he was an individual of unusually diverse interests—cartoonist, lithographer, writer, and balloonist as well as photographer. Nadar has been called the greatest photographer in French history. It is easy to understand why. He was the first photographer to work underground, taking pictures of the Paris catacombs and sewers with artificial light. He also was the first photographer to work in the sky—landscapes from a balloon. And his portraits of the artistic and intellectual elite of nineteenth-century Europe, including Liszt, Doré, George Sand, Berlioz, Delacroix, Verdi, and Balzac, are among the finest in the history of the art.

Nadar's portraits are of an entirely different nature than those of Cameron. While Cameron used a soft-focus lens to depict her sitters in a highly romanticized manner, Nadar's portraits are direct, precise, and piercing—typically posed against a plain backdrop, under the bright natural glow of a skylight. (See example on page 153.)

Most of the full-sized Nadar portraits now available to collectors are not original prints from his studio, but prints that were published in the *Galerie Contemporaine* magazine between 1876 and 1885. These *Galerie Contemporaine* prints generally sell in a price range of approximately $75 to $500 each. On the other hand, in a rare recent offering of original Nadars, seven salt and carbon prints were included in an April 1978 auction at Argus Ltd. in New York, bringing prices ranging from $850 to $1,600. At retail, original prints of some of Nadar's finest images have been offered for $4,000 and more.

In addition to Cameron and Nadar, leading portrait photographers of the wet-plate era include the following:

— Lewis Carroll (1832–1898), author of *Alice's Adventures in Wonderland* and an enthusiastic amateur photographer.
— Étienne Carjat (1828–1906), Nadar's rival as the most popular and influential French portrait photographer of the Second Empire.
— Antoine Samuel Adam-Salomon (1811–1881), a Parisian sculptor who took up photography in 1856. His poses are more elaborate and dramatic than those of Nadar and Carjat. Failing eyesight forced him to give up photography in the 1870s.

Original albumen prints by each of these three portrait artists are rare. In the case of Carjat and Adam-Salomon, as with Nadar, most of the prints coming onto the market today are from *Galerie Contemporaine*. They typically bring prices of approximately $50 to $300.

Lewis Carroll prints can be divided into two basic categories: original Carroll prints from the nineteenth century and recent reprints of eighteen images from his glass negatives. Carroll (whose real name was Charles Lutwidge Dodgson) remained an amateur and never sold his prints publicly—unlike Cameron, his contemporary. As a result, his original prints are scarce and can bring very high prices. Carroll is best known for his portraits of little girls, especially Alice Liddell, the original "Alice." In June 1977, at an auction in London, a notably erotic portrait of Alice dressed as a beggar girl sold for $8,500. That price is exceptional even for a Carroll. Most of his original prints sell in a range of approximately $1,000 to $4,000. The recent reprints, on the other hand, are being offered at an average price of about $1,000 each. A reproduction of Carroll's *The Terry Family* appears on page 163.

A third basic aesthetic movement, besides landscape and portrait photography, during the late 1850s and the 1860s was so-called "genre" or "art" photography. A number of photographers, particularly in England, took pictures with the conscious objective of imitating painting. Some of Cameron's portraits border on this style. But the three dominant personalities in the field of "painterly" photography are Oscar Gustave Rejlander (1813–1875), Henry Peach Robinson (1830–1901), and William Lake Price (1810–1896).

Rejlander was born in Sweden but lived in London most of his adult years. His 1857 photograph *The Two Ways of Life* caused a sensation in its time and helped make Rejlander one of the most popular and influential photographers of the high Victorian period. This picture, composed from more than thirty separate negatives, is an elaborate allegorical commentary on virtue versus sinfulness. While Rejlander abandoned "composite" printing (that is, printing a single image from several negatives) fairly quickly, he continued to take pictures—including portraits and figure studies for use by painters—in an artistic and romanticized manner throughout his career. (See example on page 159.) Original Rejlander prints trade actively in England, but are less well known in the United States. Price range for his work is approximately $100 to $1,500—although, as in the case of any important photographer, an exceptional work in fine condition can bring considerably more.

Robinson's work has held up much less well aesthetically than that of Rejlander. One reason is that his subject matter is more limited. While Rejlander moved on to new subject matter in the 1860s, Robinson never broke totally free from allegorical photography. Robinson is extremely important historically, but his work is less than compelling visually. Certainly a premier Robinson composite print would bring a very high price. But the few original prints which have come onto the market during the past few years have been lesser works and generally have sold for under $1,000.

In 1976, Photographic Collections Ltd. in London reprinted four of Robinson's most famous and elaborate composite works from the original negatives. These four reprints, together with separate prints from a number of the individual negatives (intended to help illustrate how Robinson made his composite prints), are being offered as a package for $6,000.

William Lake Price, perhaps the most influential of the three in their time, has fallen almost totally from sight. His work is not at all well known today—partly due to its rarity, partly due to limited public interest. One of the very few original Price prints to come onto the market recently, a fine 1855 still life of two game birds, was offered by a dealer for $2,000.

In the United States, three basic themes dominate the albumen prints of 1860 to 1880: portraits, photographs of the Civil War, and pictures of the exploration of the American West.

Mathew B. Brady (1823–1896) is the dominant portrait photographer of the late 1850s and early 1860s. He was succeeded as the most fashionable American portrait photographer by Napoleon Sarony, whose small-scale carte de visite portraits are discussed in Chapter 8.

Portrait photography in the United States never reached the same artistic apex that was achieved by Cameron and Nadar in Europe. Nonetheless, Brady was a very good portrait artist, and original prints of his best works are rare and costly. Recently, a dealer offered a 10- by 14-inch Brady group portrait of the Prince of Wales and his retinue, circa 1860, for $3,000.

In the public mind, Brady also stands as the foremost Civil War photographer. This is somewhat of a misconception. Rather than actively going out into the field, Brady was more a manager of other photographers. Even those Civil War photographs carrying the stamp of the Brady gallery generally are by photographers in his employ rather than by Brady himself.

No views of actual battle were taken during the Civil War. Wet-plate exposures were not yet fast enough to capture movement. Instead, photographers depicted the generals and foot soldiers, the sites of famous incidents, the preparations for battle and the aftermath.

Several hundred photographers took such pictures, including about twenty who worked at one time or another for Brady. From among this group, three of Brady's assistants are now considered to be the most significant in terms of both the high quality and substantial availability of their images: Timothy H. O'Sullivan (1840–1882), Alexander Gardner (1821–1882), and George N. Barnard (1819–1902).

O'Sullivan began his photographic career taking portraits in Brady's studio. He then worked in the field for Brady during the early years of the war, but left with Gardner in 1863 when the latter went into business for himself. In 1866, forty-five of O'Sullivan's images were published by Gardner in the landmark two-volume work, *Gardner's Photographic Sketch Book of the War.* It is primarily these prints, removed from that book, which are now available to collectors. Price range is approximately $100 to $1,000 per print.

One of the most powerful of O'Sullivan's Civil War photographs is *The Harvest of Death,* taken the morning after the Battle of Gettysburg and depicting bodies strewn across a bleak and forbidding field. Yet, for all the grimness of its subject matter, this image has a lyric beauty—in terms of its composition and soft, misty tones—which elevates it to far more than a specific picture about a specific battle. It becomes a moving statement about the senselessness of war in general, perhaps more so than any other photograph taken during the Civil War.

The original Gardner prints available today also are primarily those from the *Sketch Book.* Gardner included sixteen of his own images in that work. Prices tend to be a bit below those for prints of O'Sullivan's photographs.

Barnard is best known for his coverage of Sherman's march to Georgia. After the war, he published sixty-one of these images in a volume titled *Photographic Views of the Sherman Campaign. The Potter House,* from that book, is reproduced on page 165. So in Barnard's case, prints are available from two books—the Gardner *Sketch Book* and Barnard's own 1866 Sherman volume. Typical prices are $80 to $800 per print.

After the war, photographers became the eyes of an eager nation looking westward. Beginning in the late 1860s, the federal government sponsored a series of major geographic/geological expeditions, and in just about every case one or more photographers were assigned to go along. O'Sullivan, for instance, traveled with the 1867–1869 King survey of the Nebraska Territory, went to Panama with the 1870 Darien survey (searching for a possible canal site), and was attached to three separate Wheeler surveys between 1871 and 1874, exploring the Grand Canyon, Death Valley, and other areas west of the 100th meridian. After each Wheeler survey, fifty of his pictures were released to the public. These prints, plus others from his work with the

King, Darien, and Wheeler expeditions, are among the most expensive of all nineteenth-century western photographs, bringing prices of approximately $200 to $1,400 each.

Like so many of the pioneering photographers of the American West, O'Sullivan is a rather shadowy figure. Although we now know a reasonable amount about his life, for decades there was no known photograph to show us what he looked like—somewhat strange for a man who worked with cameras for more than two decades. The search for a photograph of O'Sullivan was long and controversial. It was once thought that O'Sullivan might be the individual depicted in a famous stereograph titled *Photographer at Pinogana,* but that possibility was finally ruled out when it was shown that, at the time *Photographer at Pinogana* was being taken in Panama, O'Sullivan himself was traveling in the western United States. Many collectors concluded that no picture of O'Sullivan would ever be found. Then in early 1977 collector/dealer George Rinhart, looking through the huge Alfred Waud collection of Civil War photographs he had just acquired, came across the O'Sullivan carte de visite portrait reproduced on page 157, taken in 1862 at the Metropolitan Gallery in Washington, D.C. So this unique image, uncovered among thousands of uncataloged works, emerges as one of the more significant photographic "finds" of the past few years.

Besides O'Sullivan, important photographers of the American West include Carleton E. Watkins (1829–1916), William Henry Jackson (1843–1942), Eadweard Muybridge (1830–1904), Andrew J. Russell (1830–1902), William Bell (active 1872), F. Jay Haynes (1853–1920), and John K. Hillers (1843–1925).

Watkins is best known for his early views of the Yosemite Valley. He was one of the first photographers to systematically depict a large, scenic area in its natural state, before the impact of man. His images generally are more "artistic" than those of the other leading western photographers. They tend to be taken from angles that are compositionally more complex and to stress the heroic nature of subject matter.

Jackson, on the other hand, is best known for his early photographs of Yellowstone. One of Jackson's most significant contributions to American history is his pivotal role in the establishment of Yellowstone as the nation's first national park in 1872. Nine of his Yellowstone views, distributed to every U.S. senator and representative, were instrumental in convincing Congress of the need to preserve the great natural beauty of the region. His *Calle de Guadeloupe,* taken in Mexico in the late 1870s, is reproduced on page 167.

There is an active trading market in early western photographs, especially by O'Sullivan, Watkins, and Jackson. Prices range from approximately $40 to $1,000—except, as noted, that O'Sullivan's work tends to bring somewhat more.

While western views are the dominant theme of American landscape photography between 1860 and 1880, there also were a number of photographers who documented the landmarks and topography of the eastern United States. The most important is Seneca Ray Stoddard (active 1870–1890), who photographed the Adirondack Mountain region of upstate New York. His prints sell in a price range of approximately $50 to $250 each.

Despite the fact that the wet plate represented a significant advance over previous methods for making negatives, it was by no means ideal. Only those individuals who were manually adept, and who were willing to work with smelly chemicals, could expect to be consistently successful in the making of negatives.

The *gelatin dry-plate* glass negative, introduced in 1880, resolved this problem. Dry plates were manufactured commercially in a variety of sizes and were capable of maintaining sensitivity to light over long storage periods.

Dry plates were followed nine years later by the first *celluloid roll film,* forerunner of today's roll films and a great stimulus to amateur photography.

Meanwhile, new types of prints—more resistant to fading than albumen prints—were being introduced. The many types of prints of the late nineteenth century can be divided into two basic categories: (1) those which produced original photographic prints on light-sensitive paper and (2) those "photomechanical" systems which produced high-quality photographic reproductions, printed on a press with ink.

Of the processes for making "original" prints, *platinum prints,* also called platinotypes, (1880– c. 1930) are regarded as the highest in technical quality. Platinum prints were produced with light-sensitive iron salts, through a process whereby precipitated platinum produced the final image. A platinum print can be distinguished by its delicate gray tones and the sense that the image is embedded deep in the paper fiber, rather than on the surface of the paper. There is no surface gloss whatsoever. This process was used extensively by Peter Henry Emerson and Frederick Evans, among many others, and after the turn of the century by Alfred Stieglitz, Edward Steichen, and other members of the Photo-Secessionist movement. A good platinum print tends to command a premium price because of the superiority of the process.

Gum bichromates (1884– c. 1920) were an important medium for "art" photographs, including many early Steichens and works by Heinrich Kühn in Vienna. This process generally was used to produce romantic soft-focus prints on heavy drawing paper. Sometimes pigments were employed to create subtle tints. Often, these works resemble watercolors.

Cyanotypes (1885–1910) are blue-toned photographs using a process related to the architectural blueprint. Cyanotypes are relatively rare; among the few examples are Charles Lummis's portraits of American Indians.

Carbon prints (1866–1900) were advertised as a "permanent" method for making photographic prints and were employed by Thomas Annan in printing the second edition of his photographic book *Old Closes and Streets of Glasgow* and by Jessie Bertram in the reprinting of Hill and Adamson photographs from the original negatives. Carbon prints could be made in three different colors: black, sepia, and purple-brown.

Emulsion papers (1888–1910) were mass produced and were used primarily by amateur photographers rather than professionals. So, though in great popularity around the turn of the century, they are of limited concern to the photography collector. The big drawback of early emulsion prints is that, like salt and albumen prints before them, they are extremely vulnerable to fading. This most commonly shows up, in the case of an emulsion print, as silver-toned blotches.

Then there were three major types of high-quality photographic reproductions.

Photogravures, also known simply as gravures (1879–present), were the most widely used and expensive of the three. For instance, all of Emerson's later illustrated books contain gravures, and many Edward Curtis photographs of American Indians were distributed in gravure form. A photogravure is printed with an etched copper plate and can be distinguished by its rich tones and total lack of surface gloss. The process is still popular today.

Collotypes (1865–1910) were printed with a glass plate. Their primary use was in illustrated books, including John Thomson's *Illustrations of China and Its People* and certain editions of the Eadweard Muybridge classic, *Animal Locomotion*. Impressions were limited to about 1,500 to 2,000 before the plate deteriorated. Collotypes are very difficult to distinguish from original photographic prints.

Woodburytypes (1875–c. 1900) also were used mainly for book illustrations, including Thomson's *Street Life in London* and many of the Nadar and Carjat prints from *Galerie Contemporaine*. They are similar in appearance to carbon prints and often have a reddish tint. The printing plate is metal.

The most important photographic movement of the late nineteenth century is British naturalism. The naturalists were led by Peter Henry Emerson (1856–1936), who contended that the photographer's objective should be to imitate the effects of nature. This view stood in pointed opposition to the ornate, contrived pictures of Rejlander and Robinson, whose work still was extremely popular.

A physician by training, Emerson took up photography exclusively from 1885 and also became an outspoken theorist, writer, and lecturer on photographic aesthetics. He advocated the use of a soft-focus lens, believing the camera should perceive no more detail than the human eye was capable of perceiving. His own pictures depict the marshes and simple country life of the Norfolk and Suffolk broads in eastern England. These works were published in a series of books, the most important being the first, *Life and Landscape on the Norfolk Broads*. Issued in 1886, *Life and Landscape* contains forty original platinum prints. Prints removed from that book typically sell in a price range of $300 to $2,500 each. One of these works, *The Gladdon-Cutter's Return*, is reproduced on page 171. His subsequent books all contain photogravures, which he pulled by hand. Approximate price range for the gravures is $25 to $400.

Emerson renounced his views in 1890, with the publication of *The Death of Naturalistic Photography*. But many of his followers remained faithful to his initial ideals and continued to espouse photographic naturalism.

Frank Meadow Sutcliffe (1853–1941), best known for his photographs in and around Whitby, England, is another of the leading naturalists. Sutcliffe's most famous photograph, *The Water Rats,* shows a group of nude young boys on two rowboats, one half-sunk. Although *The Water Rats* now seems quite innocent, it was widely viewed as scandalous in its time. Recently, an original platinum print of that work sold at auction in London for $850. Shortly thereafter, an original albumen print sold for $350. Other original Sutcliffe prints generally trade in a price range of approximately $50 to $600.

A third important photographer whose work generally is associated with British naturalism is G. Christopher Davies (dates unknown). Davies is not mentioned in any of the leading photographic history books, and it is only recently that collector interest in his work has blossomed. He lived in the same area as Emerson and is regarded as a forerunner of Emerson and possibly an influence on him. Davies's earliest published photographs of the Norfolk Broads date to 1883. The Davies prints which come onto the market are primarily photogravures and generally sell for somewhat under $100 each.

In the United States, the final two decades of the nineteenth century saw major advances in photography both as a documentary tool and as a fine art. Three photographers from this period stand out: Eadweard Muybridge (1830–1904), whose stop-action depictions of animals in motion are one of the great landmarks of photographic history; Thomas Eakins (1844–1916), renowned for his portraits and nudes; and Edward S. Curtis (1868–1952), who embarked in 1896 on one of the most monumental of all photographic projects, the complete visual recording of the Indian tribes of North America.

Muybridge certainly has to be ranked as one of the most accomplished and inventive photographers of any nation. As indicated earlier, he was one of the leading photographers of the American West. His western views were taken from approximately 1868 to 1873 and include some of the finest early photographs of Yosemite. He also took the first photographs of Alaska after its acquisition by the United States. And in 1875–1876 he went to the west coast of Central America, photographing Panamanian ruins and life in Indian villages.

It was in 1872, however, that Muybridge began his most significant and lengthy project: sequential pictures depicting various animals in motion. Muybridge initially undertook this project at the instigation of Leland Stanford, a former governor of California and prominent horseman. Stanford wanted to prove that a horse, while running, at some point has all four feet off the ground. He engaged Muybridge to try to prove this point with a camera.

Muybridge's first pictures were inconclusive, partly because of the slow exposures of his wet-plate negatives. By 1877, however, Muybridge had devised a more sophisticated photographic system employing dry plates and electrically controlled shutters, and with this system he established clearly that all four feet of a horse are off the ground at one phase of a gallop. These early pictures won almost immediate acclaim and were reprinted in publications throughout the world.

By 1879, Muybridge was taking photographs of hogs, dogs, oxen, bulls, and seagulls, in addition to horses, using a series of twenty-four cameras with wires attached which electrically triggered the shutters when contacted by the moving animal. He published most of this early work in 1881, in an illustrated book titled *The Attitudes of Animals in Motion*.

His most comprehensive studies were undertaken between 1883 and 1885, under the sponsorship of the University of Pennsylvania. The results of these efforts were published in 1887 in the now classic eleven-volume work, *Animal Locomotion*, containing 781 separate studies of the movements of a wide variety of animals, including humans. A detail from one of these studies, showing two men wrestling, is reproduced on page 173. The eleven volumes were offered at $600 for the set, a price only thirty-seven libraries and other institutions could afford. However, specific plates were purchased by the tens of thousands, primarily by artists and scientists, at a price of 100 plates for $100.

Individual plates from *Animal Locomotion* now trade extremely actively, at prices of about $20 to $800 each. Complete eleven-volume sets, as would be expected, are extremely rare. Recently a dealer offered one of these sets at $90,000, and subsequently one sold at auction for $60,000.

Eakins, in addition to being one of America's foremost realist painters and finest portrait photographers, had a deep personal interest in Muybridge's photographic studies. He wrote to Muybridge in 1879, suggesting that the latter superimpose a scale of measurement over the image during printing. In addition, when Muybridge was at the University of Pennsylvania, Eakins served on the university committee which supervised Muybridge's work.

However, Eakins questioned Muybridge's use of a battery of cameras instead of a single camera. The single-camera approach had been used in France by Étienne Jules Marey (1830–1904), with the multiple images of the animal in motion overlapping on a single picture—much in the manner of Marcel Duchamp's painting, *Nude Descending a Staircase,* some thirty years later. Eakins himself ended up experimenting with the photographic depiction of motion, and his works are difficult to distinguish from those of Marey.

Original Eakins prints—whether his motion studies, portraits, or nudes—are extremely rare. In November 1977, in an unusual offering of twenty-two original Eakins prints at Sotheby Parke Bernet in New York, prices ranged up to $11,000, for a classically posed study of three female nudes. Seldom do prices for Eakins prints fall below $3,000 or $4,000.

Although the career of Edward Curtis, from 1896 into the 1940s, falls mainly into the twentieth century, he generally is associated with the nineteenth century because of his subject matter and style.

There actually are a number of late-nineteenth-century photographers known for their pictures of American Indians. Just as there was a wave of photographers depicting the western landscape beginning in the 1860s, numerous photographers turned their attention to the "vanishing race"—the Indian—in the 1890s. In addition to Curtis, important photographers in this movement include Karl Moon (1878–1948), Clark Vroman (1856–1916), F. A. Rinehart (1861–1928), Charles Lummis (dates unknown), and Laton Huffman (d. 1931). Price range for their work is approximately $150 to $1,200 per print.

But of this group, Curtis clearly made the most important contribution. He set out, in 1896, to record with photographs all available information about the customs, ceremonies, and daily life of Indian tribes west of the Mississippi River, from Alaska to New Mexico. Thirty-four years later, his project finally complete, he had produced more than 40,000 negatives, nearly all glass plates. The finest of these images are reproduced in the twenty-volume work titled *The North American Indian,* which was published from 1907 through 1930. A complete twenty-volume set sold at auction for $60,000 in May 1976. Individual photogravures removed from these books generally sell for between $50 and $300 each, while original Curtis prints typically sell for between $200 and $1,500.

As the nineteenth century drew to a close, a new star had already risen on the photography horizon: Alfred Stieglitz. Stieglitz was destined to become the most influential of all twentieth-century photographers. We shall pick up on that story in Chapter 10.

Chapter 7

Stereographs

Two major areas of nineteenth-century photography still open to low-budget collectors are stereographs (sometimes called stereo views) and cartes de visite. This chapter discusses the former, and Chapter 8, the latter.

Stereographs are double-picture photographs which, when viewed through a stereoscope, create an illusion of depth. This effect, achieved because each image depicts a scene from a slightly different angle (as do our eyes), was discovered by Sir Charles Wheatstone before the invention of photography, but was seldom practiced until 1851, when stereographs were displayed at the Great Exhibition of the World's Industry in London.

Viewing stereographs was highly fashionable from the early 1850s through the 1870s, fell from favor, and then experienced a massive revival beginning in about 1887 and continuing into the early 1930s. During the two major "in" periods, virtually every middle-class family in England, France, and the United States had its collection of stereographs, mainly in card form, as well as the equipment to view these works. "No home without a stereograph" was the slogan of the London Stereoscopic Company.

Because millions of different stereoscopic views were published to satisfy public demand, stereographs offer one of the most comprehensive documentations available of nineteenth-century life and events. Subject matter—so widely varied— includes royalty, presidents, famous actors and actresses, circus performers, peoples of distant lands, war pictures, world landmarks, expeditions, well-known buildings, city street scenes, cemeteries, historic events, Biblical allegories, expositions and fairs, warships, trains, great disasters, so-called "ethnic" pictures (primarily blacks, Indians, Mormons, and Shakers), still lifes, humorous pictures, and nudes. A stereoscopic portrait of Abraham Lincoln at Antietam is reproduced on page 155.

Stereographs cut across lines in terms of process used: daguerreotype, ambrotype, glass, calotype, albumen print, collotype, and lithographic print. London dealer Howard Ricketts notes that collectors will find an extensive body of stereoscopic daguerreotypes from which to choose (although nobody has any idea just how many were made or have survived), fewer stereoscopic ambrotypes, and a tremendous number of stereoscopic cards.

Stereoscopic daguerreotypes, which for the most part represent the upper end of the price scale, typically sell for $50 to $500 or more. The record auction price for a stereograph of any type is $1,600, paid in May 1976 for a stereoscopic daguerreotype portrait by Antoine Claudet of his son Francis George Claudet. That work drew a high price for three primary reasons. First, Antoine Claudet is one of the most important early British photographers, and his stereoscopic daguerreotypes typically carry premium market values. Second, from an aesthetic standpoint the work is bold and striking. The photographer's son is standing with his arms folded across his chest, staring intently into the camera and totally free from the stiffness associated with most daguerreotype portraits. Third, the work is of a highly personal nature. Early pictures of photographers and members of their immediate families seldom were released to the public and, therefore, are extremely rare today. Especially unusual in this case is the fact that Francis George is nude from the waist up—a very "private" type of photograph for its time even though, by today's standards, there is nothing at all immodest about such a pose.

On the other hand, routine card stereographs tend to be inexpensive and are available in great quantity. Auction houses like Christie's South Kensington and Sotheby's Belgravia in London and Swann Galleries in New York frequently offer 100 to 150 card stereographs per lot, and the average price seldom goes much above $1 per card. In some cases, the average price might even work out to as little as 15¢ to 20¢. However, Ricketts warns that, when dealing with masses of run-of-the-mill stereographs, a collector often must sort through as many as 200 cards to find just one which is at all unusual or interesting.

Between these two price extremes—15¢ to $1,600—there are substantial quantities of stereographs at nearly all price levels, with the biggest market activity in card stereographs costing between $2 and $30.

The pricing of card stereographs is tricky because it involves so many variables: the identity of the publisher, the identity of the photographer (if known), subject matter, the year when the photograph was taken, the year when the specific card in question was printed, type of photographic print, rarity, and condition. William C. Darrah, author of two excellent books on stereographs (see Bibliography), has noted that cards issued before 1868 tend to be valued primarily on the basis of photographer or publisher, with subject matter secondary. For later cards, these factors tend to reverse; subject matter usually becomes primary in determining market value.

American Stereographs

Commercially produced stereographs were introduced to the U.S. market by William and Frederick Langenheim in 1854 and enjoyed immense popularity after the invention of the hand-held stereoscope by Oliver Wendell Holmes in 1859. The Langenheim brothers, whose studio was located in Philadelphia, are best known for their early glass stereographs, in which the image is printed in a thin egg albumen coating on the glass surface. Glass stereographs were widely produced in the United States until about 1862 and endured much longer in Europe, particularly in France.

Because these works are so vulnerable to breakage, some dealers and auction houses prefer not to deal in them. In September 1975, however, four hand-tinted glass stereo views of Niagara Falls, by Frederick Langenheim, did come up for sale at auction in New York and brought a combined price of $275.

The Langenheim brothers also are among the most important early publishers of stereo cards, both under their own names and under the name American Stereoscopic Company. Their card stereographs are relatively rare and sell at prices from a few dollars each on up. Recently, an early Langenheim picture of the U.S. capitol, with the dome under construction, was offered at auction. The work, in good but not excellent condition, brought $45—a substantial price for a card stereograph.

Other leading American publishers of stereographs during the 1850s included New York Stereoscopic Company, D. Appleton Company, and Stacy of New York. The work of each of these companies is today rare, although somewhat less so in the case of New York Stereoscopic than the other two.

While these very early stereo views—particularly those of the Langenheims—were popular in their time, it was left to two other publishers to produce card stereographs on a truly massive scale. These two companies were E. Anthony (also called E. & H. T. Anthony), active from 1859 to 1880, and Kilburn Brothers (also called B. W. Kilburn), active from 1865 until after the turn of the century. There is now an extensive market in the works of both of these publishers, with a wide variety of material available at various price levels.

The many views published, and republished, by Anthony illustrate the problems faced by collectors in determining the value of a specific work. The earliest Anthonys were issued in 1859, with negative number one, titled *Group of Vessels Under Sail,* photographed in July of that year. (The number of each view generally is printed on the mount or in the picture itself.) The negatives ran, with some gaps in sequence, to about 600, at which point the firm changed its name to E. & H. T. Anthony & Co. The firm continued to issue additional views under its new name, to an eventual total of about 11,000. This primary series comprises the basic views offered by the firm throughout its history.

In addition, the firm published somewhat over twenty specialized sets of views, with anywhere from 10 to 200 views per set. Typically, each of these sets has a unified pictorial theme, such as *Hills and Dales of New England* or *A Visit to Central Park in the Summer of 1863*. Most of these sets also begin with the number one. So a low number does not in any way guarantee that the card is a valuable early edition—both because new editions of views starting with low numbers were issued throughout the firm's history and because even many of the original low-number negatives continued to be printed in later years.

Other clues must therefore be studied to determine the approximate issue date of a specific card. When it entered the stereograph business in 1859, the Anthony firm at first pasted a descriptive label, approximately $2\frac{1}{2}$ inches by 6 inches, on the back of each card. After moving its quarters in 1860, the firm began pasting smaller labels, about $1\frac{1}{2}$ inches by 6 inches, on the back. The very earliest cards, then, all have the larger label.

Another key indication of issue date is the type of cardboard or paper used. In the case of Anthony, the firm initially attached the stereoscopic photographs to a cream-colored mount. In 1860, it changed to a better grade of paper, more nectarine in hue. Within another year, the firm switched over to the yellow mount which is now so familiar to collectors. Subsequently, Anthony used still other colors, including orange, red, and green.

The size and shape of the card also are important factors in determining approximate issue date. As a general rule, any card with square corners—regardless of publisher—probably dates to 1868 or earlier. Subsequently, the corners of most cards were rounded to reduce damage. These early cards are approximately $3\frac{1}{2}$ inches by 7 inches in size. Beginning in 1873, a somewhat larger card—called a "cabinet," "artistic," or "deluxe" card and either 4 inches by 7 inches or $4\frac{1}{2}$ inches by 7 inches in size—also was offered, and remained popular until about 1885. Furthermore, the curved or "warped" card was devised in 1879 to heighten the illusion of depth. By 1893, the curved card was dominant.

The point, then, is that it is the card, rather than the picture, which must be studied to determine which cards are the earliest, and therefore in most cases the rarest and most valuable. An early Anthony stereo view, titled *Floating Baths at New York Harbor* and using the cream-colored mount issued prior to 1860, recently was offered by a dealer for $20. On the other hand, later prints of Anthony stereographs— including, perhaps, a later print of that same view—typically bring prices between about $2 and $10 each, depending on subject matter, condition, and relative rarity.

Among the other important American publishers of the 1860s and 1870s are J. Gurney, F. G. Weller, William H. Jackson, Carelton Watkins, D. Barnum, W. M. Chase, James Cremer, and Ropes and Co. The work of each of these publishers, plus that of hundreds of more localized publishers from the same period, remains available in the market, with varying degrees of rarity.

Some of these publishers—such as Jackson and Watkins—were photographers who took their own pictures. Others were businessmen who employed photographers on their staffs or purchased the negatives of free-lance photographers.

During the second golden age of stereography in America, around the turn of the century, two mass-distribution publishers dominated: Underwood & Underwood and Keystone View Company. Both employed door-to-door sales forces—like the marketing of encyclopedias in our own time—and produced massive quantities of stereographs. So collectors tend to be highly selective in terms of what they buy, focusing on works of superior photographic and technical quality or unusual historic interest.

Underwood & Underwood pioneered the concept of selling "boxed sets" of stereographs, and today these sets—when complete and in good condition—can be among the most interesting collector's items from this later period of stereography. For instance, a boxed set of eighteen Underwood & Underwood views of the Grand Canyon, in excellent condition, recently was offered by a dealer for $30.

Other important American publishers during the great revival of stereography include H. C. White, Stereo Travel Company, Griffith and Griffith, and William K. Rau.

Stereographs tend to be interesting as much from a historic viewpoint as on aesthetic grounds. Many of the great epic stories of our nation can be brought to life through a sampling of stereographs, including the history of the American presidency, the Civil War, and the opening of the American West.

Nearly every president since Lincoln has sat before a twin-lens stereoscopic camera to have his picture taken. Recently a collector could have purchased the following card stereographs, which came up for sale through auction houses or dealers: Abraham Lincoln standing in semiprofile, $325; Ulysses Grant at "Tip Top House," $15; Grover Cleveland in a horse-drawn carriage on Pennsylvania Avenue, $8; William McKinley having his picture taken by a miner's daughter in Arizona, $5; Theodore Roosevelt speaking at Tipton, Indiana, $4.50; William Howard Taft at the opening of the Gunnison Tunnel in Colorado, $5; Woodrow Wilson with Clemenceau and Lloyd George at Versailles, $6; William Harding feeding a bear at Yellowstone, $6; Calvin Coolidge with his Cabinet, $8; Franklin D. Roosevelt at his desk, $20; and Dwight Eisenhower seated at a round table with an unidentified woman, $60.

While the Lincoln price is the highest, perhaps even more striking is the $60 paid at auction for the Eisenhower stereograph. But since stereoscopic photography is no longer widely practiced, portraits of more recent presidents tend to become increasingly rare.

Fine Civil War pictures also are extremely popular with many collectors. An outstanding Civil War view, such as Alexander Gardner's *A Confederate Sharp-Shooter, who has been killed by a shell at Battle of Gettysburg,* might sell for $40 or more. Other, less rare Civil War stereographs are available for under $10. One dealer recently offered various Anthony and Kilburn cards at prices from $4 to $24—the highest price being for a view, taken by photographer Timothy O'Sullivan and published by Anthony, titled *Pontoon Bridge at Mrs. Nelson's.*

O'Sullivan also was one of the leading photographers of the exploration of the American West, and his stereo views are among the most expensive in that category, sometimes drawing prices of $30 to $40 or more. As discussed in Chapter 6, O'Sullivan was the official photographer on the government-sponsored Wheeler surveys. In that role, he took a wealth of pictures, many stereoscopic, of canyons, rivers, waterfalls, Indians, old Spanish churches, and other subjects. Other photographers, such as Carleton E. Watkins and Eadweard Muybridge, specialized in pictures of early California, particularly San Francisco and Yosemite. Watkins's output includes some 2,000 stereo views of Yosemite alone.

The early railroads are still another western subject which is extremely popular with collectors. Perhaps best known are the "official" pictures of the Union Pacific west of Omaha, taken by Andrew J. Russell and William Henry Jackson. Other railroads also hired photographers to depict their trains and trestles and the views along their tracks. Alfred A. Hart served as official photographer for the Central Pacific Railroad, and the Northern Pacific engaged F. Jay Haynes. In addition, other photographers, such as Savage & Ottinger of Salt Lake City, produced stereo views without specific railroad sponsorship. Today, early stereo views of western railroads represent one of the most active sectors of the American stereograph market, at prices between about $5 and $50 per card.

British Stereographs

The stereograph actually was a British invention, and the major initial improvements were pioneered there. As early as 1858—a year before the Anthony firm was founded in New York—the London Stereoscopic Company advertised a stock of more than 100,000 views. But public demand for stereographs, while huge, proved to be more short-lived in England than in the United States. The great boom period began to fade after 1862, with the rise of the carte de visite. Then, in the second golden era of the stereograph around the turn of the century, England clearly played a secondary role to the United States.

Nonetheless, British stereographs offer many opportunities for collecting. This is particularly true of stereoscopic daguerreotypes, produced primarily in England and France from approximately 1851 to 1854. The stereoscopic daguerreotype never caught on in the United States.

Almost all the leading London daguerreotypists—Antoine Claudet, Richard Beard, Edwin Mayall, William Kilburn, and T. R. Williams—began taking stereoscopic daguerreotypes after Queen Victoria, a great devotee of photography, expressed an enthusiastic interest in stereography in 1851. At first, these photographers concentrated primarily on interior views of the Crystal Palace, where the Great Exhibition was being held. But Claudet, Williams, and Kilburn quickly branched out to the taking of stereoscopic portraits—mostly of members of the upper middle class—in their commercial studios. Today, half a dozen or more of these early portraits will generally be included in any major London photography auction. Williams also began taking fine still lifes, and other photographers turned to the depiction of statuary, nudes, and other subject matter. Recently, an excellent Williams still life of a stuffed parrot, large vase, and various other objects, arranged against a draped backdrop, sold at auction in London for nearly $600.

In 1854, the London Stereoscopic Company—in its time the greatest publisher of card stereographs in the world—was founded, and public interest in stereoscopic daguerreotypes fell off rapidly. While British card stereographs cover a wide range of subject matter, there is a particularly huge number of scenic views. Nearly every home in England had its collection of views of Egypt, the Alps, Palestine, the British countryside, and other lands around the world. Some early scenic cards, from the 1850s, are today prized as collector's items. But later cards, from the 1860s on, tend to be poorer in quality and available in huge quantities and are, therefore, often of lesser collector interest.

As in the United States, certain subjects are more in demand than others. Early pictures of steamships are among the most popular stereo views. These works are relatively rare on both sides of the Atlantic and generally command top prices. One of the few recent auction offerings of such views occurred in October 1977, when Christie's sold nine card stereographs, including seven published by the London Stereoscopic Company, of the Great Eastern. These cards brought a combined price of $360, or just over $50 each.

Most stereograph collectors own several antique stereoscopes, to view their stereographs three-dimensionally.

In addition, many collectors spend $13 a year to join the National Stereoscopic Association, R.D. 1, Box 426A, Fremont, New Hampshire 03044. That group's magazine, issued every other month to members, is filled with dealer ads for card stereographs, mostly in the $1 to $25 price range, and contains articles of interest to collectors.

Chapter 8

Cartes de Visite

In the mid-1860s, cartes de visite (small "visiting card" portraits) replaced stereographs as the most popular form of photograph for the broad public. Stereographs reached an almost manic peak in 1862, as did cartes de visite three to four years later, when an estimated 300 million to 400 million cartes were being sold annually in England alone. Cartes de visite continued to be produced—in England, on the Continent, in the United States, and in many other areas of the world—until about 1880.

Like stereographs, cartes de visite offer a wealth of opportunities for the budget-conscious collector.

Cartes de visite were produced in a standard size of a $3\frac{1}{2}$- by $2\frac{1}{4}$-inch photograph mounted on a 4- by $2\frac{1}{2}$-inch card. Two examples are reproduced on page 157. Equally important were the mass-production techniques behind the concept. Special multi-lens cameras were developed which could shoot eight, ten, or twelve different poses in rapid succession, all on the same wet-plate negative. A single print from this negative could then be cut into eight or more separate portraits, with the cutting done by unskilled labor. In this way, the production of the cameraman and printer was increased eightfold or more.

Credit for the carte de visite generally is given to André Adolphe Disdéri (1819–1890), who patented the concept in France in 1854. However, the carte didn't win much public acceptance until five years later, when portraits of Napoleon III, taken by Disdéri, were distributed throughout France to glorify the emperor as he led his troops into battle in Italy. Within weeks, hundreds of thousands of other Frenchmen wanted to have their carte portraits taken.

In England, the fad didn't take hold until the next year, when Edwin Mayall, one of the foremost daguerreotypists, published a Royal Album consisting of fourteen carte de visite portraits of Queen Victoria and her family. That album was an immediate success, and the English, like the French, began flocking to photography studios for carte de visite portraits.

The leading American exponent of the carte de visite was Napoleon Sarony (1821–1896), successor to Brady in the late 1860s as the most fashionable portrait photographer in the United States. By all accounts, Sarony was a delightful eccentric and raconteur. His portraits of theatrical and literary personalities, including Sarah

Bernhardt, Edwin Booth, and Oscar Wilde, are especially well known and are readily available to collectors.

Initially, cartes de visite were used largely in place of printed visiting cards, but soon it became extremely popular to collect cartes of celebrities and friends. Few Victorian parlors were without a carte de visite album containing pictures of the owners of the album, their relatives, and their friends, plus, in later years, pictures of actors, circus performers, freaks, and other more colorful types. Entire albums still come up for sale at auction and through photography dealers.

Although the carte format was employed primarily for portraits, enterprising publishers also issued carte-sized pictures of historic events, world landmarks, city street scenes, building interiors, trains, animals, flower still lifes, and other subjects.

The market value of a carte de visite depends on the identity of the subject, rarity, historical interest, approximate date of issue, identity of the photographer, pictorial quality, and condition.

Many cartes de visite are essentially worthless. This is especially true of routine, anonymous portraits, which generally sell for only a few cents each.

To have much market value, a carte generally must meet any one of three tests:

1. The subject must be historically important. Abraham Lincoln and James Buchanan are classic examples, and their carte portraits, when available, often command the highest prices. Carte portraits of Lord Tennyson, Kit Carson, Mark Twain, and other nineteenth-century notables also can be quite valuable.

2. The carte must be unusual or historically important in some other way. For instance, an extremely rare and emotionally painful carte de visite album containing portraits of seventy-two inmates of a nineteenth-century British insane asylum sold at auction for $2,300 in June 1976.

3. The photograph on the carte must be a fine nineteenth-century image which is the work of an important photographer and is valuable in any size print. Julia Margaret Cameron and Oscar Gustav Rejlander are prime examples of leading photographers who printed many of their images in carte de visite format. A charming Rejlander "art" picture of a young child, titled *After Raphael's Sistine Madonna* and printed as a carte, sold recently for $60. Cameron cartes sometimes sell for $10 to $50, far below the prices for her larger prints of the same images.

In the United States, cartes involving two related subjects bring some of the highest prices: Lincoln and the Civil War. In October 1977, actor Dustin Hoffman paid $700 at auction for an early, rare, and aesthetically powerful Lincoln carte. This particular carte, published by E. & H. T. Anthony and believed to have been photographed by Mathew Brady, has a federal revenue stamp affixed to the back, providing a clear indication of its early date. To help raise funds for the war, the government charged a small tax on all cartes de visite and stereographs sold between September 1, 1864, and August 1, 1866. Therefore, any carte or stereograph carrying a revenue stamp must have been sold during that twenty-three month period. On the other hand, some Lincoln portraits were reissued as cartes well after his death, and these later works tend to be worth much less than early prints.

The past few years have seen an amazing outpouring of historically important cartes from the Civil War period.

At a New York auction in September 1975, two exceptional albums compiled during the war by Representative Nehemiah Perry of New Jersey were offered for sale. These albums contain 390 cartes, including a Lincoln, a very rare Andrew Johnson, and carte portraits of virtually all leading Union officers and Union senators and representatives. Nearly half the cartes, including the Lincoln, are signed by the subject. The two albums brought a combined price of $2,800—quite reasonable, it would seem, considering their tremendous historic significance.

Two years later, at another New York auction, a Civil War album containing 1,120 cartes was offered for sale. The treasures in this album include eighteen portraits of various U.S. presidents, many from life; eighty-four Union officers; sixty-six Confederate officers; one hundred and thirty Union statesmen and authors; eleven Confederate statesmen; and forty-one actors and actresses. However, this album failed to reach the "reserve," or minimum price, specified by the owner—probably about $6,000—and was taken off the market without being sold.

More recently, an album containing sixty-six cartes, including Lincoln, Jefferson Davis, and Harriet Beecher Stowe as well as many prominent European writers and artists, was offered for sale in London. It brought $270.

And in April 1978 an album containing 191 Mathew Brady carte de visite portraits, of Lincoln, James Buchanan, Andrew Jackson, James K. Polk, Franklin Pierce, Jefferson Davis, and other prominent Americans of the mid-nineteenth century, was offered for sale in New York. This album, in near-mint condition and bearing Brady's initials on the cover, brought $2,200.

In addition, less spectacular albums have been coming onto the market fairly regularly. For instance, an album containing carte portraits of thirty-three members of the U.S. Congress during the 1860s and early 1870s sold for $300 in April 1977.

In England, there is a highly active market for carte portraits of Queen Victoria, Prince Albert, and other members of the royal family. However, because cartes of British royalty were produced in great quantity, they are not especially rare or expensive.

It is the more "artistic" cartes, by photographers like Rejlander, Cameron, and Lewis Carroll—as well as by French photographers like Nadar and Étienne Carjat—which generally draw the highest prices. For instance, a fine Nadar portrait, printed in carte format, might bring a price of between $10 and $100, depending on the subject, quality, and physical condition.

In 1867, with demand for carte de visite portraits waning, photographers began turning to the cabinet portrait in hopes of generating new business. The cabinet portrait is somewhat larger than the carte de visite, measuring $5\frac{1}{4}$ inches by 4 inches on a mount $6\frac{1}{2}$ inches by $4\frac{1}{4}$ inches. This was followed over the next decade by a series of other sizes: Victoria, promenade, boudoir, imperial, and panel.

The cabinet portrait, most important of the formats which followed the carte de visite, was an especially popular medium for mass distributing pictures of famous actors and actresses, and these pictures are regularly available to collectors today—at prices which generally are moderately higher than those for cartes de visite.

Chapter 9

The High-Priced Market in Nineteenth-Century Illustrated Books

Many of the finest nineteenth-century photographs were published in books. The earliest of these volumes, *The Pencil of Nature*, was issued between 1844 and 1846 and contains twenty-four calotype prints by William Henry Fox Talbot. It has been estimated that, over the next seventy years, more than 3,000 photographically illustrated books were published, either containing original photographic prints mounted on the pages or containing high-quality photographic reproductions, such as photogravures or Woodburytypes (see Chapter 7).

Today, photographically illustrated books in good condition are important collector's items. This is one of the most sophisticated segments of the photography market, with collectors and dealers paying substantial sums to acquire these works.

Photographic books typically were produced in limited editions, with a press run of anywhere from a dozen to several hundred copies. Peter Henry Emerson, one of the masters of the photographically illustrated book, is a case in point. Between 1886 and 1895, Emerson issued eight different volumes containing his photographs, including *Life and Landscape on the Norfolk Broads,* his finest work. Emerson originally planned to issue 100 deluxe and 750 ordinary copies of *Life and Landscape,* but actually published only 25 deluxe and 175 ordinary due to low demand.

Life and Landscape sometimes is cited as being a "small oblong folio." This refers to the size of the printed book (not the photographs mounted inside the book). Illustrated books were published in a number of fairly standard sizes, as follows:

Folio	11 by 15 inches
Quarto (abbreviated as 4to)	9½ by 12 inches
Octavo (8vo)	6 by 9 inches
Duodecimo or twelvemo (12mo)	5 by 7½ inches

These sizes are approximate. The term *folio,* in particular, is used to describe any large-dimension illustrated book.

Very few of these illustrated books have come down to us in perfect condition. Often the pages or photographs are discolored, and it is extremely rare for the binding to be in perfect condition. This is only natural, considering that wear and tear occurs every time a book is opened to view the pictures inside.

Sometimes the books have been rebound, and this creates perils of its own. One time I was visiting with a dealer when a four-volume set of John Thomson's *Illustrations of China and Its People,* published in 1873–1874, arrived at the dealer's gallery. This set was being offered for consignment by a collector. *Illustrations of China and Its People,* one of the better-known nineteenth-century illustrated works, contains 218 collotype prints of photographs taken by Thomson during the 1860s. A four-volume set in good condition might sell for approximately $3,000. In this case the four volumes had been rebound, which the dealer knew before the books arrived. That in itself would detract from market value. But on viewing the works, the dealer also discovered that the rebinding was so inept that the title pages for volumes two and three had been switched and were therefore bound into the wrong volumes and that the original gold leaf on the outer edge of the books had been trimmed off. Furthermore, on comparing these four volumes with another set which the dealer already owned, it was quite apparent that the quality of the prints in the former was inferior. The pictures had a washed-out look, due either to a poor job of original printing or excessive exposure to light over the years.

The point is that, when buying illustrated books—or any other expensive photograph, for that matter—it is important to exercise a great deal of care: Study the work (it would have been obvious, in this case, after a few minutes of study that the title pages were misplaced, since they didn't make any sense in terms of the contents of each volume) and, where possible, compare the work directly with another copy of the same work in good condition.

Among the factors influencing the market value of a photographically illustrated book are its historic importance, the identity of the photographer, aesthetic quality of the images, type of prints (platinum prints, calotypes, and albumen prints generally draw higher prices than photographic reproductions like carbon prints and Woodburytypes), rarity, and condition. While interesting volumes are available in the $50 to $1,000 range, the very finest photographically illustrated books sometimes sell for $20,000 to $30,000 or more.

Certain photographically illustrated books stand as undisputed classics. An example is *Gardner's Photographic Sketch Book of the War,* probably the most significant photographically illustrated book published in the United States. This two-volume work, issued in 1866, contains 100 images by Alexander Gardner, his son James, Timothy O'Sullivan, Barnard & Gibson, and six other Civil War photographers. Included are *The Harvest of Death, Scouts and Guides to the Army of the Potomac, Home of a Rebel Sharpshooter,* and other well-known images. Although many different photographers' negatives were drawn on in publishing the book, Gardner himself made all the prints. The works are albumen prints, each about 7 inches by 9 inches in size, mounted one to a page and accompanied by descriptive text.

Gardner was born in Paisley, Scotland, in 1821, immigrated to the United States in 1856, and joined the Brady gallery in 1858. Angered by Brady's policy of taking personal credit for all photographs by members of the gallery staff—the common practice at the time—Gardner quit in 1863 to set up his own studio. Gardner himself was meticulous about giving his assistants credit. In *Photographic Sketch Book,* the identity of the photographer is listed under each picture. The book thus serves as a unique reference work, naming several otherwise unknown Civil War photographers and enabling us to associate specific images with specific photographers.

Gardner had hoped that his *Photographic Sketch Book* would win broad appeal. But the public wanted to forget the war, and so Gardner ended up printing only about 200 copies, far fewer than planned. Of the 200, some have been destroyed or lost over the years and many others have been broken up and the photographs sold off individually. Perhaps ten to fifteen copies remain intact. Several of these copies have come onto the market in recent years, apparently flushed out by sharply rising market values.

As in the case of almost any scarce and expensive object, prices for *Photographic Sketch Book* tend to be highly sensitive both to the physical condition of the specific copy in question and to temporary supply and demand pressures in the marketplace. Recently, a leading dealer offered a copy in excellent condition for $30,000. Subsequently, another dealer offered a copy, in perhaps not quite so fine condition, for $15,000. Still another copy, which appeared to be in between the first two in relative condition, was sold at auction in February 1977 for $17,000. Two months later, another set, in somewhat poorer condition, sold for $12,000. And then in April 1978 a set in good condition sold at auction for $15,000. On the other hand, as recently as 1972 a copy lacking the title pages was auctioned for $2,500, a price we almost certainly will never see again.

One of the most important English illustrated books is *Life and Landscape on the Norfolk Broads,* containing forty platinum prints by Peter Henry Emerson, the great naturalist photographer. This work was published in 1886 and contains some of Emerson's finest images—including *Gathering Water Lilies,* perhaps his best-known photograph of all. In October 1977, a copy sold at auction in London for $19,000.

William Henry Fox Talbot's *The Pencil of Nature,* the very first photographically illustrated book, was published in six installments from 1844 to 1846. Talbot issued *The Pencil of Nature* to demonstrate the versatility and effectiveness of paper-print photography, which had yet to achieve the popularity of the daguerreotype. The work contains twenty-four calotypes depicting china, lace, a lithographic print, a drawing, a bust of Patroclus, a piece of fruit, books in a library, Westminster Abbey, three men with a ladder, the tower of Lacock Abbey in Wiltshire, the Martyr's Monument at Oxford, and other subjects. Although the original edition size is uncertain, about thirty copies, not all of them complete, are known to have survived. Recently, a leading dealer sold one privately at a price in excess of $35,000. And in July 1977 a copy sold at auction for close to $34,000.

Other important photographically illustrated books include George Barnard's *Photographic Views of Sherman's Campaign,* offered recently by one dealer at $14,500 and by another at $22,000; *The Arctic Regions,* which depicts marine artist William Bradford's 1869 voyage along the Greenland coast and carries a market value of approximately $5,000; Julia Margaret Cameron's *Illustrations to Tennyson's Idylls of the King, and other Poems,* offered recently in fine condition for $15,000; John Thomson's *Street Life in London,* which generally brings between $3,000 and $5,000 at auction; and George Robinson Farndon's *San Francisco Album: Photographs of the most beautiful views and public buildings of San Francisco,* one of the earliest (1856) and rarest (about five known copies) illustrated books and worth about $10,000 to $12,000 in excellent condition.

Although the British were most active in publishing photographically illustrated books, important volumes also were issued in France, Germany, Italy, and other countries, including the United States. One of the finest French examples is *Monographie de Notre Dame de Paris et de la Nouvelle Sacristie de Mm. LASSUS et VIOLLET-LE-DUC,* published sometime prior to 1858 and containing twelve photographs by Louis-Auguste and Auguste-Rosalie Bisson plus sixty-three engravings. A copy recently was offered by a dealer for $8,500.

In general, any significant illustrated book containing original photographic prints is likely to sell for $1,000 at the very least.

However, hundreds of less important books are available for well below that sum. Often, these works contain regional scenic views or architectural studies, such as Russell Sedgfield's *The Thames Richmond to Clifden* ($50 at a recent auction) and Theophilus Smith's *Wharncliffe, Wortley and the Valley of the Don* ($100). Many others are special editions of literary works, such as Sir Walter Scott's *Marmion,* illustrated with fifteen photographs by Thomas Annan ($90).

In addition, many illustrated books contain high-quality photographic reproductions (photogravures, carbon prints, collotypes, or Woodburytypes, for instance) rather than original photographic prints, and these works tend to be within the financial reach of many collectors. Even the most important and expensive of these volumes, such as Emerson's *Pictures of East Anglian Life,* seldom exceed $2,000 to $3,000 in price. Others are available for much less.

Increasingly, there has been a tendency to "cannibalize" photographically illustrated books and sell off the pictures individually, often at a tremendous profit over the cost of an intact volume. Dealer George Rinhart, for instance, cites the time he purchased a copy of *Life and Landscape on the Norfolk Broads* for $12,000 and was able to gross more than $35,000 by removing and selling the individual pictures. Certain of the higher-priced books lend themselves almost automatically to big profits on such "break-outs," and whenever one of these works comes up for sale at auction there is concern among some dealers and collectors about the intentions of the buyer.

The breaking up of old books is highly controversial. Book dealer Charles B. Wood III has stated that while it is not hard to justify the cannibalization of photographically illustrated books on economic grounds, "morally it is indefensible." Nonetheless, it occurs—and will keep on occurring so long as it is so highly profitable. One reason why cannibalization happens in the first place is that few people can afford, say, the $12,000 Rinhart paid for his *Life and Landscape.* On the other hand, many people want and can afford individual pictures from that work, at prices from about $500 to $2,500 each. Of course, it is easier to accept the breaking up of a book which is in poor condition than the dismantling of one which is rare, intact, and of top quality.

Chapter 10

The Photo-Secession

Twentieth-century photography can be divided into two broad areas:

- Works by the established "master" photographers, including members of the Photo-Secessionist movement in the early part of the century (discussed in this chapter) and a wide range of other leading twentieth-century greats (Chapter 12).

- Works by the current generation of "contemporary" photographers, whose reputations are, in most cases, not yet so firmly established (Chapter 13).

In approaching twentieth-century master photography, the collector is faced with a somewhat different set of considerations than in approaching photography of the nineteenth century.

For nineteenth-century works, the primary concerns include how to buy wisely in the face of a lack of documentation and well-developed research; how to sort out the really good pictures from the huge number of more mundane works; and physical condition, including the extreme vulnerability of some works to fading.

For twentieth-century photography, these specific concerns are less of a problem. Documentation is better in this field, and the market is not nearly as muddied by a large supply of lesser images. There has been more of a sorting out, in terms of price levels and in terms of which photographers are most favored by collectors.

A somewhat different set of issues tends to come into play, then, including the following:

- The issue of vintage prints versus later prints (as discussed in Chapter 4).
- Whether to buy posthumous prints, which are much more common in twentieth-century than in nineteenth-century photography.

- Whether to buy *Camera Work* gravures or original prints—or both. For Alfred Stieglitz, Paul
  Strand, Edward Steichen, Clarence H. White,
  Alvin Langdon Coburn, Baron Adolph De
  Meyer, and several other major twentieth-
  century photographers, the majority of pictures
  on the market today are gravures rather than original photographic prints. (See Chapter 11.)

Another key difference between nineteenth- and twentieth-century photography is the relatively low "historic content" of the latter. Twentieth-century photographs achieve value on the basis of aesthetic merits or the identity of the photographer or the important position of the work in the history of photography—but seldom
because of what they tell us about the history of mankind.

In general, buying well in twentieth-century master photography requires an
annual budget of at least $2,000 to $3,000 and preferably more; an understanding of
the history of twentieth-century photography, including the way various photographers and movements fit into the whole; an aesthetic appreciation of twentieth-century
works; and a good business relationship with at least one or two important dealers who
can help you find prime items as they come onto the market.

The term "master photographer" is widely used by critics, collectors, and
dealers to distinguish photographers of achievement and importance. It is a highly
subjective term, but essentially denotes an established, blue-chip quality, as opposed
to the more challenging and unsettled nature of the market in contemporary
photography.

Although there are scores of twentieth-century photographers who might be
considered to qualify for "master" status, three stand out as being at the top of the list:
Alfred Stieglitz (1864–1946), Paul Strand (1890–1976), and Edward Weston (1886–
1958), all born in the United States and highly influential in the development of photography both in the United States and abroad.

Fine original prints by these three giants are today rare, although photogravures (in the case of Stieglitz and Strand) and posthumous prints (in the case of
Weston) are readily available to anybody with a few hundred dollars to spend. Original Strands are perhaps the highest priced of the three, with an approximate range of
$2,000 to $10,000. The work of Stieglitz is a bit behind, at approximately $1,000 to
$9,000. And Weston originals are somewhat behind that, at approximately $800 to
$8,000.

Those prices indicate the upper end of the monetary scale for twentieth-
century master photography. Toward the lower end there is a wealth of quality works in
a price range of approximately $300 to $1,000—works by Imogen Cunningham,
Ansel Adams, Arnold Genthe, Nathan Lerner, Berenice Abbott, W. Eugene Smith,
Barbara Morgan, André Kertész, Brassaï, Wynn Bullock, Minor White, and many
others.

Although items also are available for less than $300 each, many tend to be of
poor quality. If you simply cannot afford to spend a minimum of approximately $300
per print, you probably are better off collecting in another, less costly area of
photography.

The Photo-Secession

The twentieth century has seen a number of important schools and movements in photography. By far the most significant is the Photo-Secession, which flourished from about 1902 to 1910 under the leadership of Stieglitz. The broad aim of the Photo-Secessionists was to advance photography through excellence. Stieglitz himself said: "Photo-Secession actually means seceding from the accepted idea of what constitutes a photograph." Stieglitz and his followers believed photography to be a separate, full-fledged, independent art form with its own ground rules and aesthetic standards, totally apart from—and in every way equal to—painting. This was a rather brash notion at the time, since photography was generally considered to be a minor art form, if one at all, to be judged by the same pictorial standards as those applied to painting. The common thread running through much Photo-Secessionist work is an emphasis on realistic imagery and the subtleties of natural light. But despite the stated goal of breaking free from vassalage to painting, one cannot help but be struck by the fact that many Photo-Secessionist pictures draw their inspiration from painting, especially from Whistler and the Impressionists, as much as did the Victorian "art" photography which the Photo-Secessionists found so nauseating. So what was stated in theory by the Photo-Secessionists as their absolute goal was not always carried out in fact.

Photo-Secessionist principles were argued through the pages of *Camera Work* magazine, a lavishly produced quarterly founded by Stieglitz in 1903 and dominated by him until its demise in 1917. And the work of many important Photo-Secessionists was exhibited by Stieglitz in his modernist Little Galleries, or "291" as it was more commonly known (for its Fifth Avenue street number).

Stieglitz himself was a small, contentious man who has been variously described as brilliant, domineering, egotistical, and visionary. Weston, upon meeting Stieglitz for the first time in 1922, wrote to a friend that Stieglitz had talked "to" him for four straight hours without giving Weston a chance to say more than half a dozen words. Nonetheless, Weston came away impressed with both Stieglitz and his work.

Today, Stieglitz's name, like that of Julia Margaret Cameron before him, is magic in the marketplace. His original platinum and silver prints are highly prized by collectors. And photogravure reproductions of his work are sought with an almost equal intensity. One of the most stunning prices ever achieved in the photography market was the $4,500 paid at auction in February 1975 for a $12\frac{1}{4}$- by 10-inch photogravure of the Stieglitz masterpiece *The Steerage* (see page 179 for a reproduction). No other *photogravure*, of any photograph, has even come close to that high level.

Like a number of other works mentioned in earlier chapters, *The Steerage* illustrates the compelling need to know exactly what you are buying. Three versions exist:

1. The original gravure version is a $7\frac{3}{4}$ by $6\frac{1}{4}$-inch photogravure published in an edition of approximately 1,000 copies in the October 1911 issue of *Camera Work*. This version is sometimes

referred to as the "small format" gravure. Market value is approximately $800 to $1,200.

2. The popularity of the *Camera Work* gravure was so great that friends convinced Stieglitz to devote an entire issue of his brief-lived magazine *291* to photography and to feature a larger gravure of *The Steerage*. This "large format" version, $12\frac{1}{4}$ inches by 10 inches in size, was published in September-October 1915 in an edition of 500 copies. However, only about 108 of those gravures were sold, and Stieglitz eventually threw away the rest. This is the version which brought $4,500 at auction in February 1975. Current market value is approximately $3,000 to $4,500.

3. Stieglitz made a very limited number of original platinum prints of *The Steerage*. The price, if one could be acquired, probably would exceed $10,000.

Stieglitz's photographic output, spanning five and one-half decades from 1883 to 1937, encompasses a variety of types of work. One of his most remarkable accomplishments was the ongoing series of more than 400 photographs of his wife, Georgia O'Keeffe, taken over nearly twenty years. With consummate photographic skill and enormous love, Stieglitz recorded O'Keeffe's face, eyes, hair, body, and especially her hands; her many moods; and her various day-to-day activities. However, pictures from this series seldom come onto the market.

Instead, his most important photographs, from a collecting viewpoint, include pictures taken in New York City and his "equivalents" — pictures of clouds taken primarily in the 1920s.

Stieglitz was among the first photographers to use a hand-held camera, which freed him to take pictures more unobtrusively. His photographs of commonplace incidents on the streets of New York were regarded in their time as the highest expression of American photographic art. The concept of "equivalency," on the other hand, was that cloud photographs could evoke emotional reactions totally unrelated to subject matter, as with the emotional response to great music. Original silver-print "equivalents" sell occasionally at auction for between approximately $2,000 and $3,500 each.

Photo-Secessionist prints are a rich and active area of collecting. Outstanding collections have been assembled devoted exclusively to these works, which are so central to photographic history.

Besides Stieglitz, Photo-Secessionists whose prints are available to collectors include Edward Steichen (1879–1973), Alvin Langdon Coburn (1882–1966), Gertrude Käsebier (1852–1934), Clarence H. White (1871–1925), John G. Bullock (1854–1939), Paul B. Haviland (1880–1950), Frank Eugene (1865–1936), and Baron Adolph De Meyer (1868–1946).

Steichen came under the influence of Stieglitz in 1902 and went on to become his friend and greatest protégé. Two men could hardly have been more different in appearance, outlook, and personality. While Stieglitz was small, quarrelsome, and (in his later years) increasingly withdrawn, Steichen was a tall, bony individual who was outgoing and talkative and, totally unlike Stieglitz, perfectly willing to take on commercial photography assignments for magazines and corporate clients.

Steichen's work can be divided into three primary phases: (1) his early, impressionist photographs taken in both Paris and the United States; (2) his activities during World War I as commander of aerial photography for the Allied Expeditionary Forces in Europe; and (3) his highly successful career in the 1920s and 1930s as a leading fashion, portrait, and advertising photographer. One of his best-known fashion photographs, *Chéruit Gown,* is reproduced on page 191.

In the pre-World War I phase, Steichen's portraits and landscapes are noted for their soft focus, their dark, hazy lighting, and their romantic manner, often resembling the paintings of Whistler. His portraits of Rodin and Pierpont Morgan are among his most famous from this period. A fine original print from this period might sell for anywhere from $1,000 to $6,000, while *Camera Work* gravures typically bring $150 to $800.

Aerial photographs from World War I involve more complex purchase considerations. There is some controversy about whether it is actually possible to identify which specific pictures were taken by Steichen and which by other photographers working under his command. Generally, it is believed that platinum prints from this period were at least printed by Steichen and perhaps taken by him. Also, works which have come onto the market from his personal collection are often attributed to him, although agreement on this point is by no means unanimous. Three aerial photographs, listed as by Steichen but with a question mark after the listing (indicating some doubt), were offered by Sotheby Parke Bernet in February 1977. They brought an average price of $250.

While Steichen's early work is all soft in focus, the wartime experience of producing pictures of the greatest possible precision for military purposes marked a turning point. Thereafter he was to become fascinated with the technical aspects of photography, and eventually he only produced pictures of utmost clarity. These later photographs, including portraits and fashion pictures taken for *Vogue* and *Vanity Fair,* generally bring between $400 and $3,000 each. One of the finest pictures from this period is Steichen's multiple-exposure portrait of his brother-in-law, Carl Sandburg, taken in 1936. A print of that work sold at auction recently for $1,900.

Coburn is best known for his photographs of men and cities. His most famous image, *The Octopus,* depicts Madison Square in New York, looking almost straight down at the park from an adjacent skyscraper. This picture emphasizes the abstract, octopuslike patterns of the walkways through the park, with the soft shadow of the Metropolitan Tower cutting across, and is considered a landmark of modern photography — one of the first truly successful abstract pictures. Coburn published a number of important books — most notably *London* (1909), *New York* (1910), and *Men of Mark* (1913) — illustrated with handmade photogravures which he pulled personally on his own press. A copy of *New York* sold at auction in November 1976 for $1,900. Individual gravures, from his books and from *Camera Work* magazine, trade very actively at prices between $100 and $700. His original photographic prints are mostly gum-platinum prints, but these rarely come onto the market. Two exceptional early Coburns were offered recently by a dealer for $5,000 each. Others have sold at prices between approximately $300 and $2,000.

Käsebier's specialty was portraits. Trained as a painter, she took up photography in middle age and soon had a thriving commercial portrait business in New York City. In contrast to the ornate, prop-filled portraits being turned out by most other photographic studios of the time, Käsebier depicted her subjects in simple, real-life settings. Many of her pictures are infused with enormous amounts of natural light. (See the reproduction of *Happy Days* on page 175.) In addition, Käsebier was distinctive in the use of gum processes and sepia tones in the making of her prints, and she mounted many of her photographs on layers of dark-colored paper. There is great charm and originality to the best of Käsebier's work. On the other hand, at their worst her photographs can become highly romanticized to the point of being maudlin.

Käsebier is an example of an important (though by no means truly major) photographer whose original work — particularly her commercial portraits — remains eminently collectible. Original prints are available, from dealers and at auction, at prices ranging from approximately $300 to $4,000 each. There is perhaps no other Photo-Secessionist for whom quality original prints, as opposed to *Camera Work* gravures, come onto the market in such variety and quantity.

White concentrated on informal portraiture and landscape studies. There is a straightforwardness and simplicity of composition to his pictures which makes them stand apart from the work of many other photographers of the same period. White's photographs tend to be lyrical and romantic, including backlit pictures of young women in flowing white gowns. He clearly was influenced by both Japanese woodcuts and Impressionist art. His original prints are mostly platinum prints and bring prices of approximately $200 to $2,500 each. *Camera Work* gravures typically sell in the $100 to $500 range.

John Bullock's body of work includes landscapes and portraits. Although a founding member of the Photo-Secession, none of his images appear in *Camera Work*. So it is primarily his original platinum prints, plus some silver prints, which come up for sale today. Price range is approximately $100 to $500.

Haviland's work is divided into three major categories: portraits, primarily of friends and colleagues; candid street scenes similar to those taken by Stieglitz; and nudes. Unlike most other members of the Photo-Secession, Haviland was a businessman rather than a professional photographer. His original prints are relatively rare. In by far the largest recent offering of his works, Lunn Gallery in Washington, D.C., marketed seventy-three original prints at prices between $300 and $1,200 each. All these prints came from Haviland's personal collection. *Camera Work* gravures, on the other hand, typically sell at prices between $75 and $200 each.

Frank Eugene, like a number of other members of the Photo-Secession, began as a painter. Eugene frequently employed the unusual technique of scratching over sections of his photographic negatives, so that his prints often appear to be a combination of photography and drawing. Twenty-eight of his photographs were reproduced in *Camera Work,* and it is primarily these gravures, rather than original prints, which come onto the market. Price range is approximately $100 to $500.

Baron De Meyer was by far the most colorful and flamboyant member of the Photo-Secession. By the time he was a young man, De Meyer had amassed a small fortune and had established friendships throughout British high society, including one with the future King Edward VII. In about 1901, he married Donna Olga Alberta Caraccio, one of the most beautiful and elegant women of her day and the goddaughter (reportedly the illegitimate daughter) of the King. The rank of baron was conferred on De Meyer by the King of Saxony so that De Meyer and Olga could attend Edward's coronation.

De Meyer's early photographs, both before and during the period of the Photo-Secession, include portraits and magnificently composed flower still lifes. Starting in 1913, he became the first important fashion photographer as well as one of the leading photographers of modern dance. Original De Meyer prints generally sell at prices between $300 and $2,500 each. *Camera Work* gravures bring about $100 to $500 each.

Still other Photo-Secessionists whose work is available to collectors, both in the form of original prints and *Camera Work* gravures, include the following:

— Eva Watson-Schütze (1867–1935), known primarily for her portraits.
— Harry C.Rubincam (d. 1941), a Denver insur-
   ance executive whose best-known photograph,
   In the Circus, is considered one of the gems of
   Photo-Secessionist art.
— Karl Struss (b. 1887), who photographed outdoor scenes and portraits. Struss later became a
   leading Hollywood cinematographer.
— Annie W. Brigman (1869–1950), whose subject
   matter includes nudes and nature studies.

In addition to the Photo-Secessionists themselves, a number of important international photographers are associated with that movement—either as members of the Linked Ring, a London group which predates the Photo-Secession, or working independently in a style closely related to the aesthetic goals of Stieglitz and his colleagues. These photographers include Frederick H. Evans (1852–1943), Heinrich Kühn (1866–1944), Robert Demachy (1859–1937), and J. Craig Annan (1864–1946).

Evans, owner of a London bookshop, took up photography in the 1880s and initially specialized in portraits of his artistic and literary friends, including Aubrey Beardsley and George Bernard Shaw. Beginning in 1896, he also photographed British and French cathedrals. These cathedral pictures are among the finest architectural studies in the history of photography.

Most original Evans prints are platinotypes. In fact, Evans so preferred this process that when his favorite platinum paper became impossible to obtain during World War I, he gave up photography, never to return to the medium. His platinum prints generally sell in a price range of $500 to $2,000 each. *Camera Work* gravures bring approximately $100 to $600 each.

Kühn's work, well known in Europe, is just beginning to gain recognition in the United States. Kühn was the leading Austro-German photographer of the late nineteenth and early twentieth centuries. He is especially important because of his pioneering technical work in multi-layered gum prints. Many of his prints are richly toned in green, blue, red, or brown. He also was among the first to exhibit full-color photographs printed in gum from three different negatives.

Landscapes and portraits are Kühn's primary subject matter. He drew great inspiration from the photographs of Hill and Adamson, and many of his own portraits are reminiscent of their work. Kühn's three-color gum-bichromate prints typically bring prices of $2,500 to $5,000 each. Other original prints generally sell in a range of $500 to $3,500 each.

Demachy, like Kühn, is known primarily for his technical work in colored gum prints. A leading French photographer, he was a founding member of the Photo-Club de Paris. In addition, he contributed photographs regularly to *Camera Work* and to exhibitions at Stieglitz's New York gallery, and he wrote extensively on the aesthetics and techniques of manipulated prints. His photographs generally are more concerned with artistic effects than specific subject matter. Price range for his original prints is approximately $800 to $2,500 each.

Annan, son of Scottish photographer Thomas Annan (see Chapter 6), is important on two counts: as an accomplished photographer in his own right and as the person responsible for bringing the works of Hill and Adamson to public attention. Annan's father had been a friend of Hill's, and it was through this association that Annan knew about Hill and Adamson's calotype prints. He rephotographed many of these works and issued photogravure prints. Twenty-five of Annan's own photographs were printed in *Camera Work,* and in terms of his own work it is primarily these gravures which are available to collectors. Price range is approximately $80 to $250 each.

Chapter 11

Camera Work Gravures

Camera Work was the quarterly magazine of the Photo-Secession, edited by Alfred Stieglitz. From 1903 through 1917, fifty issues were published. As indicated in the previous chapter, individual photogravures removed from these issues are mainstays of today's photography salesroom, at prices between about $50 and $1,200 each. In addition, complete issues trade regularly, at prices between about $200 and $4,500 each. And a rare fifty-issue set, with all gravures in place, would likely bring a price in excess of $30,000.

Rather than being original photographic prints, photogravures are high-quality reproductions printed with ink from etched copper plates. In the case of *Camera Work,* the gravures were printed by hand on high-grade paper and then "tipped" into place in the magazine.

Are these gravures worth buying? The answer is really a matter of individual choice.

The advantages of buying *Camera Work* gravures include availability and relatively low price. As in the case of *The Steerage,* the Stieglitz masterpiece discussed in Chapter 10 and reproduced on page 179, an original print would be extremely difficult—perhaps impossible—to find and would almost certainly cost in excess of $10,000. By contrast, the *Camera Work* gravure of the same image was produced in an edition of perhaps 1,000 (the exact number is unknown) and is readily available in a price range of approximately $800 to $1,200.

Stieglitz himself wrote, in the October 1905 issue of *Camera Work,* that the gravures "can in reality be considered original prints, having been made directly from the original negatives and printed in the spirit of the original picture and retaining all its quality." These photogravures are indeed of high quality. They exhibit a lushness that, in some cases, actually exceeds the quality of original prints of the same images.

Yet, the fact is that *Camera Work* gravures, being an additional step removed from the hand of the photographer, are lesser works than original prints. As recently as ten years ago, few major collectors would have considered buying gravures. Today's growing dealer and collector interest in these works is largely a result of shortages of original photographic prints from the Photo-Secession.

Probably the answer for most collectors is that buying *Camera Work* gravures makes sense as a supplement to buying original prints, but not as an end in itself. As a practical matter, certain images — such as *The Steerage* or Paul Strand's *New York (Wall Street)* — are available only in gravure form. So if you want to acquire these works you have little choice but to buy gravures.

The work of more than thirty different photographers appeared in *Camera Work*. In addition to Stieglitz and Strand, these photographers include J. Craig Annan, Julia Margaret Cameron, Alvin Langdon Coburn, F. Holland Day, Robert Demachy, Baron Adolph De Meyer, Frank Eugene, Frederick H. Evans, Paul B. Haviland, David Octavius Hill and Robert Adamson, Gertrude Käsebier, Heinrich Kühn, Harry C. Rubincam, George H. Seeley, George Bernard Shaw, Edward Steichen, Eva Watson-Schütze, and Clarence H. White. Works by Steichen, Stieglitz, Coburn, White, and Eugene were presented with the greatest frequency, in that approximate order.

In addition, many of the issues — particularly from number 30 on — contain photogravure reproductions of paintings, drawings, and sculpture by Picasso, Braque, Rodin, Matisse, and other modern masters.

It is the issues with gravures of photographs which generally command the highest prices. The most expensive and sought-after issue of all is number 36 (October 1911), which contains gravures of sixteen of Stieglitz's finest photographs, including *The Ferry Boat, The Terminal,* and *The Aeroplane.* This also is the issue in which *The Steerage* appears. Retail price of an intact issue is in excess of $4,000.

Other high-value issues include number 49/50 (June 1917), with eleven gravures of Paul Strand photographs; number 12 (October 1905), with eight gravures and two halftones of Steichen photographs and a color halftone of Steichen's renowned impressionistic picture of the Flatiron Building in New York; and number 42/43 (April-July 1913), with fourteen gravures of Steichen photographs and three color halftones of Steichen paintings.

Of the fifty issues, numbers 34/35, 42/43, and 49/50 were double issues, with two issues published as one. On the other hand, special unnumbered issues were published in April 1906, August 1912, and June 1913, bringing the total number of separately published issues back up to fifty.

Rarity is another factor for the collector to consider. In general, the later issues are much rarer than the earlier ones. Dealer Harry Lunn notes that the subscription list was about 650 when the first issue was published in 1903 and less than 50 when publication ceased in 1917. But the actual press run was greater, since more than fifty complete sets can be documented.

Camera Work actually is one among a number of photographic periodicals which have become important collector's items. Others include the following:

- *Galerie Contemporaine,* published weekly between 1876 and 1885. Each issue contains articles about a well-known French writer, composer, artist, scientist, or political leader and includes a portrait of the individual — either a carbon print or Woodburytype. In selecting these pictures, the *Galerie Contemporaine* editors drew heavily on previously published portraits by leading nineteenth-century French photographers, especially Nadar and Carjat. A complete set of *Galerie Contemporaine,* containing 132 portraits, brought $5,000 at auction in February 1978.

- *Sun Artists,* published in eight issues between October 1889 and July 1891. Each of the eight issues contains four photogravures of pictures by a leading British photographer, including Julia Margaret Cameron, Henry Peach Robinson, and Frank Meadow Sutcliffe. A complete eight-set issue, with all gravures hand signed by the photographer (except those by Cameron, who had died before *Sun Artists* came on the market), was offered recently by Colnaghi's, the London art dealers, for $4,000.

- *Camera Notes,* forerunner of *Camera Work* and published quarterly from July 1897 through December 1903 in an edition of 1,000. Stieglitz edited *Camera Notes* for the Camera Club of New York, but finally dropped the project amid widespread complaints about his authoritarian rule and his increasing tendency to reproduce works by photographers who weren't even club members. A complete set of the twenty-four issues was offered recently for $11,000.

- *291,* in effect a monthly gallery catalog published by Stieglitz from March 1915 to February 1916. A complete set of the twelve issues, in excellent condition, was offered recently at $12,000.

While each of these periodicals — and a number of others which haven't been mentioned — is interesting in its own right, *Camera Work* stands at the top of the list, in terms of its historic importance, the quality of its reproductions, and the volume of dealer activity in the market today.

One of the controversies surrounding *Camera Work,* as with nineteenth-century illustrated books (see Chapter 9), involves the increasing tendency of dealers to break up issues and sell off the individual gravures. Some collectors and dealers contend there is an integrity to an intact issue that should not be violated. But the economic forces of the market clearly are in the direction of cannibalization, since dealers can make almost guaranteed profits by breaking up an issue and reselling the individual pieces at big mark-ups.

In buying any issue of *Camera Work,* it is crucial to look through item by item to make sure none of the gravures has been removed. The standard reference book is *Camera Work: A Critical Anthology,* edited by Jonathan Green, published in 1973 by Aperture Inc. This book contains an issue-by-issue listing of the contents of *Camera Work* plus reproductions of many of the gravures.

Chapter 12

Twentieth-Century
Master Photography

The final, double issue of *Camera Work* was devoted to the imagery of an important new photographer: Paul Strand. These pictures, including semiabstractions emphasizing form and design, were "brutally direct" (in the words of Stieglitz) and stood in sharp contrast to much of the more romantic and soft-focused photography of the Photo-Secession. They exhibited a simplicity and boldness that paralleled developments in painting: a turning away from Whistlerian wistfulness and romance to the raw power of the post-Impressionists and Fauvists. And, as it so happened, they presaged the birth after World War I of the doctrine of "straight" photography.

"Straight" photography, the dominant style of the twenties and thirties, draws its name from its direct, clear-focus manner and total lack of visual trickery. The picture is the picture, carefully previsualized by the photographer and printed from the negative without cropping or other alteration. A crispness, an emphasis on structure and visual honesty, and a high level of technical skill — these are among the most important characteristics associated with straight photography.

Strand himself saw the manipulation of photographs, through gum prints, oil prints, soft-focus lenses, and the scratching of negatives, as "merely the expression of an impotent desire to paint." He argued that greater intensity could be achieved through a pure, gimmick-free approach.

Among Strand's early efforts, two of his most famous pictures are his chilling view of workers heading for their jobs on Wall Street, under the large, ominously dark windows of the Morgan Bank building, and his portrait of a blind newsstand woman. These are classics of modern photography, with their directness, patterned composition, great visual strength, and total purging of idealized romanticism. A vintage silver print of *Blind Woman* was offered recently by a dealer for $7,000.

Strand also was among the first to discover the photographic beauty of precision machines, including extreme close-ups of his Akeley motion picture camera and of lathes (see a reproduction of *Lathe, 1923* on page 185). In the early 1920s, he began a series of close-up nature studies. Then, with his Mexican trip of 1930–1932, he undertook a series of projects photographing peoples and their lands. The *Mexican Portfolio*, published in 1940 in an edition of 1,000 copies (and republished in a second edition in 1967), contains twenty gravures recalling his Mexican visit. A copy of that important portfolio, first edition in good condition, probably would bring between $2,000 and $3,000. A second edition recently was offered by a dealer for $750.

Edward Weston, like Strand, was a proponent of straight photography. But his work is less brutal and more purely aesthetic, with utmost emphasis on light and form. It was Weston, more than any other photographer, who showed that pure photography was a creative end in itself. His work has a sensuousness, clarity, and classical perfection which are unsurpassed. These qualities are illustrated in his *Nude, 1920,* reproduced on page 183.

Weston began as a commercial portrait photographer in California in 1911. Initially he worked in the soft-focus manner of the day, but by the early 1920s had turned to the precise, well-ordered style which was to make him famous. Some of his most important pictures were created in Mexico, where he lived and worked from 1923 to 1926. In Mexico he lived with Tina Modotti (1896–1942), the Italian-born movie actress whose own photographs, created primarily during those same years, were highly influenced by Weston and are today among the rarities of the marketplace. Only about 200 original Modotti prints are known to exist. One of these, a 1924 semiabstract close-up of roses, recently sold at auction for $2,100, while a 1924 Weston portrait of Modotti sold at the same auction for $5,100 — a record auction price for a Weston print. So Modotti is important to the history of twentieth-century photography both as an accomplished photographer in her own right and as one of Weston's favorite models.

Weston returned to the United States in 1926 and established a studio in Carmel, California, in 1929. It was in California that he took perhaps his most famous photographs: extreme close-ups of shells and highly sensuous pictures of peppers and other vegetables. In 1937, he was awarded the first Guggenheim fellowship for photography, enabling him to travel some 25,000 miles over eighteen months taking more than 1,500 pictures of California and the West. He then traveled through the southern and eastern states in 1941, taking pictures for a special edition of Walt Whitman's *Leaves of Grass.* With the outbreak of World War II, he returned to Carmel and continued to photograph around his home and on nearby Point Lobos until stricken by Parkinson's disease in 1948.

Group f/64

Weston was a founder, in 1932, of Group f/64, so named because its members favored a stand camera (as opposed to a hand-held camera) with a small f/64 aperture which permitted great clarity of focus and depth of field. This group has become synonymous with high standards in straight photography.

Besides Weston, important founding members of Group f/64 include Ansel Adams (b. 1902) and Imogen Cunningham (1883–1976).

To meet Ansel Adams is to have your day filled with sunshine. He is warm, relaxed, and open, so enthralled with life, so mentally alert and agile, so possessed of grace and wit. His pictures of western nature scenes, many taken in and around Yosemite, are enormously popular throughout the world. An Ansel Adams exhibition at a museum or gallery will invariably draw large and enthusiastic crowds. Perhaps no other photographer in history has so successfully broken through to the public consciousness.

For a dealer, an inventory of Ansel Adams photographs is like money in the bank. His original prints trade very actively at retail prices between approximately $1,000 and $7,000 each. Ansel Adams books also are big-selling items, as are posters reproducing his work. In December 1975, Los Angeles dealer G. Ray Hawkins published a 40- by 45-inch poster of Adams's most famous photograph, *Moonrise, Hernandez, New Mexico*. This was a blown-up, high-quality reproduction of the photograph, not an original print. However, when Adams saw a copy of the poster, he was impressed enough to hand sign each work on the back for free. Hawkins reports that these signed posters, in an edition of fifty copies on handmade paper, sold out in two and one-half days at a price of $100 each and then jumped to an open-market price of $400. An eager public stands ready to buy Adams's works in nearly any form.

But are Adams's photographs really of the quality to merit serious collector interest? The answer clearly is yes, despite the folk-hero quality of the man that sometimes obscures the virtues of the work. Ansel Adams pictures are truly delicious to behold, both for their heroic treatment of subject matter and their incredibly rich tonal finish. Adams is a master printer who seems consistently able to squeeze an extra ounce of quality out of each negative. Technically, his finished prints are as close to perfection as any photographer has ever come; this point is raised time and again by dealers who handle his work, but rather than being an overblown sales pitch it really is true. There also has been a consistency, from year to year, in the quality of his imagery. As is not the case with most other twentieth-century photographers, it is simply not possible to cite one chronological period as offering his best and most important work. In all of Adams's pictures, from 1930 to present, there is a highly dramatic and impeccable sense of timing, a sense that he has instinctively triggered the camera at the exact moment when nature was in her fullest glory. A reproduction of *White Branches, Mono Lake, California* appears on page 201.

Where Adams's work does fall short is in its lack of strong intellectual content and its limited contribution to the advancement of photographic aesthetics. While Adams has produced some of the finest, most technically perfect photographs of western nature, he will never be considered a truly innovative artist who led the way into a whole new style or school of photography — as did, for instance, Stieglitz and Strand.

Cunningham also is renowned as one of the finest nature photographers of the twentieth century. But her work tends to be more abstract than that of Adams: an extreme close-up of a leaf, for instance, or of two calla flowers. She also is known for her portraits and nudes. The four-level pricing of Cunningham's work is discussed on page 17.

A number of other important photographers, though not founding members of Group f/64, have deep roots in the San Francisco Bay area and often are associated with that group. These photographers include Minor White (1908–1970), Wynn Bullock (1902–1975), and Brett Weston (b. 1911).

White became interested in photography at an early age, but did not pursue it seriously until 1937–1938. His initial work consists primarily of architectural documentation of buildings in Portland, Oregon. After World War II, he joined the faculty of the California School of Fine Arts, where he met Ansel Adams and Edward Weston. His close ties with these two masters influenced the sharp detail and high quality of his prints, although his imagery is distinctly his own. White's works, primarily depicting nature, are poetic and often highly mystical. His prints bring prices between about $450 and $2,000 each.

Bullock began his career as a concert singer and became interested in photography in about 1929 after seeing the abstract, manipulated images of László Moholy-Nagy. He photographed for the next decade as an avocation, earning a living at other jobs. After World War II, he moved to Monterey, California, and opened a commercial studio. A 1948 meeting with Edward Weston inspired him to devote more time to noncommercial photography. His best-known images include nudes, landscapes with nude figures, and abstractions. Bullock also was a master printer who held a number of patents for technical innovations. Price range for his work is approximately $250 to $1,000.

Brett Weston, second son of Edward, is known primarily for his nature studies—landscapes as well as close-ups. His prints sell in a range of approximately $250 to $400 each.

In recent years, the traditions of Group f/64 have been extended by Paul Caponigro (b. 1932), a former student of Minor White. As with White, Caponigro's imagery tends to be imbued with mysticism. One of his favorite subjects is Stonehenge. He has photographed that great and mysterious British landmark for more than a decade and in early 1978 published a portfolio of twelve of his Stonehenge pictures at a retail price of $4,500. Individual Caponigro prints generally sell in a range of $300 to $500 each.

Charles Sheeler (1883–1965) is yet another of the important American straight photographers, although he has no relationship to Group f/64 on the West Coast. Best known for his paintings and drawings, Sheeler took up photography in 1912 as a means of support. His photographs, like his paintings, are noted for their extreme precision and highly ordered composition.

Sheeler specialized initially in architectural photography, but subsequently broadened into still lifes, the photographing of works of art, and fashion photography. In addition, much of his imagery, in both his paintings and photographs, is concerned with early American handicraft, particularly that of the Shakers. (See example on page 189.)

From a collecting viewpoint, Sheeler is considered one of the most important of all twentieth-century photographers. His work is rare and expensive. Price range is approximately $800 to $10,000. Sheeler was an exceptional photographic craftsman. In 1927, he was hired by Ford Motor Company to undertake a series of photographic studies of its plant in River Rouge, Michigan. In six weeks on that assignment he took thirty-two photographs, less than one a day. His 1929 studies of Chartres Cathedral also are among his best works.

Documentary Photography

The growing strength of straight photography in the 1920s brought with it renewed interest in documentary photography — a straightforward "factual" style intended to record, inform, or convince.

Documentary photography encompasses a variety of subject matter — for instance, the depiction of slum conditions, the recording of a city's buildings and monuments, or the broad portrayal of a race or ethnic group. The essential point is that this category includes nearly any type of photographic portrayal which is systematic, straightforward, and comprehensive.

The roots of documentary photography go well back into the nineteenth century, to John Thomson's depictions of street life in London. By the early twentieth century, a number of important photographers were working in the documentary vein — Jacob Riis (1849–1914) and Lewis W. Hine (1874–1940) in New York, Eugène Atget (1857–1927) in Paris, and Paul Martin (1864–1944) in London. However, these photographers received little or no public attention in their own time.

Atget is a classic example of an artist who labored in total obscurity, nearly destitute, and for whom recognition did not come until after death. Atget was born in Libourne, France, and at an early age went to sea. He subsequently tried acting and painting and finally, at age forty-one, turned to photography. His ambition was to photograph everything that was artistic and picturesque about Paris. To eke out a living, he sold his prints to painters and illustrators for use as studies.

Atget's equipment was of the most rudimentary nature — a large bellows camera, old glass-plate negatives, a wooden tripod, and a set of rectilinear lenses. Yet, with this equipment he created the most comprehensive and visually beautiful record that exists of early-twentieth-century Paris. His photographs depict buildings, trees, flowers, monuments, parks, prostitutes, street vendors, statues, shop fronts, and interiors of houses — all with exceptional grace, lyricism, and attention to detail. (For an example, see a reproduction of *Corset Shop* on page 181.)

Atget's work went unnoticed until 1926, when it was discovered by the Surrealists, including Man Ray. When Atget died the following year, his negatives were rescued by Berenice Abbott, a student of Man Ray and later one of America's outstanding documentary photographers. Abbott began printing from the negatives and arranging exhibitions of Atget's work. In the years since, Atget has steadily gained recognition as one of the most important photographers in the history of the medium. Virtually every major institutional collection of twentieth-century photographs includes examples of his work. The Museum of Modern Art in New York owns an especially large number of his original prints and acquired his negatives in 1969.

There are two categories of Atget prints: original prints made by Atget and posthumous prints made by Abbott. The former, generally gold in tone, are becoming increasingly rare and sell in a price range of approximately $500 to $2,500 each. The latter, identified as Abbott prints on the back, sell at prices between about $150 and $600 each.

Riis documented slum conditions on New York's Lower East Side. A native of Denmark, he came to the United States in 1870 at age twenty-one. After several years of initial hardship, he established himself as an influential muckraking newspaper reporter and, in 1888, began taking photographs to illustrate his articles on the plight of immigrants. Little was thought of the artistic quality or historic importance of these works at the time, and when he died in 1914 they were forgotten. Three decades later, free-lance photographer Alexander Alland noticed references to photography in Riis's autobiography and began a lengthy search for his negatives, eventually finding

412 of them in the attic of the old Riis family home on Long Island—just days before the house was torn down. These negatives, as well as most original Riis prints, are owned by the Museum of the City of New York. The few prints coming onto the market were made by Alland in the late 1940s. Two Alland prints, both scenes in New York tenements, sold at auction for a combined price of $250 in October 1977.

Original Lewis Hine prints, on the other hand, remain available in substantial quantity—at prices between about $50 and $400 each. In addition, the International Museum of Photography, which owns Hine's negatives, has made reprints of a number of his works and sells them at $35 to $55 each.

Hine's career as a documentary photographer is one of the most impressive and varied. A sociologist and teacher, he began to photograph in about 1905 with a series of pictures of immigrants at Ellis Island. He went on to depict the miseries of immigrant laborers on the New York State Barge Canal, child labor in factories and mines, and blacks in the ghettos of Washington, D.C. Then, in 1930, he produced a remarkable and dramatic series of pictures of the construction of the Empire State Building; some of the most breathtaking of these views were shot while Hine swung out from a crane nearly one-quarter mile above street level.

Almost all of Hine's work argues a cause, particularly on behalf of the underprivileged and downtrodden. His single most important contribution to American history was the role he played, through both his photographs and writings, in winning passage of the nation's first child labor laws.

Paul Martin had a very different sort of career. Martin was a turn-of-the-century British portrait photographer whose work in that category is essentially undistinguished. However, on weekends and holidays he would roam the streets and parks of London, taking candid portraits with a camera hidden in a brown paper bag. These "snapshots," as he called them, provide a wide-ranging documentation of the life and historic events of late Victorian England. Martin tried to sell these pictures to newspapers, but with only limited success. It was not until the 1940s and 1950s that his "snapshots" began to win the favor of collectors. Original Martin prints, mostly carbon prints, sell in a price range of approximately $150 to $600 each.

Two other early-twentieth-century photographers whose work is essentially documentary in nature are Arnold Genthe and Jacques Henri Lartigue.

Arnold Genthe (1869–1942) was a San Francisco portrait photographer who is known for his candid views of Chinatown and his pictures of the 1906 earthquake. (For an example of a rare print of one of his earthquake photographs, see page 177.) Price range for these early works is approximately $100 to $1,500 each. Genthe later became an important portrait and fashion photographer, and a photographer of the dance.

Jacques Henri Lartigue (b. 1894) is known for his incredibly witty and charming snapshots of early automobiles and airplanes and of fashionable Parisian ladies, taken when he was a child. Long admired by relatives and friends, these works did not gain public recognition until exhibited in 1962. Vintage Lartigue prints typically sell for $400 to $700 each. Modern prints, made by Lartigue in recent years, typically bring about $300 each.

The historic peak of documentary photography was reached in the late 1930s, when the Farm Security Administration embarked on an eight-year project to depict the plight of rural America in the depths of the Depression. The FSA hired

Arthur Rothstein (b. 1915), later director of photography for *Look,* to head this project and eventually added twelve other photographers. More than 270,000 negatives were produced between 1935 and 1943, and most of them are now on file in the Library of Congress.

Today, vintage prints from the FSA project—generally identified as FSA prints on the back—trade actively at prices of about $50 to $1,400 each. In addition, reprints can be ordered from the Photoduplication Service of the Library of Congress for $3.50 to $20 each, depending on print quality and size. Sometimes dealers will process these reprints to meet "archival" standards—that is, make the prints more resistant to deterioration and staining—and offer them at about $35 each.

Several noted photographers worked for the FSA. The most important was Walker Evans (1903–1975), widely regarded, together with Atget, as one of the two finest documentary photographers in history. Originally a writer, Evans took up photography in 1928 at age twenty-five. Over the next forty years he produced thousands of pictures of hand-painted signs, store windows, the rural poor, automobiles, wooden buildings in the South, urban structures, city street scenes, people riding in subways, humble interiors, run-down antebellum mansions, and Victorian houses in New England.

Evans's pictures are the epitome of documentary photography: understated, frontal, uncluttered, and direct. Particularly in the case of his pictures of the rural South, there is a strong feeling of specific time and place. His images also tend to be extremely "quiet": No action occurs, no noise can be "heard." Partly because of this overriding sense of absolute stillness, the pictures invariably treat their subject matter with great reverence and respect.

Vintage Evans prints sell in a price range of approximately $400 to $1,500 each. In addition to these vintage works, three limited-edition portfolios of his photographs have been published in recent years: the 1971 Ives-Sillman portfolio, the 1974 Selected Photographs portfolio, and the posthumous 1977 Portfolio I. Individual prints from these portfolios sell in a range of about $150 to $600 each. *Santa Monica, California,* from Portfolio I, is reproduced on page 203.

Other photographers who participated in the FSA project include Dorothea Lange (1895–1965), Ben Shahn (1898–1969), Russell Lee (b. 1903), John Vachon (1914–1975), and Jack Delano (b. 1914).

Next to Evans, Lange is perhaps the most important of the group. Originally a successful San Francisco portrait photographer, she specialized during the Depression in depicting the plight of migrants. Her most famous picture, one of the landmarks of the FSA era, is titled *Migrant Mother, Nipomo, California.* This work shows a woman, perhaps in her thirties, and her two small children. The children have buried their heads in her shoulders. The expression on the woman's face, so striking, is one of total emptiness about the future. A print of *Migrant Mother* sold at auction for $950 in November 1976. Other Lange prints sell in a price range of about $150 to $600 each.

While the FSA photographers were portraying rural America, Berenice Abbott (b. 1898) was creating a comprehensive visual record of New York City landmarks and buildings under the sponsorship of the Works Progress Administration. (A reproduction of one of these images appears on page 199.) Originally a sculptor, Abbott took up photography while working with Man Ray in Paris in the 1920s. Many of her finest photographs, primarily portraits of artists and writers, were taken during this period. She returned to the United States in 1929 and, between commercial assignments, began to document New York as Atget had documented Paris. Initially working on her own, she received financial support from the FSA between 1935 and 1939 as part of its Federal Arts Project.

Like Walker Evans's work, Abbott's pictures are exceptional in their sense of perspective, composition, use of light, and emphasis on detail. Beginning in the 1940s, Abbott extended her range of subject matter to include scientific studies intended to illustrate the normally invisible principles of physical science, including magnetism and principles of motion. Price range of Abbott's prints is approximately $150 to $800. Of all her images, her Parisian portraits tend to bring the highest prices.

The 1930s also was an important decade for documentary photography in other nations of the world.

In eastern Europe, particularly Poland, Roman Vishniac (b. 1897) undertook an extensive documentation of the Jewish ghettos. These pictures, dating from 1936 to 1939, stand as a final, moving portrait of a people about to be systematically destroyed by the Nazis. After being imprisoned briefly in a concentration camp, Vishniac immigrated to the United States in 1941 and subsequently established himself as one of the most important and imaginative scientific photographers, employing photomicroscopy to depict various organisms.

In Germany, August Sander (1876–1946) set out in the 1920s to portray the German people in their entirety, seeking the perfect individual to typify each trade or position in society. (See example on page 193.) Although his work, taken in its entirety, is not at all anti-Teutonic, the Nazis harassed Sander at every turn and eventually confiscated all the prints they could find. Chilled by this experience, Sander abandoned portrait photography and, after World War II, worked primarily on landscapes. Vintage prints of his prewar portraits sell in a price range of approximately $400 to $1,800, while posthumous prints made by his son Gunther bring about $250 each.

Manuel Alvarez Bravo (b. 1902) is the great Mexican documentary photographer of the same period. His work, beginning in the 1920s and covering four decades, offers a broad depiction of the people and art of Mexico. Individual prints of Bravo's work sell at a retail price of $200 to $300, depending on size. In addition, a 1974 limited-edition portfolio of fifteen of his images carries a retail price of $2,500.

Many other photographers have produced works of an essentially documentary nature during this century. Those whose original prints are regularly available to collectors include the following:

- Doris Ulmann (1884–1934), who photographed widely in Appalachia during the 1920s and early 1930s. Her prints sell for about $200 to $500 each.
- Helen Levitt (b. 1913), known primarily for her 35mm photographs of the people and events of the New York City streets. Her black-and-white prints sell at a retail price of $250 each and her color prints at $450 each.
- Dr. Harold E. Edgerton (b. 1903), a Massachu-

setts Institute of Technology professor known for his pioneering work in high-speed photography. Inventor of the strobe, Edgerton has employed high-intensity light and super-fast exposures to capture bullets in motion, acrobats in midair, splashing water, and other forms of movement. His original black-and-white prints retail at $250 each.

- Werner Mantz (b. 1901), a leading German architectural photographer. His work has been published widely in European architectural and trade magazines, but is not especially well known in the United States. Vintage prints sell for approximately $300 to $900 each.

- Clarence Kennedy (b. 1892), the leading photographer of Italian Renaissance sculpture. A professor of art history at Smith College, Kennedy began taking photographs initially for use in his courses. In the late 1920s and early 1930s, many of his images were issued publicly in limited editions. Prints from these editions, as well as unpublished prints which have made their way onto the market, sell in a price range of approximately $50 to $200 each.

Photojournalism

By the early 1930s, a new type of documentary photography was on the rise: photojournalism (photographs produced for use in newspapers, magazines, and books). This movement eventually became the dominant form of documentary photography, and remains so today.

While the beginnings of photojournalism can be traced back to Roger Fenton's coverage of the Crimean War in the 1850s, the father of "modern" photojournalism generally is considered to be Erich Salomon (1886–1944). Salomon, a German, originated the candid news photo in the late 1920s, including photographs of statesmen caught in unguarded moments. He was renowned for his ability to sneak into banquets and diplomatic meetings, and he often employed great resourcefulness to get the picture he wanted. At a 1932 dinner attended by Herbert Hoover, Salomon hid his camera in a flowerpot on the head table and triggered the shutter by remote control. Vintage Salomon prints today sell in a range of about $200 to $600.

Two developments were responsible for the burgeoning of photojournalism in the late 1920s. First, the combination of high-speed rotary presses and improved photoengraving techniques facilitated the broader use of photographs by newspapers and magazines. Second, hand-held cameras with fast lenses were introduced, permitting exposures with ordinary room light.

Henri Cartier-Bresson (b. 1908) was among the first photojournalists to employ the hand-held camera. Initially an amateur, he started photographing seriously in about 1930. Today he ranks as one of the most important and influential photographers of this century.

Cartier-Bresson has a special interest in photographing people and in capturing the essence of what has not previously been seen. He is famous for his theory of the "decisive moment"—that is, seizing the split second when the subject stands revealed in its most significant aspect. His modern prints sell at about $250 to $500 each.

André Kertész (b. 1894) was another early user of the small camera—as with Cartier-Bresson, a Leica. Born and raised in Hungary, Kertész went to Paris after World War I to pursue a career in photography. He undertook assignments for many leading European publications until 1936, when he came to the United States to work for Keystone and then the Condé Nast publications. Since 1962, he has photographed exclusively for himself.

Kertész also was one of the first photographers to demonstrate the tremendous photographic richness of the street. His work is known for its wit, composition, and sense of the unusual. One of his most famous bodies of work is his series of distorted nudes, photographed with warped mirrors. Retail prices for recently-made Kertész prints are $400 to $600 each, depending on size. However, his nude distortions carry an additional premium of $125. Vintage Kertész prints, generally small in size, are extremely rare and sell at approximately $2,500 each.

In 1926, a year after he went to Paris, Kertész met a young journalist who went by the name Brassaï (b. 1899). It was through this association that Brassaï (born Gyula Halász) became interested in photography. Soon he bought a camera and began photographing the night life of Paris, a subject which was to make him famous.

Brassaï's first book, *Paris de nuit,* depicts the brothels, cafés, and other "underground" hangouts and was an immediate sensation. Other books followed, but none with the impact of that initial work. Recently, Brassaï has been making prints from many of his 1930s negatives, and these are available at a retail price of $550 to $950 each. Vintage prints from the thirties generally bring somewhat more.

In England in 1938, Bill Brandt (b. 1904) published *London by Night,* a counterpart to Brassaï's volume. Brandt now ranks as the foremost British photographer of the past forty years. However, while much of his early work can be described as photojournalistic, Brandt does not fit neatly into any specific category. Particularly since World War II, he has concentrated on portraits, landscapes, and nudes. Much of Brandt's work is fantastic and surreal. His nudes often are highly distorted or placed in incongruous surroundings. Frequently he photographs from strange perspectives, such as a close-up of an ear against a landscape of Friar's Bay. Brandt's prints sell at about $450 each.

Many of the leading photojournalists of the past forty years were associated with *Life* magazine. Examples include W. Eugene Smith (1918–1978), Margaret Bourke-White (1904–1971), Alfred Eisenstadt (b. 1898), Robert Capa (1913–1954), and Andreas Feininger (b. 1906)—all of whose original prints can be acquired today by collectors.

A native of Kansas, Smith became interested in photography while in high school and began to photograph for local newspapers at age seventeen. After one year in college, he joined the staff of *Newsweek* but was dismissed when he insisted on using a 35mm camera, which he felt gave him greater freedom than the traditional large-size press camera. He subsequently worked for a number of other leading U.S. magazines, including service on the staff of *Life* in 1939–1941 and 1944–1954.

Like that of many other outstanding photojournalists, Smith's work covers a wide range of subject matter. His "photo essays" are especially well known. These include *Folk Singers* (1947), *Trial by Jury* (1948), *Country Doctor* (1948), and *Nurse Midwife* (1951). Smith was a man of great sensitivity and high standards and ideals. In preparing his most moving photo essay, *Spanish Village* (1951), he spent more than a year living with the people in order to be a friend rather than an interloper.

Many of Smith's photographs depict moments of great tenderness or pathos. Another hallmark of his work is its dramatic use of light, with extremes of dark contrasted against small patches of bright. Retail price for his prints ranges from $400 to $600 each, depending on size.

Bourke-White joined *Life* when the magazine was founded in 1936 and was, in the public consciousness, probably the best known among the dozens of photographers who were on its staff over the years. In a career spanning three decades, she traveled almost constantly to depict such subjects as the might of American industry, the hardships of the rural poor, South African gold miners, victims of Buchenwald, and life in Russia. She was one of the first photographers to understand the possibilities of aerial photography; many of her most graphically beautiful pictures were taken from airplanes and helicopters. She also was a prolific commercial photographer, working on a number of major advertising accounts. Her vintage prints sell at prices between about $40 and $600 each, while photogravures of a series of pictures taken in the Soviet Union are priced at about $200 each.

The German-born Eisenstadt has been described as a five-foot-three-inch "bundle of raw nerves and raw energy." He began his career in Berlin in the late 1920s and became one of the leading European photojournalists. In 1935, he immigrated to the United States and, the following year, joined *Life* at its founding. He soon established himself as perhaps its most versatile and trusted photographer, covering everything from sharecroppers in Mississippi to the war in Ethiopia. Original Eisenstadt prints, harder to find than those of Smith or Bourke-White, generally cost between $200 and $400 each.

Capa was the greatest war photographer of this century. He covered five different conflicts and, during World War II, was assigned by *Life* to Europe, first in London and then moving with the troops onto the Continent. He was killed in 1954 by a land mine in Indochina. His original prints typically bring prices of $175 to $350 each.

Feininger, son of the American painter Lyonel Feininger, was on the *Life* staff from 1943 to 1962, completing 346 assignments during that period. His work is divided into four major areas: early amateur photographs, including pictures of cars, buildings, and young women; architectural studies, taken primarily in Stockholm in the early thirties; photojournalism; and his precise, close-up depictions of feathers, shells, and other objects emphasizing abstraction and form. Feininger also has been one of the most influential teachers and writers on photography. His original prints sell in a price range of approximately $200 to $1,200 each.

Still another of the important *Life* photographers is Gordon Parks (b. 1912), who joined the *Life* staff in 1949. His first assignment was a photo essay on gang leaders in Harlem. He continued to depict black America for the next two decades, including major assignments on the Black Muslims, the death of Malcolm X, and the Black Panthers. Parks is outspoken and multi-talented. He wrote and directed the film *Shaft,* and he wrote, directed, and composed the score for a feature film titled *Learning Tree*. His original prints, mostly color prints, generally bring about $1,000 each.

Other leading twentieth-century photojournalists include the following:

— Josef Sudek (1896–1976), a Czech who specialized in panoramas, still lifes, nudes, landscapes, and symbolic "Remembrances." Sudek preferred to use large old cameras because of their greater sensitivity. His use of these cameras was all the more remarkable because he lost an arm in World War I. Original Sudek prints sell for about $600 to $1,200 each.

— Barbara Morgan (b. 1900), the great photographic interpreter of modern dance. Her pictures of Martha Graham, stressing form and movement, are among her most famous. Retail prices for her prints range from $350 to $450, depending on size.

— Edouard Boubat (b. 1923), a French magazine photographer who specializes in reportage and portraits. Retail price of his prints is $150 each.

— Josef Koudelka (b. 1939), known for his depictions of gypsies in Czechoslovakia and Rumania. His prints typically sell in a range of $150 to $200 each.

— Elliott Erwitt (b. 1928), an American whose pictures are filled with great wit and humor. Retail price of his prints is $125 to $175, depending on size. A limited-edition portfolio of ten of his photographs carries a retail price of $1,150.

Then there is perhaps the most popular photojournalist of them all: Arthur Fellig (1899–1969), better known as Weegee. Weegee (the nickname is a corruption of Ouija) was the last of the great old-style press photographers. A free lance, he lived in a cluttered room across from Manhattan police headquarters and always slept fully clothed, ready to speed to the scene of a crime or fire.

Weegee's photographs are a strange mixture of the humorous and the grotesque. While other press photographers focused on an event itself, Weegee learned that some of the most captivating pictures could be found in the reactions of the surrounding crowd. One of his most famous images is of a drowned man at the beach. The man's fiancée is staring into the camera with a faint smile, seemingly more interested in looking pretty for her picture than in the tragedy that has just occurred.

Weegee also was fascinated with violence, and his most gruesome pictures, of dead gunmen, do not make for easy viewing. Yet, his work has an appeal that is undeniable. Perhaps it is his eye for the unusual, or the primitive nature of the man himself, which draws so many collectors to these photographs. Weegee's prints are among the most actively traded in all of photography, at prices of approximately $100 to $800 each.

Photography for Commercial Markets

Beginning in the 1920s—and continuing to the present day—a huge market has developed for high-quality commercial photography, including fashion photography, photographs for use in advertisements, and commercial portraiture. The buyers of these photographs include manufacturers of consumer products, the leading women's magazines, and the movie industry.

In addition to making prints for their clients, photographers often make additional prints for their own files or sometimes for sale to the public. It is primarily these additional prints which are available to collectors.

Edward Steichen, whose career is discussed in Chapter 10, was one of the first well-known photographers to recognize the massive potential of the commercial market. He began accepting commercial assignments in about 1920 and remained one of the dominant personalities in this field through the late 1930s, working on such advertising accounts as Eastman Kodak and Packard automobiles and serving as chief portrait and fashion photographer for *Vogue* and *Vanity Fair*. His portraits and fashion photographs, in particular, now come up fairly regularly for sale. Recently, a dealer offered a print of his 1931 portrait of Clark Gable, taken for *Vanity Fair*, at $1,200. Baron De Meyer, also discussed in Chapter 10, is another of the leaders.

In contrast to the documentary photography of the 1930s, commercial photography is highly refined, even slick, and generally posed in studio settings.

One of the earliest masters of the sophisticated studio pose was Nickolas Muray (1892–1965), whose original prints are now relatively rare. Born in Hungary, Muray came to the United States in 1913 and within a decade had established himself as one of the most prominent of all celebrity portrait photographers. He frequently contributed to *Harper's Bazaar* and *Vanity Fair*, and his sitters included Charlie Chaplin, Greta Garbo, Eugene O'Neill, Loretta Young, Mary Pickford, Bela Bartok, and H. G. Wells, among many others. A Muray portrait is refined and flattering. Many of his photographs were retouched to eliminate the sitter's flaws. One of his most famous pictures is his 1927 portrait of Babe Ruth, bat in hand, with the smooth face of a choirboy and the massive body of a gorilla.

Beginning in the late 1920s, while continuing a limited involvement in portraiture, Muray became one of the leading advertising and fashion photographers. One of his best-known commercial assignments was his extensive work for the Seabrook Farms line of frozen foods.

Vintage prints of Muray's work, primarily his portraits, sell in a price range of approximately $100 to $450 each. His early portraits of Claude Monet are an exception. These pictures were taken at Monet's estate at Giverney, France, in 1926 and represent one of the few times Muray worked outside the studio. They generally bring prices of $500 to $1,000 each. In addition to vintage prints, a limited-edition portfolio of twelve posthumous prints was published in 1978 by the International Museum of Photography (which owns Muray's negatives) and the Prakapas Gallery in New York. Retail price of this portfolio is $375.

Paul Outerbridge, Jr. (1896–1958) is another important photographer whose vintage prints, like Muray's, are relatively rare. His imagery is among the most bizarre ever produced.

Outerbridge took up photography in 1921, after studying drawing at the Art Students League in New York for four years, and went on to become one of the most successful commercial photographers of the twenties and thirties. In addition to his commercial work, he created an important body of images which were undertaken purely for his personal pleasure and were exhibited widely at the time. Initially in this personal work he concentrated on black-and-white cubist studies in abstract form. Beginning in 1929–1930, he pioneered the use of the three-color carbro print technique, which produces full-color photographs with pastel tones. Many of his carbro print photographs are of female nudes. As the years went by, these works became increasingly erotic, until Outerbridge had created what scholar Graham Howe calls "some of the most impressive examples of color photography concerned with sexual decadence and fetishism." Outerbridge eventually was ostracized because of this work, and he left New York in 1942 to write and earn a living as a portrait/travel photographer in California.

It is only fairly recently that Outerbridge's photographs, so exceptional in their craftsmanship and composition, have begun to win renewed collector attention.

The works which come up for sale are primarily his early cubist studies, some early prints of photographs taken for *Harper's Bazaar* and *Vanity Fair,* and his carbro prints from 1930 on. His early prints, mostly small-sized platinum prints, sell in a price range of about $500 to $1,200 each. However, a platinum print with especially strange imagery can bring considerably more: An undated self-portrait — showing Outerbridge dressed in tuxedo, top hat, gloves, and turtleneck-type sweater, with a cloth hood covering his entire head like a ski mask, a folded piece of paper fitted across his nose, wearing a Lone Ranger-type mask with glass inserts that reflect all light and with three horizontal sashes across the front of his white shirt creating a striped effect — was offered recently by a dealer for $2,500.

His bizarre carbro prints can bring more than that. Two recently sold at auction for $3,000 each. One depicts a female model facing away from the camera, nude from the waist down and wearing a band leader's jacket. The other depicts a woman wearing a formal evening gown, seated in an upholstered chair. It appears that the dress has been pulled down to reveal her breasts, but it is impossible to be sure, since she is shielding herself with a fan. The fan itself bears the image of one black hen and one white hen, pecking at a snail on the bare bottom of a naked child lying face-down under a bush.

In the highly competitive commercial photography world of the 1930s, there was a great premium on creativity and style. And one of the most stylish portrait photographers of them all has been Cecil Beaton (b.1904), whose active career spans a period of forty years from the late 1920s through the 1960s.

In a Beaton portrait, there invariably is great emphasis on setting, reflecting his work as one of the leading set designers for movies and the theater. Often, in taking a portrait, he has constructed an elaborate backdrop especially for the occasion. Examples include his portrait of Mrs. Harrison Williams, a society lady, emerging through a sea of torn paper, and of Dolores Del Rio in a mock "jungle." Beaton also has been a leading fashion photographer, working for *Vogue, Harper's Bazaar,* and other publications. Prices for vintage Beaton prints range from about $150 to $800 each.

Certain photographers have specialized primarily in fashion. Examples include Erwin Blumenfeld (1879–1969) and Horst P. Horst (b. 1906). Blumenfeld is considered one of the most innovative and imaginative of all photographic illustrators. He emigrated to the United States from Germany in the late 1930s and became a great commercial success, producing more than 100 color covers for *Vogue, Harper's Bazaar, Look,* and *Cosmopolitan.* Like Outerbridge, he also pursued his personal imagery and developed great technical skill. He is best known for his pictures of female nudes, often draped in wetted muslin. Price range for his work is approximately $300 to $400.

Horst, who, like Blumenfeld, came to the United States from Germany, has worked for many leading publications, primarily in fashion, but also as a portrait and travel photographer. His prints generally sell in a range of $200 to $600 each.

Then there are a number of photographers who are known primarily as portrait artists. Examples include Arnold Newman (b. 1918), Yousuf Karsh (b. 1908), and Philippe Halsman (b. 1906).

The New York-born Newman is a free lance whose portraits of famous people have appeared in numerous publications, including *Look, Holiday, Life, Time, Fortune,* and *Esquire.* His hallmark is the use of a setting depicting the sitter's work, such as Igor Stravinsky seated at a piano or Martha Graham standing at a practice bar. Retail prices for Newman's prints are $300 to $500 each.

Karsh, a Canadian, is the leading commercial photographer working in the studio tradition. His thriving business takes him around the world, photographing business leaders, statesmen, famous writers, and other notables in a posed, studio-type setting. His original prints carry retail prices of $400 to $500 each.

Halsman, like Newman a free lance, took up photography in Paris in 1931 and fled to the United States in 1940. Among his most notable achievements, he holds the distinction of having produced more *Life* covers than any other photographer. His custom, at the end of each photography session, is to ask the subject to jump a few inches off the floor. Some of his most amusing and remarkable portraits are from this "jumping" series. Halsman's prints bring prices of about $150 to $500 each.

Still other living photographers have been successful in a range of commercial work. An example is Irving Penn (b. 1917). A native of New Jersey, Penn first came into prominence in the late 1940s as a photographer for the Condé Nast publications, particularly *Vogue.* His subject matter—whether portraits, fashion pictures, advertising pictures, or still lifes—typically is presented in a simple setting against a plain backdrop. The result, almost always, is imagery of extreme elegance. Retail prices for his prints range from $700 to $2,000.

Other important twentieth-century portrait, fashion, and/or advertising photographers include the following:

— George Platt Lynes (1907–1956), who made stylish pictures for *Harper's Bazaar* and other magazines and specialized in fashion and advertising photography for the most prestigious New York stores. His subject matter includes portraits, male nudes, the ballet, and surrealistic still lifes. Platt Lynes prints seldom come onto the market. One, a portrait of Yves Tanguy, sold recently at auction for $400.

— James Abbe (1883–1973), one of the earliest photographers of Hollywood stars. Abbe pioneered the idea of taking movie stars off the set and into a studio for their portraits, and he often used backlighting to create a heightened sense of glamour. His prints trade in a price range of approximately $300 to $600 each.

— James Vander Zee (b. 1886), the leading studio photographer in Harlem from the 1920s through the 1940s. Vander Zee's work, which has come into prominence in the past decade, offers a wide-ranging portrayal of the life of middle-class blacks. Price range for his prints, mostly modern prints by Richard Benson, is about $150 to $400 each.

In recent years, a new generation of commercial photographers has come to the fore. The most prominent of this group is Richard Avedon (b. 1923). Avedon achieved his initial fame as a fashion photographer. But it is his portraits, stark and penetrating, which have won the greatest acclaim among collectors. Avedon has photographed famous people from nearly every stratum of society—from Gerald Ford to Oscar Levant, from General William Westmoreland to the Chicago Seven. Retail prices for his 8- by 10-inch prints are $300 to $900. Huge "photomurals," on the other hand, are priced as high as $25,000.

Dada and Surrealism

These important international art movements—Dada from approximately 1916 to 1922, and Surrealism from the 1920s forward—have resulted in the creation of a substantial body of photographs as well as other art forms.

Dadaism, one of the most nihilistic and antiaesthetic movements in art history, grew primarily out of the disillusionment of many artists during World War I. The Dadaists rejected traditional art, ideas, and morality in favor of works that were accidental and incongruous in nature. Man Ray's "ready mades," including the urinal he exhibited in 1917, are prime examples.

Surrealism provided an answer to the nihilism of the Dadaists: It stresses fantasy and the imagination and is based on a belief in the omnipotence of the dream. Examples include the paintings of Salvador Dali and Joan Miró.

In photography, these two movements were dominated by Man Ray (1890–1976), one of the greatest of all photographic experimentalists. Born in Philadelphia, Ray moved to New York as a young man and became a leading member of the American avant-garde. He began to photograph in 1920 and the following year moved to Paris, where he supported himself by establishing a commercial fashion and portrait photography business.

In the early 1920s, Ray accidentally discovered the "Rayograph"—a cameraless type of photography in which objects are placed on photosensitive paper and then strafed with light. Ray would typically employ a series of exposures to create these works—casting the shadow of a glass on the paper during one exposure, for instance, and then using other objects and different types of light. While similar to the photogenic drawings produced in the earliest years of photography, this technique had not been practiced in any significant way for nearly a century. Because each Rayograph was created directly on photographic film—rather than being a positive print made from a negative—it is a unique image that could not be produced in multiple copies. Ray made these works throughout the 1920s, and in 1931 produced a portfolio of photogravures of his Rayographs as a promotion for the electric utility serving Paris. (These photogravures, unlike the Rayographs themselves, were produced in a multiple edition.) A copy of this portfolio, which is entitled *Electricité* and contains ten gravures, sold at auction for $2,600 in February 1977.

Ray also was one of the earliest experimenters with photomontage—the photographing of paper collages. And beginning in 1929 he experimented with the use of solarization. This is a technique, also discovered accidentally, in which the negative is reversed during exposure. The process tends to produce a highly dreamy effect.

In addition, Ray experimented at various times with multiple-exposure techniques and with prints which combine photography and drawing. The most famous example of the latter is his *Violon d'Ingres,* with the sound holes of a violin drawn on the back of a nude female model.

Ray returned to the United States in 1940, settling in Los Angeles, where he was active both as a painter and photographer. He once again moved to Paris in 1951, but thereafter took few photographs.

In general, it is Man Ray's Parisian images, particularly his Rayographs and solarized prints, which draw the highest prices—sometimes up to $6,000 or more. A fine portrait of a famous sitter, taken in Paris, might sell for $2,500 to $5,000. A lesser portrait from the Paris years might sell for $1,000 to $2,000. His photographs from the 1940s, taken in California, usually are priced somewhat below comparable Parisian works. The above prices are for vintage prints. Later prints typically bring less. As an example, a dealer recently offered a vintage print of Ray's 1923 portrait of Eric Satie at $3,500 and a later print, circa 1950, of the same work at $2,500. One of Ray's early Parisian works is reproduced on page 195.

At about the same time Man Ray invented the Rayograph in Paris, László Moholy-Nagy (1895–1946) was inventing, totally independently, the "photogram" in Berlin. The two processes are essentially the same.

Although generally considered to be a member of the "Constructivist" school of art—a post-Cubist movement which sought to translate Cubist painting into three dimensions, and to create works which incorporated time and movement— much of Moholy-Nagy's photography relates directly to Surrealism. Like Ray, he has been one of the most influential artists of this century, in photography as well as in other media.

Moholy-Nagy was born in Hungary and as a young man briefly attended law school. After World War I, he abandoned the law for art, moving to Vienna in 1919 and to Berlin the following year. In 1923, he joined the faculty of the Bauhaus at Weimar and there became one of the world's foremost photography teachers and theoreticians. He left the Bauhaus in 1928, and in 1934 he left Germany. After spending three years in Holland and England, he settled in 1937 in Chicago, where he founded the new Bauhaus (now the Institute of Design).

As an artist, in both his constructions and photographs, Moholy-Nagy was preoccupied with the effects of light and of light in motion. His photographic work is divided into three major categories: photograms; photographs of collages (see example on page 187); and his more standard images, emphasizing light, patterns, and form.

Moholy-Nagy was not a prolific artist. His original prints, therefore, are among the rarest of any major photographer. A vintage print of his earliest photogram, *Der Spiegel,* was offered recently at auction. The presale price estimate of the auction house was $10,000 to $12,000. But the work failed to reach its "reserve," or the minimum price specified by the owner, and so did not sell. Other Moholy-Nagy photographs trade occasionally at prices of about $1,000 to $5,000 each.

In addition to Ray and Moholy-Nagy, other important photographers who have worked in a Dadaist or Surrealist style include Christian Schad (b. 1894), Herbert Bayer (b. 1900), Nathan Lerner (b. 1915), John Heartfield (1891–1968), and Francis Bruguière (1879–1945).

Schad, a German expressionist painter, cofounded the Dada movement in Zurich in 1916. In 1918, in connection with Dada experiments with new mediums and techniques, he began producing "Schadographs"—cameraless photographs which predate the Rayograph and photogram. Schad's work rarely comes up for sale in the United States, but does trade occasionally in Europe in a price range of about $600 to $1,000.

Bayer is an Austrian-born architect, designer, painter, and sculptor who, like Moholy-Nagy, was associated with the Bauhaus, the foremost design school of the 1920s. Many of his works are photomontages in which geometric shapes—including cones, cubes, and spheres—have been placed, incongruously, in natural landscapes or imaginary environments. He has described his technique as follows: "Photographs are cut out, their parts are put together in a new form and occasionally retouched. Then the finished montage is rephotographed." Bayer's most renowned image is his 1932 self-portrait, a photomontage made partially with a mannequin. In this amusing picture, Bayer appears to have pulled a slice out of his left arm, and he stares, startled, at the resulting gap. Price range of Bayer's work is approximately $500 to $1,100.

Lerner was one of the first students, in 1937, at the new Bauhaus in Chicago. He subsequently taught there, and then became dean of faculty and students. Like the work of Moholy-Nagy, many of his photographs are concerned with the effects of light, including early time-exposure studies of moving automobile lights. Lerner also invented a device called the "light box," which allows the selective introduction of light into the camera to create montagelike effects. His work sells at about $250 to $500 per print.

Heartfield, a native of Berlin, was born Helmut Herzfelde, but anglicized his name to protest anti-British propaganda in Germany during World War I. He was a political activist and radical, and a master of satire in art. One of his classic works, titled *Hurrah, die Butter ist alle!* (Hurrah, the butter is finished!), shows a Nazi family eating a bicycle. It was inspired by Goering's statement, "Iron always makes a country strong. Butter and lard only make people fat."

Heartfield's photographs, mostly pictures of his collages, come onto the market only occasionally. One, titled *Krisenfestes Rindvieh* (Depression-resisting Bull), was offered recently by a dealer for $2,400. This work, a collage depicting a bull devouring itself with a fork and carving knife while shedding two big tears, first appeared in a German newspaper in 1934. It was accompanied in the newspaper by the following caption: "The long campaign to breed the ideal bull has ended successfully. The import of expensive cattle-destroying machines has therefore become unnecessary. This has resulted on the one hand in a significant surplus for livestock-producing countries, while on the other hand seriously complicating the export of standard cattle in machine-producing countries. Due to the machinations of exportation, several governments have already failed as a result of the new hybrid. Pictorial report by our correspondent John Heartfield."

Bruguière is regarded as the first important photographer of pure abstraction. Born in San Francisco to wealthy parents, he went to Europe in his early twenties to study painting. In 1905, he returned to the United States, met Stieglitz, took up photography, and joined the Photo-Secession. One of his images, a portrait, was published in the October 1916 issue of *Camera Work*. He began to experiment with multiple exposures in 1912, and in 1919 opened a studio in New York, where he became well known for his photographs of Theatre Guild productions. Then, in 1926, he began what is now considered his most important work: experiments with cut-paper abstractions, photographed with strong light playing across the surface. These are strange and eerily beautiful works, often difficult to comprehend at first look. Price range for Bruguière's work is approximately $150 to $600 per print.

Still other important twentieth-century avant-garde photographers include the following:

> — Alexander Rodchenko (1891–1956), a Russian photojournalist who was also a leading Constructivist painter and photographer. Rodchenko was, like Ray, Moholy-Nagy, and Heartfield, one of the earliest experimenters in photomontage. However, few of his photographs have ever come out of Russia, with the result that his work is extremely rare. His prints, when they do come on the market, typically bring prices of about $4,000 to $6,000.

> — Maurice Tabard (b. 1897), who worked in Paris as a free-lance photographer during the 1930s and applied many of Man Ray's discoveries and

ideas to illustrative and advertising photography.

— Hans Bellmer (1902–1975), best known for his photographs of dolls which have been taken apart and reassembled to form strange geometric configurations.

— Lotte Jacobi (b. 1896), a portrait photographer who has experimented extensively in photomontage and photogenic drawings.

A number of important twentieth-century photographers have worked outside any clear-cut photographic movement.

An example is Alphonse Marie Mucha (1860–1939), a leading Art Nouveau painter and printmaker. Mucha often made photographic studies of female models for use in his paintings, and vintage prints of these photographs today trade in a price range of about $200 to $1,000 each. In addition, a dealer recently offered a rare Mucha study of a male model in female costume, circa 1900, for $1,350. Modern reprints from fifteen of Mucha's negatives also are available, at a price of about $125 each.

In New Orleans, E. J. Bellocq (1873–1949) was a commercial photographer who was considered a rather bizarre and reclusive individual of modest professional accomplishment. But when he died, a surprising discovery was made: Bellocq had, in mid-career, spent his leisure hours taking portraits of New Orleans prostitutes. Nearly 100 glass-plate negatives, dating from about 1912, were found in his desk. Photographer Lee Friedlander acquired the negatives in 1966, and he now makes prints from them using a process in wide use at the beginning of the century. Retail price is $300 to $350 per print.

More recently, Clarence John Laughlin (b. 1905) has developed an imagery that is highly personal and sensory. Laughlin was born in Louisiana and lived on a plantation as a small boy. In about 1925, he began reading Baudelaire and the French Symbolists and started writing his own poetry and gothic fiction. He took up photography in 1934 and made his living until 1969 as an architectural photographer.

Laughlin, who has said that his photographs can be divided into twenty-three distinct bodies of work, is best known for his photographs of run-down southern mansions enveloped in shadows. In almost all his pictures there is a sense of piercing through a veil of mystery to begin to see the unseen. Retail price of his prints is $250.

Frederick Sommer (b. 1905) has produced a body of work that is both small and diverse. Sommer, a painter, took up photography in 1938. His earliest images include horizonless Arizona landscapes, photographs of embryos, and his junkyard series. By the mid-1940s he was making and photographing assemblages of "found" objects. He also has worked in cameraless photography, using cellophane and glass as a ground for pigment-laden oils or grease stained by smoke. Negatives created in this manner are then contact printed or enlarged. And he has created portraits which are blurred through movement of the camera and detailed photographs of folded reproductions of Dürer wood engravings. Sommer often takes months to plan, execute, and print an image, and so it generally requires great patience to acquire a Sommer. He seldom makes more than a few prints of any image. Some of his prints are unique. Retail prices range from about $1,000 to $5,000.

Chapter 13

Contemporary Photography

The term contemporary photography refers to the forward edge of current photographic activity—works by photographers who are taking the medium in new aesthetic and conceptual directions, often pursuing a highly personal vision.

We live in an age of great ferment and change in photography. A new generation of university-trained photographers is increasingly abandoning the aesthetic structure inherited from painting—and even the traditional aesthetics and content of photography itself. It is a long way, for instance, from Edward Weston's classical nudes (see example on page 183) to the social landscapes of Robert Adams (see page 213).

Often, as in the case of Adams, it is necessary to study a body of a contemporary photographer's work to appreciate the imagery and understand the photographer's intentions. Knowing something about Weston and his range of work is helpful in viewing the photograph reproduced on page 183, but not at all essential to enjoying the work or perceiving its exceptional purity of light and form. The Adams photograph on page 213, by contrast, means very little by itself—unless you understand Adams's objective of documenting the Colorado landscape, including the grace of the land and the man-made squalor upon it.

Furthermore, the Adams photograph—unlike the Weston—cannot really be described as "beautiful." But that isn't the point. Few contemporary photographers are concerned with traditional issues of visual attractiveness. (For an exception, see the Lilo Raymond photograph reproduced on page 215. There *always* are exceptions in contemporary photography.) Instead, photographers are increasingly seeking to explore the uniqueness of photography as a medium. While the apparent subject matter of a contemporary photograph may be a tree, chair, or landscape, the real theme often is photography itself—its possibilities and limitations; relationships between shapes, tones, lines, and depths; and the effects of monocular ("one-eyed") vision. In other words, many contemporary photographers are more interested in photographing things to see how they will appear in photographs than in evoking meanings beyond the photographs themselves. Thomas Barrow, in his well-known "cancellation" series of photographs of buildings and open fields, has gone so far as to draw a large X across each image, pointedly questioning the meaning of content.

It will take years to evaluate fully most of today's contemporary photography. For this reason, the collecting of contemporary photographs tends to be the most unsettled, challenging, and personally involving sector of the photography market—and, for many collectors, the most gratifying.

"There's a huge market for contemporary works," says Victor Schrager, director of Light Gallery, one of the leading New York galleries specializing in contemporary photographs. "It's growing and it's going to keep growing. People love these works. They're very accessible and they're inexpensive and you can collect them. If you could look through our invoice book you would see that the buyers run the whole range. There are a lot of institutional [museum and corporate] collections. But there are also individuals who spend $50,000 to $75,000 a year here and people who save up for six months to buy the one print they love and go out the door hugging it. There is so much material and there is such a range to look at, and you can really make a collection with any focus you want. It becomes sort of a diary, a reflection of your interests. And it will mirror very directly the amount of time and energy—and sometimes money—you put into it."

Price range for most contemporary works is $100 to $350 per print. However, in a few cases, such as the work of the late Diane Arbus, prices go as high as $2,500.

Although there is great diversity of content, form, and tenor in contemporary photography, much of the work fits into two broad, contrasting trends:

> 1. *Documentary* or straight photography. Robert Adams's images are an example. Other photographers whose work generally is considered to be documentary in nature include Arbus, known for her portraits of freaks, transvestites, and nudists; Lee Friedlander (b. 1934), who uses a 35mm camera to capture seemingly insignificant bits of the everyday world (monuments, tree branches, shop windows, street scenes, etc.); Garry Winogrand (b. 1928), who has an unusual eye for finding human gestures and juxtapositions in the chaos of urban streets; and George Tice (b. 1938), who takes "straight" pictures of traditional subjects, including nature, urban buildings, and portraits. Sometimes, in this "new" documentary photography, subject matter is trivial, even boring. But this reflects, in many cases, a conscious desire to find "neutral" content in order not to interfere with the pure exploration of the potential of the camera—that is, how photographic vision differs from the perceptions of the unaided human eye. As opposed to earlier documentary photographers like Lewis Hine and Dorothea Lange, the objective of today's docu-

mentary photographers is not so much to persuade as to explore and understand. Many of the photographers, including Friedlander and Winogrand, are noted for their "found" images — those which they have perceived amid the jumble of life, capturing these images in a snapshotlike way with a hand-held camera.

2. *Conceptual* photography, including prints which have been "manipulated" through double exposure, the addition of words, the scratching of the negative, hand coloring, or other techniques. The Duane Michals photograph reproduced on page 211 is an example. These are essentially "staged" works which have been conceived in advance, or in which the print has in some way been doctored. While documentary photographers are concerned with catching a finished picture at the "decisive moment" of snapping the shutter, conceptual photographers are equally concerned with what happens before or after that moment. In addition, in contrast to the cool aloofness from subject matter which characterizes much of today's documentary photography, conceptual work tends to represent a highly personal outpouring of dream and fantasy. Jerry Uelsmann (b. 1934), who "composes" his photographs by piecing together various negatives in the darkroom, is among the best-known conceptualists. One of Uelsmann's photographs depicts a cathedral rising magically from a majestic old tree stump. Other leading photographers who manipulate their imagery include Benno Friedman (b. 1945), who applies solarization, bleaching, toning, drawing, airbrushing, crayon, watercolor, and even nail polish to his prints; Naomi Savage (b. 1927), who treats photoengraving plates with acid to achieve a relief effect and then displays the metal plates as "photographs"; and Robert Heinecken (b. 1931), who prints his images on shaped linen and employs a variety of other manipulative techniques.

A third major trend is the rapid acceptance, since the early 1970s, of color photography as a major medium of artistic expression. Color photography is discussed in the next chapter.

One reason for the tremendous changes taking place in photographic aesthetics is that the market for photographs has changed so dramatically. When the great pictorial magazines, particularly *Life* and *Look,* were in their prime, photojournalism was the dominant movement, offering leading photographers a practical means for earning a living. But photojournalism has declined. So today's photographers typically make a living by selling their original prints and by producing photographic books—and also, in many cases, by teaching photography at a university. Going back to Robert Adams as an example, four books of his work have been published: *White Churches of the Plains* in 1970, *The Architecture and Art of Early Hispanic Colorado* in 1974, *The New West* in 1974, and *Denver* in 1977. In addition, his prints are marketed by Castelli Graphics in New York.

Earning a living by selling books and prints is more difficult financially than travelling around the world for *Life* or *Look*. But it also has given today's photographers total freedom to pursue whatever imagery they wish. Partly because photography has become such a wide-open alternative to traditional media, it has emerged as one of the most fertile and creative art forms of this decade.

Some photographers bridge the gap between the great twentieth-century "masters" and the more iconoclastic younger generation. Two such photographers are Aaron Siskind (b. 1903) and Harry Callahan (b. 1912). Besides being important masters in their own right, both are teachers whose students include some of the outstanding members of the new generation of contemporary photographers.

Siskind, like so many contemporary photographers, has developed a highly individualistic style which doesn't really fit into any narrow definition. He began in the early 1930s in the documentary vein, but since the early 1940s has evolved a kind of flat, symbolic, abstract imagery based on close-up pictures of details from man-made objects: cracking walls, peeling billboards, graffiti, broken windows. In essence, he takes ordinary objects and transforms them into something different. Often, specific subject matter becomes totally incomprehensible, due to the closeness with which the picture has been taken. Siskind himself has written that his photographs show "the detritus of our world which I am combing for meaning." Price range for Siskind's work is $250 to $400 for modern prints and approximately $750 for vintage prints, made before 1950.

Callahan's subject matter includes pictures of his wife Eleanor, cityscapes, nature views, and time-exposure studies of moving flashlight beams. There is an elegance of line and structure that establishes his photographs as perhaps the most classically beautiful in all of contemporary photography. One of his photographs is reproduced on page 209. His prints sell in a price range of $450 to $600 each.

Robert Frank (b. 1924) is another key transitional figure—an individual whose work has been highly influential in the tremendous burst of photographic creativity over the past two decades. A native of Switzerland, Frank apprenticed with commercial photographers in Geneva, Basel, and Zurich in the early 1940s. He came to the United States in 1947 and worked for *Harper's Bazaar* and other magazines. In 1955, he received a Guggenheim fellowship to travel throughout the United States photographing for his book, *Les Américains*, which was published initially in Europe in 1958. The photographs in this book are blatantly opinionated and antiheroic, depicting America as an emotional wasteland filled with ugly shopping centers, lonely highways, and dehumanized people. The work became an immediate "underground" best-seller in the United States and a cult symbol of the "beat generation."

In this book, Frank showed other photographers that they could pursue their creative impulses totally free from commercial pressures. In addition, his rejection of traditional American values was a shocking departure in its time from the then-existing standards of documentary photography and photojournalism. Retail prices for original Frank prints, mostly images from *Les Américains*, are $500 to $1,200. Since 1970, Frank has concentrated almost entirely on filmmaking.

Diane Arbus (1923–1971) is still another of the most influential photographers. Originally a prominent fashion photographer, Arbus produced—in the final nine years of her life, before her suicide at age forty-eight—an unparalleled body of portraits of freaks, nudists, and transvestites. Her work seems to argue that any subject matter, regardless of how grotesque or chilling, is appropriate for the camera. A number of photographers before Arbus depicted individuals on the fringes of society. But it is the way in which Arbus portrayed her subjects which was so revolutionary.

In an Arbus portrait, the subject is an active and willing participant, almost always posed frontally and looking straight into the camera. (See example on page 205). The effect is to present the subject as being in every way "normal," clashing directly with our notion that the subject actually is grotesque. It is this conflict—between the normalcy of presentation and our queasiness, even repulsion, in viewing the subject—in which the tension and power of an Arbus portrait lie.

Vintage Arbus prints, made and signed by her, sell in a price range of $500 to $2,500 each. Posthumous prints made by Neil Selkirk, one of her students, fall into two categories: (1) those from a ten-print portfolio selected by Arbus before her death and subsequently printed in a limited edition of 50 by Selkirk ($400 to $500 each) and (2) those from a broader selection of her work printed in varying edition sizes from 25 to 100 ($200 each).

At about the same time in the early 1960s when Arbus was beginning her series of renowned portraits, Lee Friedlander and Garry Winogrand were launching a new style of documentary photography, using the 35mm camera not to capture "significant" images, but bits and pieces of everyday life—people, store windows, animals, buildings. Friedlander's images, in particular, often seem an irrational jumble in their multiple intersections and strange juxtapositions. For instance, *Phoenix, Arizona,* 1975, shows a barbed-wire fence stretching from left to right against a disordered background of desert shrubs and cacti. The sharp edge of a shadow bisects the image from lower left to upper right, dividing the photograph into two contrasting triangles of underexposed dark and overexposed light—like yin/yang, or emphasizing the ability of the camera to capture darkness and brightness at the same time (as opposed to the human eye, which would be forced to pan from one to the other). In the upper left corner, the branches of a tree thrust helter-skelter in various directions—like a Japanese print in the finding of graphic complexity in the simplest of subject matter. The overall character of this photograph is, in fact, very much like a Japanese print, with its compressed flatness and emphasis on contrasting lines, forms, and tonal values.

Friedlander also is known for his self-portraits, contained in a 1970 book published by Haywire Press. He always appears circuitously in these photographs—as a shadow cast across a bush, for instance, or as a partial reflection in a car mirror. There invariably is great ambivalence between the description of these works as self-portraits and the overriding feeling that Friedlander is intruding into the image. This sense of intrusion, in turn, often implies alienation. On the other hand, these works can be viewed as a playful little game in which Friedlander is exploring ways to document his presence as the man behind the camera. They also can be viewed as an investigation into the visual effects of reflections and shadows—and even as a wry commentary on amateur "snapshot" photography, in which shadows and distortions often intrude inadvertently. Still further, they are a kind of travelogue, since they were taken over a period of years throughout the United States and almost always project a sense of the local environment.

Friedlander's work, because it involves such complex and private observations, often takes time to understand and appreciate.

Other documentary photographers have developed their own themes, concerns, and styles.

Danny Lyon (b. 1942) is known for his photographs of motorcycle gangs and agricultural workers in the Southwest.

Geoff Winningham (b. 1943) specializes in photographs, often humorous, of the offhanded moments surrounding the spectacle of Texas sports—moments which probably would not be perceived without the camera. One of his most famous images is a broad, majestic view of the interior of the Houston Astrodome between innings of a baseball game. An American flag hangs from the roof; the message board flashes a picture of a jazz band; five members of the grounds crew, wearing astronaut helmets, smooth the infield; and a lone baseball player, head down, walks off the field toward his team's dugout, balancing against the movement of the grounds crew in the opposite direction. Another of Winningham's photographs shows high-school football players breaking through a large paper banner as they rush onto the field before the game—an image that, because of the speed of action, probably simply could not be captured by the unaided human eye.

Lewis Baltz (b. 1945) photographs factories and office buildings, stressing semiabstract form and the bathing of buildings in sunlight.

Mark Cohen (b. 1943) is known for his candid "street" photographs taken in Scranton, Pennsylvania.

Nicholas Nixon (b. 1947) is a New England landscape photographer whose images are marked by great visual complexity. In a Nixon photograph, successive layers of branches, trees, flowers, bushes, and buildings typically progress from front to back, with each layer partially obscuring the layers behind it.

Hilla (b. 1934) and Bernd (b. 1931) Becher photograph old industrial buildings—"anonymous sculpture," as they call these structures.

Of the conceptualists, Uelsmann is perhaps the most influential and outspoken. A teacher at the University of Florida in Tampa, he is a master of the darkroom and the first important photographer since Henry Peach Robinson in the nineteenth century to use combined printing—the making of a single image from many negatives. He considers the darkroom a "visual research laboratory" in which he spends long hours experimenting with various combinations of negatives. Often, he makes "sandwiches" of negatives and prints them all at once.

A Uelsmann print invariably challenges a viewer's perceptions and calls for the suspension of disbelief. Trees hover in midair; faces are superimposed on the sides of mountains; giant hands reach out of the ocean. His is a psychological art, suggesting the world of the subconscious. Sometimes, there is a vague sense of foreboding. Retail prices are $250 for black-and-white prints and $500 for hand-colored images.

Another photographer known for his staged or manipulated imagery, Les Krims (b. 1943), photographs bizarre scenes which often depict sexual fantasies or make satirical comments about society. Many of his photographs are pointedly aimed at destroying our middle class "illusions"—such as pictures of his topless mother making chicken soup. What, after all, is more motherly—particularly for a Jewish mother—than making chicken soup? And what could be more inconceivable than her doing so only in white panties—particularly while being photographed by her son? As might be expected, Krims's work is among the most controversial in contemporary photography and often generates highly charged emotional responses.

John Baldessari (b. 1931), a painter as well as a photographer, is a conceptualist who depicts parables and "ideas." Often, he employs sequential photographs which emphasize deductive reasoning and schematic presentation. For instance, *Repair/Retouch Series: An Allegory About Wholeness (Plate and Hand)* consists of two parallel sequences of three images each. In the top sequence, from left to right, a broken plate is repaired, and in the bottom sequence a severed hand is restored.

Paul Berger (b. 1948) photographs the blackboards of the mathematics department at the University of Illinois, where he teaches photography. He advances the film only partially between images, creating complex and mysteriously symbolic multiple exposures—"illusions of form, depth and scale," he has said.

William Wegman (b. 1943) is a master of the absurd and the ironic. In one sequence, a large dog crawls under an upholstered chair half its size and disappears. In addition, Wegman often challenges our perceptions through small transformations in two similar images to call attention to the differences. In one such diptych, a saw lies, teeth downward, on a wooden desk in one image and teeth upward in the other.

Then there are important contemporary photographers whose work does not fit into either the documentary or conceptual trend—or lies on the outer fringes of one of these two movements.

Emmet Gowin (b. 1941) has created a highly personal imagery depicting his wife Edith, other loved ones, and objects and places that help define life in and around Danville, Virginia. One of his photographs is reproduced on page 209. Like a number of other contemporary photographers, Gowin loves old as well as new cameras. He sometimes uses a wooden box camera which, together with a wide-angle lens, results in haunting, circular-shaped images.

Judy Dater (b. 1941) is one of the finest of today's portrait photographers. She is particularly well known for her powerful, vibrant portraits of women.

Deborah Turbeville (b. 1938) is a leading fashion photographer, depicting alienated models in dreamlike settings.

Ralph Gibson (b. 1939) initially achieved fame with a series of books, including *The Somnambulist* in 1970. His early works are surreal and poetic—a hand silhouetted against an open door, a face pressed against a rain-streaked window. More recently, Gibson has depicted large, graphically bold details which often symbolize his dreams and fantasies—a close-up of the back of a head, for instance, or of white venetian blinds.

Except where noted otherwise, prices for prints by the photographers named in this chapter are $350 or less.

It is worth pointing out that in addition to these photographers, there are hundreds of others who regularly sell their prints to collectors. The individuals discussed in this chapter are among the most prominent. But only time will tell which photographers, from among those mentioned and those whose names have not been mentioned, will retain lasting significance. And, of course, that is part of the challenge and fun of collecting contemporary photographs—making your own choices without benefit of the sorting-out process of history.

Contemporary photography is a dealer-dominated market. Very little of this work comes up for sale at auction. Furthermore, retail prices tend to be firmly established, with little variation from one dealer to the next.

The system typically works this way: A major dealer—perhaps in San Francisco, Los Angeles, Houston, Chicago, New York, or Boston—will hold exclusive national distribution rights to a photographer's work and will establish a sales network of three or four other dealers located strategically throughout the nation, giving each dealer a discount from retail of approximately 30 percent. Each participating dealer will, in turn, be bound by contract to resell only at the stated retail price.

Understandably, there is great competition among dealers to sign up the best-selling photographers, as well as to spot emerging new talent. However, each gallery, rather than necessarily seeking to enlist any contemporary photographer of significance, tends to have a specific focus.

Take the contrasting examples of Light Gallery and Castelli Graphics, both in New York. Along with Witkin Gallery, Light and Castelli are perhaps the most influential of all dealers in contemporary photography. Light represents about thirty photographers and Castelli about fifteen—but with divergent emphases.

Light is especially committed to promoting photography as a specific, separate medium and to encouraging the more conceptual and manipulated types of imagery. There is an emphasis on exhibiting photographers who are very personal in their imagery (Gowin, for instance), who are concerned with resolving structural "problems" in photography (Michael Bishop, Stephen Shore, and other color photographers who are discussed in the next chapter), and who have developed a startling new imagery by manipulating their negatives or finished prints (Friedman, Heinecken, and Berger).

The imagery presented at Castelli, on the other hand, tends to be more unified in concept and appearance, broadly related to art in general rather than photography in particular, denser and sometimes more mysterious, and often more difficult to understand at first viewing. Castelli is especially strong in its representation of documentary photographers, although that is by no means its only focus. Adams, Baltz, Cohen, and Gibson all sell their work through Castelli.

The point is that in collecting contemporary photography—more so than in any other sector of the market—it is important to pick a dealer whose viewpoint you find compatible, since different dealers can have totally different opinions about which work and trends are most significant.

Fortunately, there are many dealers in contemporary photography, and you should be able to find locally at least one whose perspective fits your own. For the names of dealers in your area, check the listing in Appendix II.

Chapter 14

Why Color Photography Is Gaining Favor

Interest in the possibilities of color photography dates back to the beginnings of photography in the late 1830s and early 1840s. But not until 1907 were the first practical color plates marketed by Lumière of France. In November 1907, both Alfred Stieglitz and Edward Steichen exhibited color prints made with these Lumière Autochrome plates. Manufacture of Autochrome plates was halted in 1932.

During the 1930s, a number of leading commercial photographers employed the three-color "carbro" process to make color prints for advertising and fashion clients. Paul Outerbridge and Nickolas Muray were, in particular, masters of this difficult technique (discussed in Chapter 12), and their carbro color prints today sell occasionally at about $3,000 or more each.

It was not until 1935, however, that Kodak made a more lasting breakthrough in color photography with the introduction of Kodachrome film. Kodachrome proved to be the first in a family of color films now in wide use, particularly among amateurs.

Despite the important technical advances achieved by Kodak and other film manufacturers, professional photographers have, until recently, tended to shun color photography, for several reasons:

- The pigments used in color films often deviate from real-life colors and are difficult to control. Traditionally, photographers have considered these pigment tones to be "vulgar."
- Color adds another visual element to an image, making the picture-taking process more complex.
- Color prints are vulnerable to fading and unpredictable changes in hue over a period of years.
- Color film is more expensive than black-and-white.

Eliot Porter (b. 1901) and Ernst Haas (b. 1921) are among the few living photographers who have been working continuously in color for more than ten years. Porter is noted for his bird pictures, and Haas for his brilliantly hued close-ups of nature and city streets.

Since about 1975, however, color has suddenly begun to catch hold as an important, broadly based medium of artistic expression. One-person color shows are becoming increasingly frequent in both galleries and museums, and color prints keep popping up among the black-and-white images in exhibitions of established photographers.

One of the most comprehensive recent surveys of color photography was held in June 1977 at the Castelli gallery in New York. This survey included the work of twenty-nine photographers—ranging from such well-known artists as Man Ray and Andy Warhol to a number of younger photographers who work exclusively in color. This latter group included William Eggleston (b. 1939), Joel Meyerowitz (b. 1938), Stephen Shore (b. 1947), and Neal Slavin (b. 1941).

Subsequently, the Sidney Janis Gallery staged its own major survey exhibition of color photography. And in April 1978, New York's Light Gallery, which has been extremely active in support of the colorists, sponsored the first public exhibition of color photographs by Harry Callahan, one of the greatest living photographers.

In addition, at least three New York galleries now deal exclusively in color photographs—Images, K&L Gallery, and The Space.

Why all this recent activity? More than any other reason, growing interest in color seems to reflect the burst of creativity throughout photography. Photographers are experimenting with all sorts of new visual techniques—color being among them. And while the technical problems that have plagued photography in the past—especially the inability to control exact hues—have not been fully resolved, many younger photographers are working within the confines of these problems and even seeking to exploit variations in film color as part of the creative process.

From a collecting viewpoint, color photography represents one of the most fluid and challenging of all sectors, largely because it is still so new and there is no clear body of critical opinion as to which photographers are important and which are not.

William Eggleston illustrates the wide diversity of critical judgment surrounding the work of even the most prominent of today's color photographers. A native of Memphis, Tennessee, Eggleston became seriously interested in photography in 1962 and since the late sixties has worked almost exclusively in color. However, he remained essentially unknown until the summer of 1976, when he gained national prominence with a one-man exhibition of his work at the Museum of Modern Art in New York.

That exhibition—which some collectors believe marks the beginning of serious market acceptance of color photography—drew a flood of critical coverage, some enthusiastic and some disparaging. Writing in *Artweek*, critic Joan Murray termed Eggleston's photographs "the most exciting color work" she had ever seen. Sean Callahan, in *New York* magazine, termed Eggleston's photographs "a masterful achievement." And Roberta Hellman and Marvin Hoshino, in *The Village Voice*, said, in praising the work, that "Eggleston may be one of the first photographers to understand the lesson of TV"—that is, his ability through "casual imprecision" to "neutralize the unnaturalness of color photography, which would otherwise disrupt his pictures." On the other hand, Max Kozloff, in *Artforum,* said the photographs elicited "a random bliss here, yawns there." And Hilton Kramer, art critic for *The New York Times,* dismissed the photographs as "perfectly boring."

Eggleston's photographs depict suburban life around Memphis and in northern Mississippi—houses, children playing, dogs, interiors, suburban streets, automobiles, bushes. But specific subject matter actually is relatively unimportant in his work. The emphasis clearly is on form and color—including color for its own sake, relationships between colors, and the ways in which color influences pictorial composition.

One of Eggleston's best-known photographs, untitled and dated 1973, depicts an unshaded lightbulb in a socket mounted on a glossy bright-red painted ceiling. The photograph is shot at an angle pointing up into a corner of the room, so that the picture is divided into three broad patches—the ceiling and two walls, all the same bright red. However, because of the direction of the lighting, the ceiling appears to darken in color as it approaches the walls—an illusion which probably would be missed without the aid of a camera. Three white electrical cords, plugged into the overloaded socket, extend across the ceiling in different directions toward the walls, dividing the picture into thirds in a totally different way. There is a small, bright reflection on the ceiling, just to the near side of the light socket. At first, this reflection appears to be from the lightbulb. But the viewer quickly notices that the lightbulb isn't on. The reflection is coming, instead, from the photographer's flash—which has bounced off the chrome-plated base of the light socket, onto the ceiling, and back to the camera. Two black forms intrude into the predominantly red tones of the picture—the thick top of a door frame in the lower left, and three drawings of sexual positions hanging on a wall in the lower right. All we see of this room are part of the ceiling and the tops of two walls. Yet, the photograph has captured enough—the makeshift electrical cords tacked across the ceiling, the red paint slapped on everywhere, the drawings, and a missing piece of molding where one of the walls meets the ceiling—to enable us to visualize the room in its entirety as being disordered and garish, and inhabited by someone who is extremely energetic, perhaps a little bizarre. Through color, Eggleston has made a "boring" view come to life. In black and white, this photograph would be nothing.

That is a key test of any color photograph: whether color serves any purpose beyond merely making the image "pretty." Color should be more than decorative. It should play a central role in defining a picture's meaning or content. Color photography is always more interesting when it accomplishes things that black-and-white imagery cannot accomplish.

Another example is the work of Michael Bishop (b. 1946)—which, like Eggleston's, is quite controversial. Bishop's photographs, of common objects and ordinary landscapes, are defined almost entirely by their harmonies of bright color. One of his best images is a wooded landscape dominated by the subdued tones of late fall. In the middle of the landscape is a tourists' welcome sign on which is painted a similar landscape, shown in early fall with the leaves in full color. The painted view contrasts brightly with the real world behind; each version of nature comments on the other.

Bishop's prints are "type-C" prints, priced at $150 each. Type-C prints are the kind you receive when you send your film to Kodak or any other high-quality processor.

The second major type of color print being sold to collectors is the so-called "dye-transfer" print, made with special dyes absorbed from three matrices. Dye-transfer prints are considered to be more resistant to color changes and fading than type-C prints, but also are more expensive.

Typically, type-C prints sell in a range of about $150 to $300 each, depending on the photographer, and transfer prints for about $500 to $700 each. The point is that in buying any type-C print, you should be aware that the work may begin to fade or change color within a decade or two. For dye-transfer prints, no one is really sure whether colors will prove to be "permanent," but there is at least a feeling that the risks of fading are greatly reduced.

In either case, common sense and proper handling will help prevent unnecessary deterioration. The big enemies of color are moisture, light, and heat. Ideally, then, you should keep color prints in a dry, dark, cool place. Temperature should be below 70 degrees Fahrenheit and relative humidity between 25 percent and 50 percent. Humidity below 25 percent may make films brittle and cause them to crack when handled.

Color prints on display should be mounted, framed, and protected by glass. They should not be placed where direct sunlight or fluorescent light will fall upon them, nor should they be illuminated continuously. The best approach is to "rotate" color prints—on display for a period of a few months and then returned to darkness for several more.

In addition to type-C and dye-transfer prints, a number of leading photographers have been making color prints with a Polaroid SX-70 camera, producing one-of-a-kind images which recall the daguerreotype in the earliest years of photography. Walker Evans, the late documentary photographer whose work is discussed in Chapter 12, shocked many of his contemporaries when he announced about a year before his death in 1975 that he was working with a Polaroid. Ansel Adams, the western nature photographer, has been using a Polaroid on occasion for nearly five years, and these images—generally close-ups of flowers and plants—sell at prices in excess of $1,000 each. Emmet Gowin, the contemporary photographer, is still another individual who has experimented with the SX-70.

However, the "Photo-Transformations" of Lucas Samaras (b. 1936) are probably the most original of all work being done with the SX-70. Samaras, a sculptor turned photographer, first began experimenting with the SX-70 in 1973. He creates strange, sometimes terrifying self-portraits by manipulating the print just after it comes out of the camera. Working quickly, he rubs the still-moist developing fluids to distort or obliterate the image, and he sometimes then scratches or gouges the surface to eliminate all but a few selected fragments. The finished works are mounted in recessed plexiglass frames designed by Samaras himself.

In *Photo-Transformation 11/1/73,* a lone, penetrating eye—precise in detail but manipulated to a greenish tone—stares out from a squiggle of lines that vaguely suggest a head. In other Photo-Transformations, teeth, eyes, legs, or hands emerge from swirling masses of color. Sometimes the artist's face or nude body is transformed into an apelike or reptilian creature.

Helen Levitt (b. 1918) was one of the earliest converts to color. A prominent "street" photographer who worked originally in black and white, she began using color in about 1970 and has been influential in leading the way toward acceptance of bright, gaudy colors as natural. She photographs principally in the tenement neighborhoods of New York City and captures the vibrance of cheap clothing and enamel paint on the fronts of buildings.

Joel Meyerowitz is, like Levitt, a colorist known for his photographs of street life. But his photographs are of a different sort, in terms of both content and use of color. Meyerowitz has an opportunistic, prying eye and catches split-second episodes in the hustle of urban life. He often stands on street corners in fashionable Manhattan shopping districts and photographs people going by. One of his best-known pictures is a mocking portrait of an overdressed woman, probably in her fifties, wearing a pink hat, blue-tinted sunglasses, a pearl necklace, and white gloves, and smiling effusively as she looks into the camera. The background is almost entirely black, with just a hint of Fifth Avenue behind her. Apparently Meyerowitz has highlighted the woman through the use of a flash—a technique employed by a number of colorists to isolate foreground from background.

The colors in a Meyerowitz photograph are more subdued and even-toned than those in a Levitt—one indication of the variations in style that have been developed by different photographers in their handling of color. In other words, it,is not color itself, but the photographer's use of it, which should be creative. In a Meyerowitz, there typically are surprising relationships between people, just as there are surprising relationships between colors. In one photograph, taken in Paris, a workman steps gingerly around a businessman who has fallen to the sidewalk at the top of a Métro entrance and who lies on his back with his arms extended over his head. Other people rush by, looking back. But no one gets involved.

Other well-known color photographers include Stephen Shore, whose photographs are filled with swatches of color that seem to draw their inspiration partly from the distorted hues of television; Neil Slavin, who specializes in portraits of large groups and gatherings whose character often is defined by color; and William Larson (b. 1942), who combines images from different photographs into "color landscapes" which lie halfway between reality and fantasy.

Dozens of contemporary photographers are now working in color. Some of the most advanced and creative work is being done by the colorists. Meyerowitz has written: "Color is going to take over; its destiny is written large in the future.... If description is the name of the game, color does it. We've been trained to feel in black and white, but color is going to put us in touch with emotions that we've negated all these years."

Whether color "takes over" remains to be seen. But we certainly are in the beginnings of an important growth period for color photography.

Chapter 15

The Pros and Cons
of Limited-Edition
Portfolios

Limited-edition portfolios, exceedingly popular over the past ten years as a mechanism for marketing photographs, are something akin to the photographically illustrated books of the nineteenth century.

Like the illustrated book, a photographic portfolio combines a number of images by one photographer in a single package. This number usually is anywhere from four to twenty. Typical edition size is between 25 and 100. Generally, the photographs are sold in a custom-made box. The photographs themselves, inside the box, are sometimes placed in white museum-board mounts to facilitate framing, sometimes not. If loose, they generally are signed and numbered by the photographer in the margin or on the back; if mounted, they may be signed and numbered on the mount rather than on the photographic print itself.

Important twentieth-century photographers whose work has been issued in portfolio form include Ansel Adams, Edward Weston, Walker Evans, Paul Strand, Brassaï, August Sander, Minor White, Berenice Abbott, Jacques Henri Lartigue, Karl Blossfeldt, Andreas Feininger, Lisette Model, Harry Callahan, Arnold Newman, Tony Ray-Jones, Duane Michals, George Tice, Paul Caponigro, and Lee Friedlander, among numerous others.

Many dealers like portfolios because they are big-ticket items that sell for high prices, and because they create a rich source of new supply for photographers whose work is in demand but scarce. Paul Strand is an example of a photographer whose original prints, now extremely rare, have been supplemented by two posthumous 1976 portfolios of his work.

In addition, portfolios free dealers and collectors from making difficult aesthetic judgments. The images in a portfolio have typically been chosen by an authoritative expert—the photographer, the portfolio publisher, or a photography historian knowledgeable in the photographer's work—and hopefully provide a good overview of the photographer's style and subject matter.

However, Don Fuller, director of the Gallery of Photographic Arts in North Olmstead, Ohio, notes that many portfolios contain three or four lesser photographs which a buyer may not want. The tradeoff is that the combined price for the images in a portfolio generally is substantially lower than if the works were acquired individually. One possible strategy, according to Fuller, is to sell the images you don't like. Sometimes it's possible to recoup the full purchase price by selling all but two or three of the best prints—ending up with these prints at no cost.

On the other hand, there are portfolios which any collector would love to own in their entirety. Fuller cites Minor White's *Jupiter* portfolio as an example. This portfolio, containing twelve of White's finest images, originally came onto the market at a price of $1,600 in 1975. The edition size was projected at one hundred. However, only seventy-five of the portfolios had been printed when White died in 1976. Today, individual prints from the portfolio sell at $600 to $750 each, and a complete portfolio would bring about $6,000 at retail. Even at $6,000, Fuller believes a collector might be able to sell all but two or three of the prints and recover the entire purchase price.

Corporations and smaller museums are especially disposed toward the acquisition of portfolios, since a portfolio will enable such an organization to create an "instant collection" of a photographer's work with little in-house expertise or effort.

Individual collectors represent a more limited market for portfolios. Some dealers report that individuals generally are unwilling to spend the $1,000 to $10,000 it usually takes to acquire a portfolio and would prefer, in any case, to choose specific pictures on their own. However, portfolios often are broken up by dealers and sold print by print, and individuals are very active in buying these separate prints.

Dealers sometimes contend that portfolios are an automatic financial bargain, since they almost always combine a number of images at a price lower than if the works were being sold individually. But this advantage can at times prove illusory. The Ansel Adams *Portfolio VII,* published in 1976, is an example. That portfolio, containing thirteen images (including one unique Polaroid per portfolio), was offered initially at a retail price of $10,000. Meanwhile, the individual pictures from a disassembled portfolio were being quoted by one dealer at a combined retail price of $13,500, indicating that the $10,000 portfolio price was a bargain. However, when a copy of the portfolio was sold at auction in London in March 1977 it brought only $6,000—showing that even the $10,000 price was higher than a collector need have paid.

In buying almost any portfolio price above $2,000, a collector should be wary about paying the stated retail price and would do well to attempt to bargain the dealer down by at least ten per cent.

Ultimately, the appeal of any portfolio is based on the identity of the photographer, the quality and cohesiveness of the images, the technical quality of the prints, and whether the photographer personally made the prints. Paul Caponigro's 1978 *Stonehenge* portfolio is an example of a portfolio which, because of its cohesive visual theme, has a special appeal to many collectors. *Stonehenge* carries a retail price of $4,500.

There are all sorts of variations from one portfolio to the next in terms of (1) whether the photographer made the prints or they were made by a technician hired by the publisher; (2) whether the negatives were canceled or destroyed after the edition was printed; (3) if the negatives were not canceled or destroyed, whether the photographer will be able to make additional prints of the same images beyond those in the numbered edition; and (4) whether the portfolio was made during the photographer's lifetime or posthumously (some portfolios are, indeed, a sort of posthumous recapitulation of the photographer's career, seemingly published by the photographer's estate as much to cash in on the value of the negatives as to satisfy collector demand).

Often, publisher and photographer will view the portfolio as a presentation that stands on its own, with the limited-edition concept applying only to the portfolio itself. In other words, it is only the prints in the portfolio that will have been limited to the stated number; earlier prints, future prints, and even future, separately numbered portfolios will not be considered to have in any way violated the integrity of the numbering of the portfolio. In these cases, which are fairly common, buyers should be aware that they have no protection against large numbers of additional prints.

On the other hand, some photographers deface or destroy the negatives after completing the printing of a portfolio as a guarantee that no additional prints of the same images will be made. Ansel Adams, for instance, punches holes in his negatives with an old Wells Fargo check canceling machine.

Reputable publishers will generally document the number of portfolios made, the identity of the printer, any rules governing continued printings from the same negatives, and other pertinent data. But the buyer must know to ask for such information. It is especially true that many promotional brochures do not specify whether the photographer did the printing and whether the negatives have been "retired", and you must ask to find out.

Another basic issue to consider is the technical standards followed in making the prints. Collectors favor portfolios which meet "archival" standards and are mounted on all-rag, acid-free board. The term *archival* refers to the finest printing techniques, using acid-free materials and free from other impurities which may destroy the photographs over a period of decades. Prints contained in a portfolio box should be interleafed with acid-free paper.

Portfolio publishing is big business. All sorts of people and organizations are getting into the field: museums (the Metropolitan Museum and International Center of Photography in New York, for instance), publishers of fine prints (that is, publishers who print and distribute works for artists like Miró and Rauschenberg), photography dealers, and dozens of photographers who have self-published their own portfolios. There are very few major living photographers who have not yet entered into some kind of arrangement for the publication of at least one portfolio of their work.

One leading dealer/publisher cites two basic approaches as typical of the kinds of deals he has entered into:

"*Plan A*." The dealer agrees to pay an "important" photographer $20,000 for rights to publish a portfolio of ten of his pictures. The portfolio will be published in an edition of seventy-five, plus fifteen "artist's proofs" which will be given to the photographer as additional payment. The dealer will retain all seventy-five numbered portfolios, will pay all production and distribution costs, will not owe the photographer anything beyond the $20,000 and fifteen portfolios, and will assume all financial risk as underwriter of the project. The dealer will then work with the photographer to select ten specific images and will retain a master printer to make all prints. Production costs, including the hiring of the printer, will come to about $20,000—so that the dealer will have a total investment of $40,000 (production costs plus the photographer's fee). The portfolios will carry a retail price of $2,000 each, with a 40 percent discount to dealers. So, minus the 40 percent, the publisher will theoretically gross $90,000 on a $40,000 investment if and when all the portfolios have been sold. But the dealer figures he generally can end up making more, by himself selling some of the portfolios at retail and by increasing the retail and wholesale prices after perhaps two-thirds of the portfolios have been sold. While the potential profits on this type of transaction are extremely high, the publisher feels they are justified because it may take two years or more to sell all the portfolios and because he is assuming all financial risk in the transaction. "If this market doesn't develop as well as I expect, I could be up the creek," the publisher contends, noting that he currently is at risk with a number of portfolio projects. "On the other hand, if it does develop as well as I expect, I will make what some people consider unconscionable profits."

"Plan B." Under this arrangement, the publisher pays all production costs but does not pay any "up-front" money to the photographer. Instead, publisher and photographer share the proceeds as individual portfolios are sold.

Another major publisher says his firm generally enters into contracts which run three to five years and cover a specified number of portfolios—maybe two or three—to be published during that period as well as exclusive wholesale distribution rights to all individual prints made by the photographer during the period. Generally, the photographer is paid an advance—like an advance an author receives for writing a book—against future income from the arrangement; for an "important" photographer, the advance might be anywhere from $20,000 to $40,000. The publisher generally further agrees to pay the photographer between 40 and 60 percent of the retail price on individual prints (which the photographer will almost always continue to make himself) and between 7 and 15 percent of the retail price on portfolios (which will often be printed by someone else). On a portfolio, the distribution of the retail price might break down as follows: 10 percent to the photographer, 10 percent for marketing costs, a 40 percent discount to dealers, 10 percent set aside for instances where a middleman helps sell to dealers, and 30 percent for production costs and profits.

Chapter 16

_____

Buying from a Dealer

There are more than 200 U.S. galleries now dealing exclusively in photographs and perhaps an equal number that, while dealing primarily in other types of art, hold occasional photography exhibitions.

For the collector, this means there is great diversity of source for the acquisition of photographic prints, but also a degree of challenge in choosing a dealer or dealers from among the growing crowd. And, of course, some collectors may question whether it is worthwhile to buy from dealers at all, since dealer prices tend to be higher than those at auction.

But dealers actually can be very helpful to any collector, novice or expert. The three big advantages of buying from a dealer, versus at auction, are as follows:

1. Dealers provide information and guidance. A good dealer will listen to a novice collector; answer the collector's questions; find out what types of photographs interest the collector most; offer guidance in selecting specific works; suggest periodicals and books to read; help establish a direction and unity for a collection; and, after a period of months, help track down rare or unusual pieces which the collector has been unable to find on his or her own. However, do not expect hours of help from a dealer until you have developed a focus, in terms of the types of photographs you want to buy, and have done some work on your own, in terms of reading and looking.

2. Dealers generally are able to offer a greater variety of quality items than are available at auction. Only rarely does a representative selection of the finest works come up for sale at auction. More

often, these blue-chip photographs pass through the hands of important dealers. If any dealer you are buying from consistently lacks superior items, perhaps you should consider taking your business elsewhere.

3. Dealers, unlike auction houses, usually offer extended payment terms. This is very informal and subject to negotiation. Dealers sometimes are willing to let collectors take several months to pay, take items home on approval, return any purchased items for a period of months or even years or even indefinitely with full refund of the purchase price, and/or bargain down the stated retail price by 10 to 20 percent or more. However, rarely will a collector be able to negotiate all the above concessions. For instance, if you want to take six months to pay, you cannot realistically expect the dealer to give you a 20-percent price discount. A 10-percent discount from stated retail price is fairly standard on items above approximately $500, but only if you agree to pay within a reasonable period of time. Some dealers do not like to give first-time customers any discount. On the other hand, one dealer says that collectors who spend substantial sums of money at his gallery—$20,000 to $40,000 annually—generally receive discounts ranging from 10 to 40 percent. So bargaining over price is a highly subjective matter, involving the dealer's individual policies and your business relationship with the dealer.

Novice collectors typically work closely with one or two dealers, buying solely from them until they feel comfortable to go out on their own, while experienced collectors generally are more catholic in their acquisition sources—several dealers, auctions, photographers, and other collectors.

The initial choice of dealers is not unlike selecting a doctor or lawyer. Much depends on the interaction of personalities. But in general it is smart not to spend a great deal of money with a single dealer until you are sure of the dealer's integrity, as well as your own sense of taste in picking items which will have lasting appeal. It's also generally best to keep in touch with other dealers, monitoring their available merchandise and quoted prices.

Asking the advice of other collectors is a logical starting point in finding a capable local dealer. You might also ask dealers about their competitors, or contact the photography curator at a local museum and ask for some names. Or you can simply look around on your own.

The following questions also might be considered in choosing a dealer: Does the dealer handle the specific types of photographs which interest you most? Do prices seem reasonable—after checking other dealer catalogs and auction records? Is the dealer genuinely open and helpful in answering your questions? Does the dealer stand ready to guarantee, in writing on the invoice, the authenticity of any items you purchase? Do you personally like, and have confidence in, the individual?

One of the traditional roles of any art dealer is to help clients upgrade their collections as their tastes and objectives change. A dealer is not necessarily under any obligation to buy back works for cash. But a good dealer should always be willing to take back works as trade-ins toward other works, giving full credit for the original purchase price. One way to test the reliability of a dealer—before becoming heavily committed financially—is to seek after several months to trade back one or two items. If the dealer is not totally cooperative, you should consider going elsewhere with your business.

Both dealers and collectors tend to view a good dealer—collector relationship as a partnership, where there is mutual respect and an interchange of ideas. Most leading dealers greatly prefer to work with knowledgeable collectors, and you cannot really expect to get the best merchandise if you don't do your homework and develop a strong background in photography. Almost invariably, the most knowledgeable and active customers are given first crack at prime vintage items.

Aside from these general rules, different dealers tend to have their own specific styles of doing business. At Witkin Gallery in New York, for instance, photographs are left in open bins for the convenience of browsers. Witkin actively encourages people to drop in, and there is no pressure to buy.

By contrast, Lunn Gallery in Washington, D.C., is primarily a wholesaler, distributing photographs to other dealers and conducting a limited business with individual collectors. At Lunn, casual browsing is not really encouraged—at least to the extent that the great majority of the merchandise is stored in locked drawers upstairs.

At most galleries, even Lunn, it isn't necessary to make an appointment. However, if you are prepared to spend more than a few hundred dollars, an appointment or personal introduction may be helpful in assuring personal attention. Most galleries are open from about 11 A.M. to 6 P.M., Tuesday through Saturday. A few galleries are open by appointment only, as indicated in the listing of galleries which begins on page 223.

Chapter 17

Buying at Auction

Auction activity in photographic prints has expanded sharply in the past few years. Periodic sales are now held in at least five cities—New York, San Francisco, Los Angeles, London, and Augsburg, Germany—and occasional sales in a number of other cities.

Sotheby Parke Bernet, the big New York auction house, is fairly typical in its recent thrust into photography. Parke Bernet (pronounced with the *t,* as in "net") held its first photographic auction in 1967 but then undertook such sales only sporadically until February 1975, when it began scheduling photographic auctions on a regular basis. One sale was held at Parke Bernet in the 1974–1975 auction season, two in the 1975–1976 season, and three beginning with the 1976–1977 season.

Besides Parke Bernet, other leading auction houses which deal regularly in photographs include the following:

Argus Ltd., Swann Galleries, and Christie's in New York.
California Book Auction Galleries in San Francisco.
The Sotheby Parke Bernet branch in Los Angeles.
Christie's South Kensington and Sotheby's Belgravia in London.
Augsburger Kunst-Auktionshaus Petzold in Augsburg.

The tendency toward lower prices is the primary advantage of buying at auction versus from a dealer. Dealer prices generally are viewed as retail prices, auction prices as wholesale—although occasionally the auction price for a specific item will jump way above retail. The drawbacks are lack of guidance and advice and unavailability of extended payment terms. At Parke Bernet, most buyers must pay within three days and cannot take possession of any item until full payment has been made.

Understandably, the price advantage is enough in itself to draw many sophisticated individual buyers—those who can readily judge the merits of works without dealer help and have the time to inspect a range of items in advance of the sale—into the auction arena. A few Americans even go regularly to the big London auctions in October, March, and June of each year. Auction prices in London have traditionally been well below those in New York, and some buyers believe that any trip to London will pay for itself if at least $10,000 of material is acquired at London prices. In fact, both Philippe Garner of Sotheby's Belgravia and Stuart Bennett of Christie's South Kensington estimate that up to 80 percent of the material in a typical London sale goes to American buyers—an indication of the continued U.S. domination of the world-wide photography market.

The major difference between the London and New York auction houses, besides price differentials, lies in the types of material offered for sale. In London, the emphasis is very strongly on nineteenth-century photographs: daguerreotypes; stereo-graphs; cartes de visite; Victorian art photography; topographical pictures of Egypt, Palestine, and other distant lands; and late-nineteenth-century naturalist photography. In New York, by contrast, there is an emphasis on *Camera Work* gravures and twentieth-century master photography, in addition to nineteenth-century works.

Of the two big London firms, Sotheby's held its first specialist photography sale in May 1973 and quickly established its local leadership. Christie's concentrated initially on antique cameras and other equipment, rather than photographic prints, but since mid-1976 has come on strongly in prints. Conveniently for visiting Americans, Sotheby's and Christie's often hold their photographic sales on successive days.

It is very easy for any collector to keep track of material coming up for sale at Parke Bernet, Argus, Sotheby's, and Christie's simply by subscribing to those firms' auction catalogs (see list on page 217). However, other auction houses which sell photographs do not offer their photographic catalogs as a specific subscription category, so collectors must keep in touch otherwise to learn when future sales are planned.

Typically, an auction catalog will arrive two to three weeks in advance of the sale. This provides dealers and collectors with a basic working document. The would-be buyer should look through the catalog, see what types of material are of interest, make notes if necessary in the margins, and check the estimated prices in the back of the catalog. (These estimates are the auction firm's best guess as to what each item will bring at sale, but should not be taken religiously, since they are sometimes far wide of the mark. One of the most striking recent examples was a book of photographs and drawings by Edward Steichen which the auction house estimated would bring $500 to $800, but sold for $19,000.)

Generally, the auction house will open its doors for inspection of the material for two or three days immediately preceding the sale. It is essential to inspect each potential purchase carefully in advance or to have a dealer or other collector do so for you if you cannot—or short of either circumstance, not to buy. Photographic auction catalogs are notorious for not describing items in very much detail, and so you are on your own to check quality and condition. One recent example involved a Julia Margaret Cameron photograph which the auction catalog described as having a "sub-stantial tear at bottom of image." But rather than merely being torn, it turned out that a whole chunk of the photograph was gone.

Once you have inspected an item, you should establish in your own mind a firm bidding limit which you will not exceed. Stick to this limit even in the heat of action. If you feel that you may catch "auction fever" and overbid, submit your bid in writing in advance and don't attend in person at all.

Such "order bids" are executed honestly by reputable auction firms around the world. A bidder can submit a maximum bid in writing and the auction house will bid up to that limit on the buyer's behalf without going any higher than is necessary to secure the item.

It also is possible to submit bids by cable or mail without ever setting foot in the auction house. This can be done, in either the London or New York auction houses, by looking through the catalog, deciding what is of interest, and submitting maximum bids in writing. The problem, of course, is that you will not have inspected the items firsthand. However, if there are one or two items you find especially appealing, you often can phone or write the auction house and receive a fairly detailed written or oral description of condition. But Bennett of Christie's warns that this generally should be done only in cases of major items or when the catalog seems to indicate that the condition of an item is in question. He notes that certain works probably should never be bought without personal inspection—Julia Margaret Cameron pictures, for instance, where subtle variations in appearance can have tremendous impact on value.

Part of the fun of attending an auction is to watch the crowd and to sit back and take in all the zaniness. Although secret signals often are used at art auctions by bidders, this is not nearly as common in photography, where items go for relatively modest prices in relation to other major types of art and secrecy therefore is not as meaningful. If, however, you do have any intention of using secret signals to bid, you must arrange these signals in advance with the auctioneer.

It also can be interesting to try to figure out which bids the auctioneer is "pulling off the wall." Most items in an auction are subject to a "reserve"—a minimum sale price whose amount is known only to the auctioneer and seller. Parke Bernet says its own reserves are typically equal to about two-thirds of the median of the high and low presale price estimates and never exceed the high estimate. The auctioneer, controlling all activity, must achieve at least the reserve price or not sell the object. So if there is only one real bidder on an item, the auctioneer will pretend there actually is a second bidder and will alternate these phantom bids with the real bidding from the floor until the price reaches the reserve level and he is free to let the item go for sale. Some auctioneers are virtuoso performers; others are not. So when an auction enters a boring spell, as most auctions do, a collector may garner some small measure of enjoyment by trying to figure out which bids are phantom bids "off the wall" and which are real bids from the floor. Items which never reach their reserve are said to be "bought in"—that is, are bought back by the auction house and returned to the seller. Knowing which and how many items are being bought in during a sale helps a collector gauge the mood of the market and get a feel for whether the sale is going as well as expected. The auctioneer will try to pretend that items being bought in are actually being sold to someone on the floor. Some auctioneers pull off this ruse better than others. Whem items are bought in, the tendency among auctioneers is to announce in a rather loud voice that the piece has been sold to "Archer" or "Cocksmith" or some other fictitious individual who, for whatever reason, invariably is assigned an extremely Anglo-Saxon name. Three or four weeks after the sale, when the printed list of price results is mailed out to all catalog subscribers, confirmation will be possible, since items which have been bought in are omitted from this final price list.

At any auction house where you are buying for the first time, it is wise to establish your financial standing in advance by visiting the cashier so there will be no delay in receiving items once you have paid. Payment by check is acceptable at some auction houses, but cash is required at others. Ask in advance.

Buying in London has its special problems. Some items, as indicated in the catalog, will be subject to a value-added tax of 8 percent or $12\frac{1}{2}$ percent on top of the actual bid. Sotheby's Belgravia also charges a buyer's commission of 10 percent above the winning bid; Christie's South Kensington does not.

In addition, any item more than seventy years old and costing £100 or more must receive an export license before being removed to the United States. Such licenses are only rarely denied; one of the very few cases involved the album of Julia Margaret Cameron photographs discussed on page 50. However, obtaining an export license does add to the hassle. American dealers making major purchases in London sometimes stay over a few extra days to walk their acquisitions through the appropriate authorities. Alternatively, the auction house will handle all details and ship the materials to the United States once the export license has been approved; at minimum, this will cost about $40 for a group of several items.

Keep in mind, finally, that auction houses are great levelers. There is a commercial flavor much more direct than at the typical dealer gallery. Everybody is welcome. Reservations are unnecessary. Money is all that counts. Your bid is as good as the next person's, and all you have to do to win an item is bid more than anybody else. After bidding once or twice at auction, you will likely find it a simple process, and sometimes a marvelous way to acquire excellent items at bargain prices.

Chapter 18

Proper Physical Care
of Photographs

Photographic conservation is a relatively new field with contradictory viewpoints and no firm answers.

Many collectors and dealers are concerned about the fragility of photographs and would like to preserve them in the best possible condition. And while there are some general rules to follow, definitive answers on optimum care are at least several years away. Collectors must keep this point in mind in asking the advice of dealers and curators and in reading the information presented in this chapter. Five or ten years from now, the rules on proper care may have changed somewhat.

However, a basic amount of attention to proper care, even within the confines of the limited information now available, should assure the survival of photographs in good condition for several decades and probably much longer. One positive sign is that some nineteenth-century photographs have come down to us in fine condition despite a consistent lack of clear guidelines on the handling, storage, and framing of photographic prints.

Certainly we do know that the big villains in harming photographs are light, dampness, excessive heat, air pollution, careless handling, and improper framing and storage. Resulting damage may include fading, discoloration, and/or cracking.

Light and humidity are — in the current view, at least — the most dangerous environmental conditions. Photographs should *never* be hung in direct sunlight, illuminated with bright fluorescent light, or subjected to humidity above 65 percent. Special UF-3 plexiglas, which filters out most ultraviolet rays, often is recommended for protection against the effects of light. But as scholar Doris Bry has pointed out, plastics themselves are controversial and have not been studied sufficiently to know their long-term effects on photographs. Clearly a better solution is to display photographs only in dim light, to store them properly in darkness when not on display, and to rotate prints regularly from display to storage so no one picture is exposed to light for more than a few months at a time.

Both heat and humidity tend to speed up chemical processes and increase any instability present in a photograph. But given a choice between a cool or dry environment, dryness appears to be the more important of the two, since it is humidity which creates the greater risks. Individuals with substantial collections would do well to store their pictures only in rooms that are air-conditioned and dehumidified. Ideal is an atmosphere with humidity below 50 percent and temperature below 65 degrees Fahrenheit.

Air pollution is another problem. Sulfur dioxide, common in industrial and urban areas, can be especially harmful by resulting in possible discoloration, embrittlement, and eventual disintegration. Some collectors favor placing their photographs in sealed frames to keep out pollutants; others believe that frames should not be airtight because photographs need to "breathe." There is no clear resolution of this point —except, perhaps, that in areas of high air contamination the risks involved in sealing frames are worth taking.

Proper handling is largely a matter of care and common sense. *Always* wash your hands before picking up a photographic print, and then pick up the work with both hands, not one, supporting it from underneath. *Never* touch the surface image of a photograph. Oils and chemicals in the skin will react with the chemicals in a photograph and produce stains or fingerprints. At all times treat a photograph as a delicate object — which it is.

The mounting and framing of photographs raise questions of their own. Clearly, photographs should *not* touch the protective glass (they should be set back perhaps a quarter of an inch lest condensation on the glass ruin the print); touch any paper which is anything but all-rag and nonacidic in quality; be mounted or held down with ordinary cellophane tape, Elmer's Glue-All, rubber cement, or any other common household adhesive.

Ideally, a frame will both enhance the appearance of a photograph and protect it physically. Ultimately, though, protection is the more important of the two, and there may be times when appearance will have to be sacrificed to meet absolute archival standards.

The frame itself should not be made from a resinous wood, because fumes from such a frame can eventually contaminate and harm the photograph. Metal frames generally are preferred. However, be careful of frames which come with their own mats. These mats often are made of poor-quality paper that can eventually be ruinous.

The mat (the paper "window" which typically surrounds the photograph within the frame) should be of acid-free, 100-percent rag board— available at many photographic shops and art supply stores. Many of the framing materials currently in use are not acid-free. So you must absolutely insist, in taking any photograph to a framer, that your instructions be followed and only acid-free materials be used. If you are unsure about finding a quality framer who can be trusted to meet archival standards, ask the print or photography department at a local museum or university. Acid-free mounting board is sometimes referred to as "museum board." Two leading suppliers of acid-free materials are Charles T. Bainbridge's Sons, 20 Cumberland St., Brooklyn, New York 11205, and Process Materials Corporation, 329 Veterans Blvd., Carlstadt, New Jersey 07072.

Photographs are backed in various ways. One of the most common methods, subject to some dispute in terms of its conservatorial qualities, is dry mounting. This process uses a paper-thin dry-mounting tissue that is impregnated with an adhesive and becomes sticky, to form a lasting bond, when heated between the print and mount. The first question is whether dry mounting itself may damage a photograph. There is little if any evidence to date to show that it indeed does, but some collectors and curators worry that damage may begin to show up in time. The second question involves the type of mounting board which backs the dry-mount tissue; it is best to use only museum board, since there is no assurance that impurities from lower-grade boards will not eventually seep through the tissue and damage the photograph. Again, you must go to the best framers and insist that only the proper materials be used.

A presumably safer method for mounting photographs to their backings is the use of hinges made from Japanese mulberry paper and then fastened with a vegetable-base paste to both the original and the backing board. Gummed linen tapes also are commonly used, but are somewhat less desirable.

When not on display, photographs must be stored with maximum possible protection in mind. They should never be stacked directly on top of each other without being separated by acid-free sheets of Japanese tissue or Mylar-D. Solander boxes have traditionally been used by museum print and photography departments for the storage of works of art on paper. These are made of light, well-seasoned wood covered with fabric and lined with acid-free paper. A major supplier is Spink and Gaborc, 26 E. 15 St., New York, New York 10003. Increasingly, however, opinion is swinging toward the use of steel cabinets, with baked-on enamel or synthetic lacquers, for the storage of photographic prints.

For more information on the conservation of photographs, send a self-addressed, stamped envelope to Sotheby Parke Bernet, Department AH, 1425 York Ave., New York, New York 10021, and ask for a copy of "An Approach to the Care of Photographs," a brief guide written by Doris Bry specifically for Parke Bernet.

Caring for Photographs, published by Time-Life Books in 1972 as part of the Life Library of Photography, is very strong on the restoration of old photographs and fairly strong on storage but weak on general conservation. It may be available at a local bookstore or library.

Preservation of Contemporary Photographic Materials, a long-awaited volume that is expected to be the definitive book to date on photographic conservation, was yet to be issued as this book went to press. For information, write to East Street Gallery, 723 State St., Box 68, Grinnell, Iowa 50112.

Louis Daguerre often is thought to be the inventor of
photography. But actual credit is not so clear-cut.
Daguerre merely was fortunate enough to be first with
the news of his invention. Many historians date the
true beginnings of photography to a rather blurry
image produced by Nicéphore Niépce in either 1824 or
1826. Another Frenchman, Hippolyte Bayard, began
experimenting with photography in 1837. And across
the channel in England, a mathematician named William Henry Fox Talbot achieved his first faltering success with photographs on paper in 1835. For the next
four years Talbot devoted long hours to perfecting his
invention, only to have Daguerre beat him to the punch
by announcing the daguerreotype on metal in January
1839. To establish the originality of his own delicate
paper prints, which he had until then kept secret,
Talbot rushed samples to the Royal Institution in London. For the next fifteen years, these two processes—
the daguerreotype on copper and the calotype on
paper—competed for supremacy, only to give way to
newer and more commercially feasible photographic
techniques in the mid-1850s. Talbot's pioneering pictures still can be purchased for anywhere from about
$250 to $3,000 each. *Building With Carriages* is an
outstanding image in its own right. Adding to the collector appeal is the unusual border of brushed silver
chloride, a visual demonstration of the handmade
nature of the calotype. Photosensitive paper was not
yet being produced commercially. Photographers
made all their materials by hand. Sheets of ordinary
paper were brushed, one by one, with photosensitive
chemicals. Normally the rough border would be
trimmed after the image had been printed, but in this
case Fox Talbot apparently just never got around to
doing so. Approximate retail value of *Building With
Carriages* is $2,500.

David Octavius Hill (1802–1870) and Robert Adamson (1821–1848):
Horatio McCulloch, circa 1845, carbon print made circa 1916, 8 by 6 inches. Collection Lee D. Witkin, New York.

Among very early photographers, none are more esteemed for the high aesthetic quality of their work than the Scottish photographic team of Hill and Adamson. The two met when Hill, a painter, was commissioned to undertake a massive group portrait of 474 ministers attending the first convention of the Free Church of Scotland. Realizing the impossibility of painting such a work from life, he hired Adamson, a young Edinburgh portrait photographer, to capture the likeness of each minister with a camera. That initial project, so successful, was followed by a four-year collaboration, ending only when Adamson became terminally ill in 1847. More than 1,500 images were produced during this period, mostly portraits and architectural studies. For years, historians gave all the credit for the team's photographic output to Hill, arguing that Adamson was no more than a technician who did as Hill told him. Recent evidence has caused a dramatic revision of that theory. A number of historians now point out that Hill attempted to continue taking photographs with other collaborators after Adamson's death, but with no success whatsoever. Eventually, Hill gave up photography. So Adamson is increasingly being credited as an equal partner. Reproduced here is a carbon print made in about 1916 from the Hill and Adamson negative by Scottish photographer Jessie Bertram. Its retail value is approximately $500. An original Hill and Adamson calotype print of the same portrait, in good condition, would bring three to four times that amount.

Rufus Anson (active 1850–1867):
Portrait of unidentified couple, circa 1850, half-plate daguerreotype, 5 by 3½ inches. Courtesy Daguerreian Era, Pawlet, Vermont.

The era of the daguerreotype lasted some twenty years, from 1839 through the end of the 1850s. These were exuberant times in photography, as the public took an immediate fancy to this most unusual of inventions: a process which, through the marvels of chemistry, could imprint an exact likeness on a small silver-coated plate of copper. Thousands of daguerreotype studios were established around the world, and people signed up by the tens of millions to have their pictures taken. Routine daguerreotype portraits of now-anonymous individuals remain available in substantial numbers at prices from approximately $8 to $10 on up. But then there is a relatively small quantity of really good daguerreotypes which command more. Reproduced here is such a work, a classic daguerreotype studio portrait: straightforward, fairly relaxed, well posed. Retail price is a moderately high $75, reflecting the quality of the image, the good physical condition of the work, its large size, and the fact that the work remains in its original case. At its very best, a daguerreotype portrait will reveal something of the character of the subject and will portray the sitter in a direct (perhaps bold), gimmick-free manner. While this work does not meet the highest standards (very few daguerreotypes do), it is nonetheless a good example of a fine daguerreotype portrait—the type which still can be collected on a moderate budget.

Platt D. Babbitt (active 1853– c. 1870):
A man stranded on the rocks in the Niagara River,
1853, quarter-plate daguerreotype, $2\frac{1}{2}$ by $3\frac{1}{2}$ inches.
Courtesy Daguerreian Era, Pawlet, Vermont.

This is a terribly difficult picture to write about, because of its wrenching emotional content and the issue it raises so pointedly about whether photographers can go too far in portraying moments of extreme human anguish. As related by Helmut and Alison Gernsheim in *L. J. M. Daguerre: The History of the Diorama and the Daguerreotype,* Platt Babbitt was one of the earliest "tourist" photographers, taking daguerreotype portraits of visitors to the U.S. side of Niagara Falls. Soon after he obtained his concession in 1853, two men boating on the Niagara River were sucked into the rapids and their boat smashed on the rocks. One of the men was swept over the falls at once. The other, named Avery, grabbed onto a log stuck in midstream. All attempts at rescue failed, the current being too swift to negotiate, and after eighteen hours Avery was swept away. Babbitt took several pictures of Avery's struggle; the picture reproduced here is apparently the only one to have survived. The work is of great historic importance and recently was acquired by the Library of Congress for its collection of prime historic rarities. (Although the price was not disclosed, exceptional daguerreotypes of this sort typically sell in a range of $5,000 to $10,000 and higher.) More important than its historic merits, the work raises an issue central to photography and to photographylike media in general (including movies and television): whether the depiction of real-life desperation abstracts and therefore diminishes, even exploits, that desperation. The bombardment of visual imagery in our own era has tended to dull our senses and block out the deep emotional power of photography and TV. All too often, photographs are viewed as little more than "pretty pictures," devoid of meaningful content. Yet, the Babbitt picture simply cannot be ignored: a lone man facing a certain death. While painful to look at and absorb, this picture can perhaps put us more directly in touch with the tremendous power of photography and the living, breathing nature of the people it depicts.

Photography, among its other early virtues, provided a quick, inexpensive means of exact portrayal—everything from the first criminal "mug shots" to aerial photographs for use in mapmaking. *Horse Artilleryman,* from a series of pictures depicting British soldiers in various regimental dress, falls into the same general category—an early functional use of photography, replacing engraving. Certainly in its time the work was intended as no more than that: a precise visual presentation, front and back, like a scientific drawing. But time has given us a different perspective. Some old photographs take on new character and meaning with age, transforming themselves almost magically like fine wine. *Horse Artilleryman,* with its charm and decorative beauty, is such a picture, a most collectible of photographs. Retail price is $200. Thousands of offbeat nineteenth-century photographs like *Horse Artilleryman* are available to collectors who have the energy to search about—at flea markets, antique shops, auctions, and dealers' galleries—and the self-confidence to buy whatever they like, regardless of its formal standing as "art."

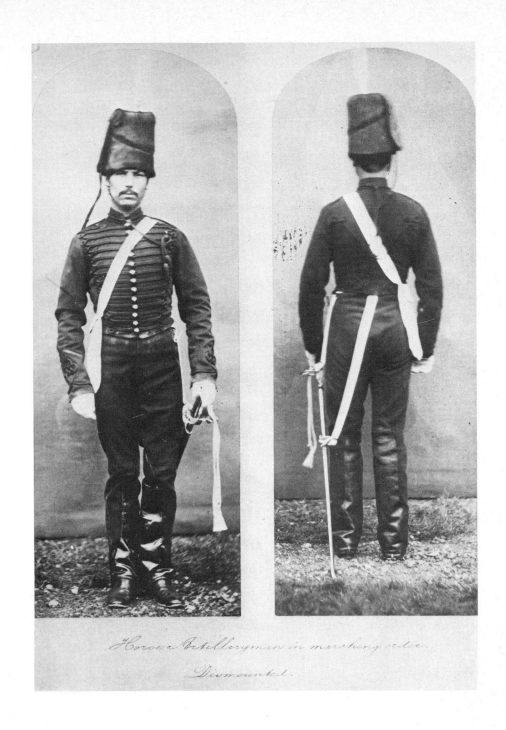

Horse Artillerymen in marching order.
Dismounted.

Roger Fenton (1819–1869):

Composition of Fruit and Flowers, circa 1858, albumen print, 14½ by 17⅝ inches. Collection The Art Museum, Princeton University, Princeton, New Jersey.

Roger Fenton was a successful British attorney who turned to photography with great enthusiasm, soon abandoning his legal career to take up the new medium full-time. His arch-topped pictures were a wonder in their era for their large size and high quality. Fenton first achieved public acclaim with a series of calotype photographs taken on a visit to Russia in 1851. Subsequently, he photographed art works for the British Museum, British cathedrals and ruins, and still lifes. In 1855, he was commissioned by Thomas Agnew & Sons to cover the Crimean War; he produced nearly 400 pictures and, in doing so, became the first successful war photographer — a fact that, in itself, would earn him a position of great importance. However, it is his still lifes which are today most prized by collectors. Retail value of a large still life like *Composition of Fruit and Flowers* probably would exceed $5,000. But, sadly, these works were the product of an era that was not to last for long. The large, grand photographs of the late 1850s — so exceptional in every way — fell victim in the early 1860s to a public frenzy for the mass-produced carte de visite. Fenton, like many other important photographers of the fifties, despised the carte and was unwilling to see his work printed on such a small scale. In 1862, some four years after creating *Composition of Fruit and Flowers,* he gave up photography at age forty-two and returned to the law, never to photograph again.

147

Louis-Auguste (1814– ?) and Auguste-Rosalie (1826– ?) Bisson:
Untitled Alpine View, circa 1860, albumen print, 9½ by 15½ inches. Courtesy Marcuse Pfeifer Gallery, New York.

A large Bisson Frères Alpine view is a glory to behold. Few early photographers achieved the aesthetic grandeur and technical perfection of the brothers Louis and Auguste Bisson. Their first Alpine landscapes, landmarks in the history of photography, were produced in 1855. It is said that when the Bissons ascended Mont Blanc in 1861 to take the first photographs from its 15,781-foot-high summit, a team of twenty-five porters was required just to carry their wet-plate chemicals, equipment, and portable darkroom. Yet, working under the most difficult of conditions, the firm of Bisson Frères obtained some of the smoothest, most detailed, most defect-free pictures, regardless of subject matter, in the first twenty years of photography. Early French photographs are rarities. Some collectors theorize that in France, unlike England and the United States, photography was essentially viewed as an aristocratic avocation; few prints were made because there was no commercial market. Bisson Frères prints, though rare, are somewhat less so than those of Gustave Le Gray, Henri Le Secq, Charles Marville, and Charles Nègre, important contemporaries. Approximate retail value of this picture is $1,200.

Saché (dates unknown):
Untitled Indian Landscape, circa 1860, albumen print, 9$\frac{1}{4}$ by 11$\frac{1}{4}$ inches. Courtesy Marlborough Gallery, New York.

Saché is one of the many mystery photographers of the nineteenth century. His work often appears in albums of Indian photographs along with that of his contemporary, Samuel Bourne—perhaps the greatest of the nineteenth-century photographers of India. But little is known of Saché himself. One possibility is that Saché's first name was John. But there also is a theory that there were actually two or three Sachés working in India. The only definitive clues are the signature and the code numbers in the prints. Perhaps someday we will learn more about Saché, perhaps not. Meanwhile, his work, some of which is very good, remains inexpensive, largely because collectors tend to shun photographs which are not well documented. Approximate retail value of this fine early landscape is $150.

Nadar (1820–1910):
Portrait of Félicien Rops, 1861, albumen print, 8 by 6 inches. Collection The Metropolitan Museum of Art, New York; gift of Michael Wilson, 1977.

Nadar (professional name of Gaspard-Félix Tournachon) has been called the greatest photographer in French history. Flamboyant and energetic, he depicted the artistic, literary, and political personalities of nineteenth-century Europe in a style distinctively his own. A Nadar portrait is direct and penetrating, taken against the simplest of backdrops. By traditional standards, this portrait of Félicien Rops, a maker of erotic prints, might be considered a bad picture. A whole section of the image is out of focus. But part of the genius of Nadar was his willingness to ignore tradition, and to bend to each sitter's personality and will. Rather than asking Rops to move his left arm, Nadar has chosen to photograph him as he stood—capturing Rops as an individual of self-assurance and eccentricity. Furthermore, Nadar clearly considered this portrait to be a major work; it has been hand signed and dated, something he seldom did. Most of the Nadar portraits available today are carbon prints or Woodburytypes from *Galerie Contemporaine* magazine. Original albumen prints, such as the work reproduced here, are rare and expensive. Retail value of this work is at least $2,000 to $3,000.

153

Alexander Gardner (1821–1882):
Stereographic portrait of Abraham Lincoln at Antietam, 1862, albumen print mounted on card, each image 3 by 3 inches. Collection George R. Rinhart, New York.

Lincoln portraits are the ultimate in stereographs. Only two copies of this Antietam portrait, taken during the darkest and bloodiest days of the Civil War, are known to exist (one owned by collector/dealer George Rinhart, the other by the American Antiquarian Society). Five other stereograph poses of Lincoln have been documented, ranging in rarity from about eight copies of a seated portrait slightly in profile to a single known copy of the so-called "Lincoln flat top" (so named because Lincoln's hair shoots straight up as if he had stuck his finger in an electric socket). The great rarity of Lincoln stereographs is a mystery to collectors. Lincoln was photographed often, and his portraits, unlike most old photographs, have always been cherished objects that have been preserved in fairly substantial numbers. Rinhart, one of the premier stereograph collectors, searched nearly twenty years before acquiring his first two Lincoln stereographs within weeks of each other in early 1977. (He also once owned the only known Robert E. Lee stereograph, but sold that unique item several years ago—much to his current regret.) Part of the fun of owning a group portrait like this Antietam stereograph is to attempt to identify everybody in the picture. General McClellan is the second person to Lincoln's left; General McClernand stands directly to Lincoln's right. The man in the light suit may be John Dix, later governor of New York. The officer to Lincoln's far left is from a Massachusetts brigade—a point established by Rinhart when he spotted the same individual in an 1864 group portrait with General Sherman in Atlanta. Everybody else in this stereograph remains unidentified. Determining retail market values of historically important rarities is always difficult. Possible value of this work: $1,000.

Entered according to act of Congress, in the year 1862, by Alexander Gardner, in the Clerk's Office of the District Court of the District of Columbia.

Cartes de visite:
Portraits of Timothy O'Sullivan (left), circa 1862, and
Alexander Gardner, circa 1863, albumen prints, each
image 3½ by 2¼ inches. Collection George R. Rinhart,
New York.

The Rasputin-like individual pictured on the right,
Alexander Gardner, is the photographer who took the
Lincoln stereograph reproduced on the preceding
page. It may seem strange that such a rough-hewn person could create such a moving photograph. But early
photography was not an easy art and required, above
all, great force of personality—including a willingness
to work with messy chemicals and (in the case of
landscape and war photographers) the courage and
physical strength to travel long distances with heavy
equipment. Gardner, like Timothy O'Sullivan (pictured on the left), is one of the most important of all
nineteenth century American photographers. Yet,
although each spent his entire adult life working with
cameras, neither seemed to have much inclination to
pose in front of a lens. Each of these images is believed
to be unique—the only known portrait of either individual. When they did have their pictures taken, both
chose the carte de visite format. Cartes were small-
scale "visiting card" photographs produced in a standard size of approximately 3½ by 2¼ inches. Throughout the early 1860s it was extremely fashionable in the
United States and Europe to present carte portraits of
oneself to friends—a rage that began after Napoleon
III posed for a carte portrait in 1859. Most carte poses
are stiff and lifeless. The O'Sullivan carte is somewhat
above average in its capturing of the sitter's personality. On the other hand, the Gardner carte is exceptional, with its sense of the sitter's rugged individual-
ism and its use of the ornate chair (which imparts a
princely quality to Gardner). Market value of these
two photographs? Owner Rinhart declines to give a
figure, terming the works "unique and priceless." A
possible range, however, is $500 to $800 each.

Oscar Gustave Rejlander (1813–1875):
Full-figure study of a young woman standing, circa
1864, vintage albumen print, 9 by 6 inches. Courtesy
Thackrey & Robertson, San Francisco.

Little known in the United States, but held in high
esteem and actively traded in England, works of the
great Victorian art photographers—particularly O. G.
Rejlander and, to a lesser extent, Henry Peach
Robinson—offer opportunities for collectors at prices
from about $300 on up. Victorian art photography rep-
resents the historic peak of photographic "pictorial-
ism," a doctrine which emphasizes picturesque,
staged, even theatrical imagery. Rejlander, a native of
Sweden, became a painter and went to Rome in the
1840s to study the old masters. There he married an
Englishwoman and subsequently settled in London. In
about 1853, he took up photography and set out to rescue the medium from the reproach, often made by its
critics, that it was merely a mechanical art. At first,
Rejlander composed elaborately staged "allegorical"
photographs, often pieced together from as many as
thirty different negatives. These works were enormously popular in their time. But he soon tired of making them, and by 1860 he turned to a simpler type of
photography that has, more than his early work,
retained its visual charm and sense of vitality over the
years: studies intended for use by artists. The image
reproduced here, a rare full-figure study in near-mint
condition, is an example of Rejlander at his best.
Approximate retail value is $2,000.

159

Julia Margaret Cameron (1815–1879):
The Turtle Doves, circa 1865, albumen print mounted on card, 5 by 4 inches. Courtesy Sotheby Parke Bernet, New York.

Julia Margaret Cameron was the "ugly duckling" among six sisters noted for their talent and beauty. But what she lacked in appearance she more than made up for in enterprise and intellect. She married well, bore six children, adopted several others, and had energy to spare for social, humanitarian, and literary activities. When her daughter and son-in-law gave her a camera in 1863, she plunged into photography with characteristic enthusiasm. Working out of a chicken coop which she converted to a photographic studio, she portrayed many of the most prominent British literary, artistic, and scientific figures of the era, including Tennyson, Browning, Carlyle, and G. F. Watts. She strove to capture the personality of each of her sitters, sometimes making them pose for hours at a time until she was satisfied with the results. When Tennyson brought Longfellow to her studio, he is reported to have said: "I will leave you now, Longfellow. You will do whatever she tells you. I will come back soon and see what is left of you." Cameron also had a special interest in pictures of children. Some of her most charming works, often posed like Renaissance paintings, fall into this group. Her pictures were extremely popular with the Victorians and were marketed actively by Colnaghi's, the London art dealers. The print reproduced here carries the Colnaghi blind stamp, indicating it was made specifically for public sale. This print brought $625 at auction in September 1975.

The Turtle Doves

Lewis Carroll (1832–1898):
The Terry Family, 1865, modern gelatin-silver print,
7$\frac{13}{16}$ by 9$\frac{15}{16}$ inches. Courtesy Lunn Gallery/Graphics
International Ltd., Washington, D.C.

Carroll, best known as author of *Alice in Wonderland,*
was a fierce devotee of amateur photography. His
favorite subjects were portraits of families and little
girls. Unlike Julia Margaret Cameron, who sold her
work commercially, Carroll never did so, with the
result that vintage prints are extremely rare. Recently,
eighteen of Carroll's original glass-plate negatives
were purchased from his descendants by an American
publisher, and newly made prints are now being issued
in limited edition—an increasingly frequent occur-
rence with major nineteenth-century photographers.
Approximate retail price for this modern print of *The
Terry Family* is $1,000. A vintage print, if one could be
found, would likely sell for at least five times that sum
in good condition. Should a collector buy modern
prints from nineteenth-century negatives? While caution is advised, there ultimately are no definitive
answers. Several factors should be considered in
reaching a decision: quality of the modern prints,
price, reason for their being published, importance of
adding the photographer's work to your collection, and
availability of vintage prints. The overriding point is
that, whatever the final choice, the collector must go in
with open eyes and an awareness of just what is being
acquired.

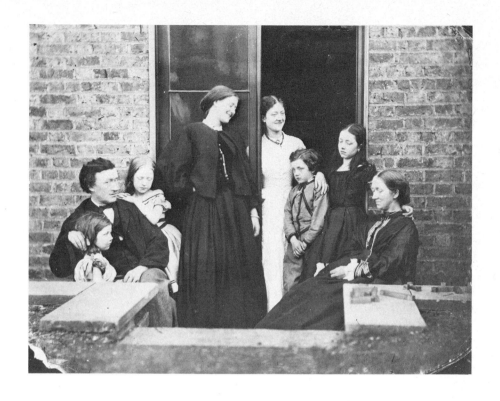

163

George N. Barnard (1819–1902):
The Potter House, Atlanta, 1864 or 1865, from
Photographic Views of the Sherman Campaign,
published in 1866, albumen print, 10 by 14 inches.
Courtesy Robert Schoelkopf Gallery, New York.

War photography in the era of the wet-plate negative
was largely a conceptual art. Since the preparation and
exposure of a wet plate was a slow and laborious process, photographers were forced to follow in the wake
of battle and depict its aftermath rather than the battle
itself. George Barnard's *Photographic Views of the
Sherman Campaign,* containing sixty-one albumen
prints, documents the destruction left by Sherman's
troops in their march to Georgia and is considered
(along with Alexander Gardner's two-volume *Photographic Sketch Book of the War*) one of the classic
illustrated books to emerge from the Civil War. There
is a haunting quality to the best of these pictures. As in
The Potter House, the calm after the storm can be as
moving as the storm itself. The devastation depicted
by Barnard is absolute. In addition to the huge hole in
the side of the house, there are dozens of smaller holes,
the damage to the roof of the outbuilding, the damaged
chimney, the fallen tree, bricks strewn throughout the
yard, and the gouged land in the foreground. One can
only imagine the damage, emotional and physical, to
the people inside. An intact volume of the Barnard
book sold recently at auction for $8,500 and has been
offered privately for as much as $22,000. This individ-
ual picture carries a retail value of approximately
$700.

William Henry Jackson (1843–1942):
Calle de Guadeloupe, Chihuaha, late 1870s,
albumen print, 17 by 21 inches. Collection Lee D.
Witkin, New York.

William Henry Jackson was one of the most colorful
and beloved American photographers of the nineteenth century. He won wide acclaim for his early
views of Yellowstone, taken in the 1870s, and went on
to photograph throughout the American west and in
Mexico. Jackson Canyon, Jackson Lake, and the city
of Jackson in Wyoming all are named after him, as is
Jackson Butte in Colorado. Like many of his contemporaries, Jackson had his own distinctive style of photography. While Carleton Watkins's photographs are
almost always heroic and picturesque, often taken
from low angles which emphasize the towering scale
of waterfalls and mountains—and William Bell
favored high angles looking down from cliffs or into
deep canyons—one of Jackson's hallmarks is the contrast of near and far objects. The branches intruding
into the upper-left corner of this photograph are highly
characteristic of his work. So is the rider posed against
a deep, diminishing background. Such contrasts
enabled Jackson to create a sense of scale and depth
and to heighten the drama of his photographs by
adding to their visual complexity. The subject of this
photograph clearly is the landscape rather than the
horse and rider. Nonetheless, the horse and rider play a
central compositional role. Without them, the trees
would lose their grandeur and the work would become
just another mundane image. Most original Jacksons
sell in a price range of about $100 to $1,000. However,
this unusually large print, in fine condition, carries a
retail value of approximately $1,500.

Francis Frith (1822–1898):
Durham Cathedral, 1880s, vintage albumen print,
$8\frac{1}{2}$ by 11 inches. Courtesy Marlborough Gallery,
New York.

The career of Francis Frith, one of the leading British topographical photographers of the nineteenth century, was lengthy and extremely prolific. Frith achieved his initial fame in the late 1850s with a series of photographic expeditions to Egypt, Nubia, Palestine, and Syria. Many of his finest pictures from this period were taken with unusually large 16- by 20-inch glass-plate negatives, extremely difficult to handle in high temperatures. Following these early successes, Frith photographed throughout continental Europe and produced a large body of landscapes and architectural studies in rural England. Moving into the business side of photography, he became one of the leading photography publishers, selling both his own images and those of others. Frith's work is among the most difficult to evaluate, due to its huge quantity and the wide variations in subject matter and aesthetic quality. Some early Friths sell for $1,000 or more, other works for as little as $10 or $15. The photograph reproduced here is a good Frith, but not a great one, and carries a retail value of about $150. What does this picture lack? At least three factors hold down its value: its relatively small size; the fact that it is a late Frith rather than from his prime early period; and the aesthetic quality — the picture, while compositionally strong, falls short of being truly insightful or penetrating.

Peter Henry Emerson (1856–1936):
The Gladdon-Cutter's Return, 1886, vintage platinum print, $9\frac{1}{16}$ by $11\frac{1}{4}$ inches. Courtesy Robert Schoelkopf Gallery, New York.

Is photography art? Peter Henry Emerson, the leader of the "naturalist" school of photography in England, was one of the first important photographers to argue that it was. Furthermore, Emerson developed one of the earliest theories of photographic aesthetics. He believed that subject matter should be drawn from the real world, particularly man in nature, and he favored the use of a soft-focus lens, contending that a photograph should depict no more detail than that perceived by the unaided human eye. Although Emerson renounced his views in 1890, they continued to win adherents and led to the birth of the Photo-Secession in the United States shortly after the turn of the century. Emerson's photographs are extremely popular today with collectors. Two basic categories of his prints exist: more expensive platinum prints (such as *The Gladdon-Cutter's Return*) from his 1886 illustrated book, *Life and Landscape on the Norfolk Broads;* and less expensive photogravures from the seven illustrated books he published between 1887 and 1895. Approximate retail value of *The Gladdon-Cutter's Return* is $1,400.

171

Eadweard Muybridge (1830–1904):
Detail from plate 346, *Animal Locomotion,* published in 1887, collotype, $4\frac{1}{2}$ by $5\frac{3}{4}$ inches (size of detail). Courtesy Helios, New York.

Certain achievements stand as landmarks in the history of photography. The early stop-action photographs of Eadweard Muybridge are a prime example. Muybridge was a well-known photographer of the western wilderness who was asked in 1872 by Leland Stanford, a former governor of California, to prove photographically that a horse, while running, has all four feet off the ground at the same time. Initially Muybridge used wet-plate negatives, which were too slow to capture anything but a blur speeding by. Then in 1877, with improved dry plates and an elaborate system of electrically controlled shutters, he showed that all four feet are off the ground—tucked beneath the horse's body—at one phase of a gallop. These photographs were extremely controversial at first, since they clashed directly with the spread-leg "hobby horse" convention of painting. Over the next decade, Muybridge went on to photograph hundreds of other stop-action sequences of moving animals—from this classic study of male wrestlers (retail value about $800) to flying birds, dashing antelope, and lumbering elephants. These pictures are important in two ways: They have greatly influenced the course of painting, and they led directly to the first motion pictures.

Gertrude Käsebier (1852–1934):
Happy Days, circa 1902, vintage platinum print,
8 by 6 inches. Courtesy Lunn Gallery/Graphics
International Ltd., Washington, D.C.

Much like Julia Margaret Cameron three decades earlier, Gertrude Stanton Käsebier took up photography
relatively late in life and then pursued it with total
devotion. Born of frontier Quaker parents in Iowa, she
moved in her early twenties to New York, where she
married Eduard Käsebier, a German-born importer.
Motherhood, which was to form a major theme in her
photography, forced deferral of her interest in the visual arts. Finally, at age thirty-six, she entered Pratt
Institute to study portrait painting. Five years later, in
1893, she went to France to paint, and there fell upon
the beauty of photography while experimenting with
time exposures on a rainy day. "The result was so surprising to me that from that moment I knew I had found
my vocation," she later wrote. Returning to New York
in 1897, she opened a studio at a fashionable Fifth Avenue location. Soon she became one of the most successful portrait photographers in the world, rejecting
the traditional use of painted backdrops, palm trees,
artificial flowers, and other props for a more natural
and light-filled style of portraiture that was revolutionary in its time. Her work was greatly admired by the
Photo-Secessionists, and six of her pictures, along
with two by Alfred Stieglitz, comprised the first issue
of *Camera Work. Happy Days* is one of her best-
known images. Approximate retail value of this
vintage platinum print is $2,000. By contrast, a
photogravure of *Happy Days,* from the April 1905
issue of *Camera Work,* would sell at retail for about
$300.

Arnold Genthe (1869–1942):
Watching the Approach of the Fire, San Francisco,
1906, vintage silver print, 14 by 10 inches. Courtesy
Thackrey & Robertson, San Francisco.

What a strange and enchanting picture this is—people
fleeing the aftermath of the 1906 San Francisco earthquake, but appearing for all the world to be on a
Sunday picnic. The photograph was taken with the
simplest of amateur equipment—a Kodak box camera
and roll film—by Arnold Genthe, the leading San
Francisco portrait and documentary photographer of
the early twentieth century. Genthe's own cameras had
been destroyed immediately after the earthquake when
his studio was dynamited to prevent the spread of fire.
So he borrowed a Kodak and took about 150 photographs from various vantage points around the city.
Approximate retail value of this rare vintage print is
$1,500.

Alfred Stieglitz (1864–1946):
The Steerage, 1907, photogravure published in 1915
in *291*, 12¼ by 10 inches. Courtesy Lunn Gallery/
Graphics International Ltd., Washington, D.C.

The Steerage is a landmark in modern art and perhaps the most famous photograph in history. It was
Stieglitz's own favorite among all his pictures, and he
liked to relate how the work had been praised by
Picasso. Out of a jumble of people and shapes on an
ocean liner heading for Europe, Stieglitz discerned
an image of exceptional order, form, and strength—an
image that subsequently has been described as being
Cubist. Filled with excitement, he rushed to his cabin,
grabbed his camera (which contained a single remaining unexposed plate), and returned to find the scene
just as he had left it. The work is typical of the Photo-
Secession in its emphasis on everyday subject matter
and photographic excellence. The gravure reproduced
here is the so-called "large format" *Steerage*, from the
publication *291*. Approximate market value is $3,000
to $4,500. The "small format" *Steerage*, published
four years earlier in *Camera Work* magazine, generally
sells for between $800 and $1,200.

Eugène Atget (1857–1927):
Corset Shop, circa 1909, vintage print, gold chloride printing-out paper, $8\frac{3}{4}$ by $6\frac{7}{8}$ inches. Collection The Museum of Modern Art, New York.

Eugène Atget, who died in obscurity more than half a century ago, is now recognized as one of the greatest of all documentary photographers. Atget went to sea as a young man, then tried acting and painting. Finally, at age forty-one, he turned to photography. He proceeded, through the first quarter of this century, to create an unparalleled visual record of Paris—its buildings, shops, monuments, parks, gardens, and street vendors. These pictures are noted for their quiet self-assurance, lyric beauty, and sense of detail. John Szarkowski, director of the department of photography at the Museum of Modern Art in New York, has stated that Atget's photographs have not been surpassed in their "purity and intensity of vision" and that these works stand as "a bench mark against which much of the most sophisticated contemporary photography measures itself." Vintage Atget prints are becoming increasingly rare and expensive. Retail value of this vintage print of *Corset Shop,* one of his best-known images, is approximately $2,500. Also available, at much lower prices, are posthumous prints made from Atget's negatives by photographer Berenice Abbott.

Edward Weston (1886–1958):
Nude, 1920, posthumous silver print, $9\frac{1}{2}$ by $7\frac{1}{2}$ inches. Courtesy Cole Weston, Carmel, California.

This is an early Weston photograph, illustrating the classical form, beauty of line, and purity of light which were to make him famous. It also is a key transitional photograph, taken as he was beginning to move toward absolute precision of focus—but was not yet all the way there. The year 1920 was an important one for Weston. Essentially a commercial portrait photographer, he decided at that point in his career to undertake a critical reevaluation of his work. The result, over the next decade, was a tremendous creative outpouring, including nudes, abstractions, and his well-known vegetable still lifes. The print reproduced here, made from the original negative by Weston's son Cole, has a retail price of $200. A vintage platinum print of the same work, if one could be found, might cost in excess of $5,000.

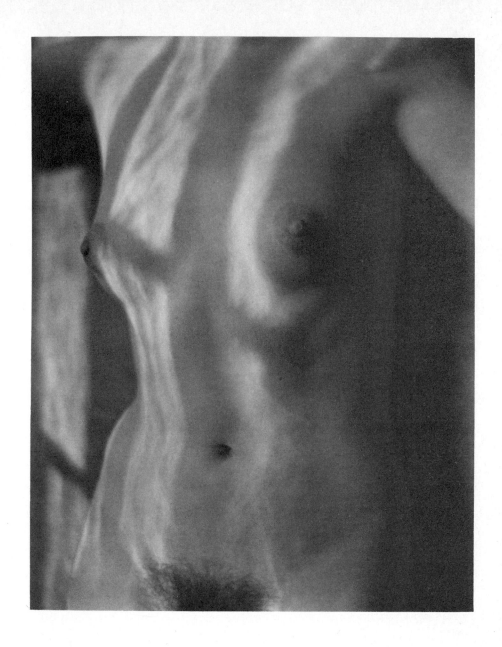

Paul Strand (1890–1976):
Lathe, 1923, toned silver print, $9\frac{1}{2}$ by $7\frac{1}{2}$ inches.
©1971 by Paul Strand. Courtesy the Estate of
Paul Strand.

Throughout the history of photography, there have
been maybe half a dozen photographers of towering
influence—individuals like Daguerre and Stieglitz
who have contributed the most essential technical
inventions to the medium or have dominated photographic aesthetics for an entire generation or more.
Another such individual is Paul Strand, who broke
from the soft-focus manner of the early twentieth century and reestablished the virtues of "straight" photography. In his bold, direct pictures, Strand stands as the
first major photographer to successfully lift photography to a totally independent art form, exploiting its
uniqueness rather than in any way imitating painting.
His influence on photography, following publication
of eleven of his pictures in the final two issues of *Camera Work* in 1917, was immediate. That influence con-
tinues today. Befitting Strand's status as a great among
greats, vintage prints of his pivotal early works are
now among the most expensive in the market, in some
cases approaching $10,000 per print. Reproductions
cannot do justice to Strand's early photographs. The
craftsmanship and tonal details are exceptional. It is
said that Strand sometimes spent three days making a
single print. *Lathe* is a truly remarkable photograph,
finding form and beauty where none had been seen
before.

László Moholy-Nagy (1895–1946):
Farewell, photomontage, 1924, vintage silver print,
11 by 8½ inches. Private collection.

Thinker, writer, sculptor, photographer, filmmaker, and teacher, László Moholy-Nagy stands as one of the most influential figures in twentieth-century art. Born in Hungary, he moved to Berlin after World War I, then in 1923 joined the faculty of the Bauhaus, the experimental design school that flourished briefly during the Weimar Republic. Fascism drove him in 1934 to Holland. In 1937, he came to the United States, founding the new Bauhaus (now the Institute of Design). There is an almost childlike joy to Moholy-Nagy's photographic experiments, including his work in photomontage—the photographing of paper collages. Perhaps to distinguish his own work in photomontage from that of Alexander Rodchenko, Herbert Bayer, John Heartfield, Max Ernst, and other artists, Moholy-Nagy termed his prints "fotoplastiks." These images are notable for their wit, satire, and sense of the absurd, and for their emphasis on formalist composition. They can be seen, further, as an extension of his interest in "constructivist" painting and sculpture—that is, the creation of art works through the assemblage of existing materials. Moholy-Nagy photographs are rare and relatively expensive. Approximate retail value of *Farewell* is $3,000 to $3,500.

Charles Sheeler (1883–1965):

Untitled Shaker Interior, circa 1925, silver print, $7\frac{1}{4}$ by $9\frac{1}{4}$ inches. Private collection.

Charles Sheeler is a prime example of a historically important painter who ranks also as one of the most significant photographers. Other examples include Edgar Degas and Thomas Eakins. Sheeler took up photography in 1912 as a means of support and continued to photograph sporadically for more than forty years—sometimes because he needed money, sometimes as studies for paintings, and sometimes purely for pleasure. His paintings and photographs are very much akin. Both are noted for their superior craftsmanship, extreme precision, bold emphasis on semiabstract form, and depiction of visual beauty in common subject matter. Shaker interiors represent one of the classic themes of Sheeler's career, in both his paintings and photographs. Because of their key position in the development of twentieth-century American art, Sheeler's photographs tend to be very expensive. One print, a 1938 still life, sold recently at auction for $8,750. Retail value of this Shaker interior is approximately $5,000.

189

Edward Steichen (1879–1973):
Chéruit Gown, 1927, vintage silver print, 10 by 8 inches. Courtesy Helios, New York. Reprinted with the permission of Joanna T. Steichen.

Fashion photography is a rich and varied field of collecting. The photograph reproduced here was taken for *Vogue* magazine and appeared in the issue of May 1, 1927, in an article titled "The Paris Mode, as New York Likes It: Seven Pages of Outstanding Fashions." In its elegance and sophistication, it is typical of the style which helped establish Steichen as one of the most prominent and successful of all fashion photographers. While the dark, shadowy lighting may seem at first to obscure rather than highlight the gown, this technique has enabled Steichen to emphasize the gown's appearance of "glittering jet," in the words of the *Vogue* caption. The model in this photograph is Marion Morehouse, wife of e.e. cummings. Morehouse was one of the first great fashion models. Tall and willowy, she posed often for Steichen and brought to his images a sense of personality and wit. Later, she herself took up photography and in 1962 published a volume of her pictures under the title *Adventures in Value,* with text by her husband. Retail price of this print of *Chéruit Gown* is $3,000.

August Sander (1876–1964):
Konditormeister, 1928, vintage silver print, $8\frac{5}{8}$ by $5\frac{1}{2}$ inches. Collection Eugene M. Schwartz, New York.

Ah, the pride of a German pastry chef. This portrait is one from a series taken by August Sander in the 1920s and early 1930s in his goal of depicting the German race in its entirety, position by position in society and trade by trade. Sander's portraits are classics of documentary photography. However, as the Nazis rose to power they began to harass him with increasing viciousness, confiscating all the prints they could find. Sander eventually gave up portrait photography and, after World War II, devoted himself primarily to landscapes. Retail value of *Konditormeister* is approximately $1,800.

Man Ray (1890–1976):
Portrait of Kiki, circa 1930, vintage silver print, 6 by
8½ inches. Private collection.

Man Ray, the American expatriate artist who lived in
Paris most of his adult life, was an enormously inventive photographer. He experimented with a wider
range of styles and technical methods than practically
any other photographer in history. Yet, for all the variety of his imagery, the work reproduced here is atypical and shows that Ray sometimes extended himself
even beyond the many styles we generally associate
with him. What makes this work so unusual is its
emphasis on pattern and texture, as opposed to Ray's
more characterisitc concern with bold patches of light
and shadow. There also is a casualness of structure,
almost like a snapshot, that stands in contrast to the
formalism generally associated with Ray's imagery.
Atypical works can be extremely rewarding to the student of photography. They challenge our understanding of the qualities which set the photographer's work
apart, and they often provide us with new insights into
the photographer's overall aesthetic concerns. Retail
value of this portrait probably exceeds $3,000.

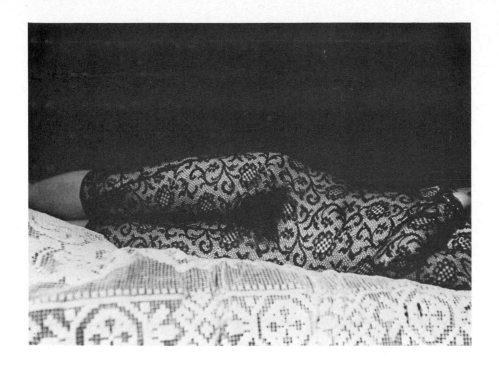

Alfred Stieglitz (1864–1946):
Poplars, Lake George, circa 1932, vintage silver print, 9½ by 7½ inches. Courtesy Sotheby Parke Bernet, New York.

Original Stieglitz prints are extremely rare. When they do come up for sale, prices tend to be quite high, reflecting both this rarity and Stieglitz's standing as the most important photographer of the twentieth century. Stieglitz made few prints to begin with, and when he died in 1946, his widow, Georgia O'Keeffe, divided the prints from his estate into various logical groupings and donated the lots to museums around the United States. The few original prints which do come onto the market, then, are mainly those which Stieglitz presented to members of his family and to friends. The scarcity of prints has made it difficult to evaluate Stieglitz's work thoroughly. Many of his early photographs are well known because they were reproduced in *Camera Work* magazine, which ceased publication in 1917. However, some collectors believe Stieglitz's "mature" period (after 1920) was his most creative, and pictures from this period are seldom seen. Even more than his earlier prints, pictures from the mature period have skyrocketed in value. (*Poplars* brought $4,100 àt auction in November 1976.) By the early 1930s, Stieglitz was deeply involved in the taking of his famous "equivalents"—photographs of clouds meant to generate an emotional response unrelated to subject matter. *Poplars,* with its dense and almost mysterious imagery, can be viewed in a similar vein: an attempt not so much to depict the trees themselves as to go beyond subject matter to a triggering of human emotions. Especially striking is the upward thrust of the branches, highly passionate and arush with life force.

Two major government-sponsored projects of interest to photography collectors were carried out during the Depression—one by the Farm Security Administration, the other by the Works Progress Administration. In the former, more than a dozen photographers were employed to document the plight of the rural poor. In the latter, approximately 4,000 artists working in all media, including some photographers, were given financial support to create as they saw fit. This photograph was taken as part of the latter, the WPA's Federal Art Project. Berenice Abbott had been documenting New York City—its buildings, piers, elevated subways, trolley cars, bridges, and other landmarks—on her own since about 1930. Beginning in 1935, she received financial assistance from the WPA. She took approximately 300 photographs between 1935 and 1939, when these images were published in a book titled *Changing New York.* It has been written that Abbott's documentation of New York is so thorough and intelligent that it might be possible to reconstruct the essential city on the basis of these photographs alone. Almost all her pictures of New York have a strikingly graphic quality, emphasizing the interplay between light and shadow. Retail value of this vintage print of *Warehouse, Water and Dock Streets* is approximately $500.

Ansel Adams (b. 1902):
White Branches, Mono Lake, California, 1950, silver print made in 1975, 20 by 16 inches. Courtesy Lunn Gallery/Graphics International Ltd., Washington, D.C.

Perhaps no other photographer during this century has captured the public imagination like Ansel Adams, master of the western landscape. Adams actually started out to be a concert pianist, photographing purely as a hobby. But at age twenty-eight, after meeting Paul Strand, he changed his mind and turned to photography as a full-time career. His work is noted for its superb technical quality and heroic subject matter—majestic rock formations, towering storm clouds, and broad rays of sunlight streaming down from the sky. One of the more interesting visual aspects of the photograph reproduced here is its extreme "depth of field"—its sharpness of focus in both the near foreground and far distance. This would be impossible with the unaided human eye, which would be forced to "scan" the scene from spot to spot. Simultaneously precise focus in all ranges of depth is a hallmark of Adams's work and is achieved through use of a small-aperture lens. Approximate retail value of *White Branches* is $2,500.

201

Walker Evans (1903–1975):
Santa Monica, California, 1953, modern silver print,
6⅛ by 6 inches. © Estate of Walker Evans.

Walker Evans, one of the most important and prolific documentary photographers, is best known for his spare pictures of the rural South taken in 1935–1937 under the sponsorship of the Farm Security Administration. But his subject matter actually was extremely varied and included portraits, Victorian houses in New England, Chicago street scenes, shop windows, New York doorways, Cuban dock workers, candid "snapshots" of subway riders, and much more. His body of work is so great that many of his pictures, such as *Santa Monica,* have seldom been exhibited or reproduced. Since Evans's death, the executors of his estate have attempted to broaden public knowledge of his full oeuvre. *Santa Monica* is one of fifteen photographs— some familiar, others not—published in 1977 in the posthumous Portfolio I. Retail value of this posthumous print of *Santa Monica* is approximately $300. Vintage prints of Evans's work, on the other hand, bring about $400 to $1,500 each.

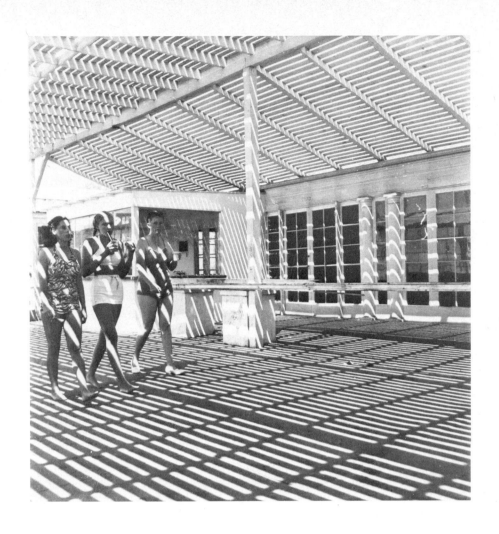

Diane Arbus (1923-71):
Female Impersonators Backstage, N.Y.C., 1962,
posthumous silver print, 8½ by 5¾ inches.

Diane Arbus is a towering but controversial figure in contemporary photography. Her work has been written about extensively, and exhibitions of her photographs invariably draw large crowds. Arbus is best known for her portraits of freaks, transvestites and nudists. As in *Female Impersonators Backstage,* these portraits are almost always direct and unflinching, presenting "strange" people in a "normal" manner. Yet, despite the straightforwardness of presentation, an Arbus often cuts two ways, with competing sensibilities tugging in opposite directions. In *Female Impersonators,* for instance, there is an irreconcilable conflict between the extreme tenderness of the subjects and their presentation as mannequin-like figures which could have no feelings at all. Arbus has, in effect, shown us two people of great human warmth, and then pulled back from this very quality. In particular, she has employed bright, frontal lighting to isolate the two figures from the background and to emphasize their highly stylized facial makeup. This would be a very different photograph if Arbus had chosen to illuminate the background, or to portray the impersonators in full costume—instead of in this phantasmal "halfway" world between their public lives on stage and their private lives at home. The price of a vintage Arbus print of *Female Impersonators Backstage,* if one could be found, probably would exceed $1,500. The posthumous print reproduced here, made by Arbus student Neil Selkirk, carries a retail price of $200.

Emmet Gowin (b. 1941): *Edith, Danville, Virginia 1967,* silver print made in 1975, 6 by 6 inches. Courtesy Light Gallery, New York.

Few photographers in the history of the medium have been so highly personal in their imagery, to the point of invasion of self-privacy, as Emmet Gowin. His pictures, evincing a strange, dreamlike entanglement between life and art, include portraits of his wife Edith, and other loved ones, as well as pictures of objects and places that help define life in and around Danville. His subjects are presented with a combination of bluntness and loving care. Many of his pictures are provocative, even disturbing. (Note in this picture the intensity of Edith's eyes and the outstretched arms, cut off at the wrists and with hands seemingly turned outward toward the viewer.) *Newsweek,* while stating that Gowin's photographs often are difficult to understand, has asserted that he "stands on the edge of young-master status." In addition to the acutely personal imagery, Gowin's work is noted for its extreme attention to photographic craft. He himself distinguishes between what he considers to be his very finest prints and others not up to the same standards of superiority—unusual among contemporary photographers. Written on the back of the print reproduced here is: "Print #3 of 3, 1975—A Very Good Print." Reflecting that judgment, the retail price of this print is $300. By contrast, two other 1975 prints of the same picture are priced at $200 each.

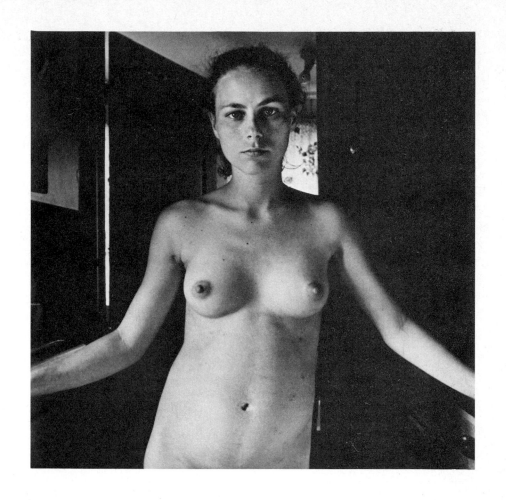

Harry Callahan (b.1912):
Cape Cod 1972, silver print made in 1975, $7\frac{1}{4}$ by $7\frac{1}{4}$ inches. Courtesy Light Gallery, New York.

More than any other photographer, Harry Callahan stands as a key transitional figure between the classicism of Paul Strand, Edward Weston, and Ansel Adams and the contemporary scene. Teacher as well as photographer, his pictures are greatly admired by collectors, critics, and curators but are not particularly well known to the public because, unlike many of his contemporaries, he has never worked as a photojournalist or, unlike an Ansel Adams, has never produced spectacular images of broad public appeal. His pictures are of a more subtle bent, more difficult to grasp, but ultimately very rewarding. Callahan took up photography in 1938 and has produced an enormous body of work. He himself has said that he might take a thousand photographs in a single month but that only one of them will mean anything. He typically devotes himself with great energy to a specific environment—Detroit, Chicago, Cuzco, Providence, wherever—for weeks, months, or even a few years. He explores that environment with penetrating eye, probing its light, spaces, and breadth. He has written of his work: "It's the subject matter that counts. I'm interested in revealing the subject in a new way to intensify it. A photo is able to capture a moment that people can't always see. Wanting to see more makes you grow as a person and growing makes you want to show more of life around you.... I do believe strongly in photography and hope by following it intuitively that when the photographs are looked at they will touch the spirit in people." Callahan's primary dealer, Light Gallery, follows a unique pricing structure for his work. The first dozen prints of an image sell for $450 each, then the price jumps to $500, and eventually, as more prints are sold, to $550, and finally to $600. As of this writing, the price of *Cape Cod 1972* was $550.

Duane Michals (b. 1936):
Self Portrait With My Guardian Angel, 1974, silver print, 4¾ by 7 inches. Courtesy Sidney Janis Gallery, New York.

Visiting an exhibition of Duane Michals photographs can be great fun—grappling with the ambiguities in his work, taking in the humor, and contemplating the metaphysical overtones. To Michals, the physical world is not real. Ideas and fantasies—the inner self—are. "What I cannot see is infinitely more important than what I can see," he has written. Michals's photographs are filled with mystery and bizarre happenings. In *People Eat People,* a six-photograph staged "sequence," a man devours a woman in successive blurred movements until all that's left is her horrified face. Michals also can be extremely playful. In *Take One and See Mt. Fujiyama,* a man takes a pill and immediately shrinks to 6 inches in height. A gigantic nude woman then comes through the door and sits on him. Mt. Fujiyama turns out to be his undershorts, bulging up from his erect penis as he awakens from his dream. Recently, Michals has turned to single-image prints with explanations written on the borders—"photographs with text." But these written explanations, as in the case of *Self Portrait,* often complicate the riddle rather than resolving it. Who is this guardian angel? Why a seaman? Is this picture based in any way on actual experience, or is it total fantasy? Retail price of *Self Portrait With My Guardian Angel,* printed in a limited edition of twenty-five, is $300.

SELF PORTRAIT WITH MY GUARDIAN ANGEL

My guardian angel's name is Pete. He was born in 1891 and died in 1932 in a terrible storm in the North Atlantic. He had been a merchant seaman all his life. During his lifetime, Pete never became what he might have been. He guides me and watches over me.

Robert Adams (b. 1937):
Untitled Denver Landscape, 1973–1974, silver print, 6 by 7¾ inches. Courtesy Castelli Graphics, New York.

Robert Adams photographs the western landscape with fineness, precision, and care. As with many other members of the new generation of "social landscape" photographers, his work portrays random fragments of a man-made squalor spreading across the foothills and plains. Best known are his pictures of tract housing in Colorado. His work relates directly back to that of Timothy O'Sullivan and William Henry Jackson, who photographed many of the same territories a century ago as unmapped virgin land. Adams has written of his work: "Many have asked, pointing incredulously toward a sweep of tract homes and billboards, why picture *that*? The question sounds simple, but it implies a difficult issue—why open our eyes anywhere but in undamaged places like national parks? One reason is, of course, that we do not live in parks, that we need to improve things at home, and that to do it we have to see the facts without blinking." While Adams's pictures are intended to inform and persuade, they stop short of blatant moralizing. He avoids high, romantic angles and sensationalized imagery. Ultimately, Adams has deep faith in the land: its life-supporting qualities, its grace, its persistence. There is, in fact, a constant undercurrent of tension in his work between the strength and permanence of the land and the transience—frequently the shoddiness—of man's additions to it. Retail price of his prints is $300 each.

Lilo Raymond (b. 1922):
Curtain and Vase, 1977, silver print, 9 by 13¼ inches.
Courtesy Marcuse Pfeifer Gallery, New York.

As contemporary photography has moved off in diverse (and sometimes arcane) new directions, Lilo Raymond is one of the few photographers who has remained true to the classical still life, infusing this most basic of genres with a highly personal vision. Raymond took up photography in the early 1960s, but received little recognition until her first major New York exhibition in April 1977. In the short period since, her work has been displayed widely and has won growing critical acclaim. A Raymond photograph is distinguished by its great warmth, refinement, and purity of light. Writing in *The Village Voice,* critic Alexandra Anderson has stated: "Simply composed and yet highly ordered, these photographs capture those rare moments when time seems to stand still and the sight of a pitcher against a doorway or rain on a windowpane becomes transcendental." Retail price of *Curtain and Vase* is $125.

Appendix I

Resource Materials

An increasing variety of catalogs, newsletters, and other publications serve the informational needs of photography collectors. These are some of the more helpful publications. Prices and subscription rates are those in effect as this book went to press.

Auction Catalogs

At minimum, any active collector — except perhaps collectors specializing exclusively in contemporary photography — might subscribe to the Parke Bernet and Argus Ltd. catalogs as a means of monitoring price trends and learning in advance of specific items as they come up for auction sale. Subscription rates include post-sale price lists, generally mailed to subscribers about four weeks after the sale, as well as the catalogs themselves.

Sotheby Parke Bernet
Auctions are held two to three times a year. Annual catalog subscription rate is $15. For a subscription application, write to Sotheby Parke Bernet, 980 Madison Ave., New York, N.Y. 10021.

Argus Ltd.
Argus is a new firm which deals exclusively in photographs. Subscription rate is $7.50 per catalog. Write to Argus Ltd., 525 E. 72 St., New York, N.Y. 10021.

Sotheby's Belgravia
This branch of Sotheby Parke Bernet holds about three photography auctions annually. Catalog subscription rate, airmail from London to the United States, is $15.50 per year. For a subscription application, write to the U.S. division of Sotheby Parke Bernet (see address above) or to Sotheby's, Catalogue Subscription Department, 36 Dover St., London W1X 3RB, England.

Christie's

Photography auctions are held at two locations—at Christie's South Kensington in London and at the firm's new branch in New York. Annual subscription rate is $16 for the London auction catalogs, and $10 for the New York catalogs. In addition, catalogs for auctions of antique cameras and other photographic equipment, held at Christie's South Kensington, are $25 annually. Write to Christie's Catalogue Subscription Dept., 502 Park Ave., New York, N.Y. 10022.

Swann Galleries

Catalogs and post-sale price lists available individually, rather than by annual subscription. For information, write to Swann Galleries, 104 E. 25 St., New York, N.Y. 10010.

California Book Auction Galleries

As with Swann, catalogs are sold individually rather than by annual subscription. Address is 356 Golden Gate Ave., San Francisco, Calif. 94102.

Sotheby Parke Bernet Los Angeles

Catalogs are automatically mailed to all subscribers to photography sales at Sotheby Parke Bernet New York, as well as being available individually. Address is 7660 Beverly Blvd., Los Angeles, Calif. 90036.

Dealer Catalogs

Increasingly, major photography dealers are publishing annual catalogs reproducing representative works from their inventories and listing prices. Collectors would do well to purchase catalogs from all dealers specializing in their field or fields of interest.

Light Gallery

Light's catalog, describing the works of approximately forty photographers (mostly contemporary photographers, plus a few established masters like Paul Strand and Ansel Adams), is one of the finest. Each two-page entry provides a brief biography of the photographer, describes the photographer's body of work, reprints two to five pictures, discusses rarity factors, lists past exhibitions, and cites published references. Available for $5 from Light Gallery, 724 Fifth Ave., New York, N.Y. 10019.

Witkin Gallery

The latest Witkin catalog, titled *Photographs: A Selected Offering,* reproduces 250 works by masters from all periods. Available for $5, plus $1.75 for first-class postage, from Witkin Gallery, 41 E. 57 St., New York, N.Y. 10022.

Lunn Gallery/Graphics International

Lunn's most recent catalog, titled *The Quality of Presence,* is especially strong on nineteenth century French photographs. Available for $3 from Lunn Gallery/Graphics International, 3243 P St., N.W., Washington, D.C. 20007.

P. & D. Colnaghi & Co.

Colnaghi's, the big British art firm, though not especially active in photography on an ongoing basis, in fall 1976 held a major exhibition of 431 prime nineteenth- and early-twentieth-century photographs and illustrated books. The catalog from that exhibition, titled "Photography: the first eighty years," is a landmark reference work. Available in the United States for $15 from Lunn Gallery (see address above).

Janet Lehr Inc.

Lehr issues a four-part catalog at a total price of $18. The major emphasis is on nineteenth century photographs and illustrated books. Write to Janet Lehr Inc., Box 617, Gracie Station, New York, N.Y. 10028.

Daguerreian Era

Top-quality paper prints, daguerreotypes, and photographic literature from the 1840s through the Photo-Secession. Available for $4 from Daguerreian Era, Pawlet, Vt. 05761.

Weston Gallery

Works by twentieth-century American master photographers, including Edward Weston, Wynn Bullock, and Ansel Adams, plus nineteenth-century works. Available for $7.50 from Weston Gallery, Box 655, Carmel, Calif. 93921.

Charles B. Wood III Inc.

One of the finest and most handsomely produced catalogs of nineteenth-century images and illustrated books. Available for $6 from Charles B. Wood III Inc., South Woodstock, Conn. 06267.

Stephen White's Photo Album Gallery

Images from all periods, from the 1840s to present, with a brief biographical entry for each photographer. Available for $5 from Stephen White's Photo Album Gallery, 835 N. La Cienega Blvd., Los Angeles, Calif. 90069.

Panopticon

An extensive offering of contemporary photographs, supplemented by a lengthy discussion of the proper physical care of photographic prints. Available for $4.50 from Panopticon Inc., 187 Bay State Rd., Boston, Mass. 02215.

The Family Album

Images from all historic periods. Available for $5 from The Family Album, 283 Post Road East, Westport, Conn. 06880.

Allen & Hilary Weiner

Daguerreotypes, stereographs and antique cameras. A three-issue subscription available for $5 from Allen & Hilary Weiner, 80 Central Park West, New York, N.Y. 10023.

Graphic Antiquity

Bimonthly catalogs—emphasizing inexpensive daguerreotypes, ambrotypes, tintypes, stereographs, and early paper prints—available by annual subscription for $10. Write to Graphic Antiquity, P.O. Drawer 1234, Arlington Heights, Ill. 60006.

Periodicals

Several key specialty publications are available to photography collectors. The following list does *not* include the major art magazines *(ARTnews, Art in America, ARTFORUM,* and *Arts)* which regularly devote part of their space to photography or the photography magazines like *Popular Photography* and *Modern Photography* which, though oriented primarily toward technical developments in photographic equipment, give some coverage to photography as art.

printletter

This is a trilingual (English, German, and French) newsletter published six times a year. It is good in its coverage of auction activity, dealer exhibitions, dealer prices, photographer interviews, etc. Available in the United States, by airmail, for $22 annually. Write to Marco Misani, P.O. Box 250, CH-8046, Zurich, Switzerland.

Afterimage

This is the monthly publication, in tabloid format, of the Visual Studies Workshop in Rochester, New York. It offers news, reviews, and other information of interest to both collectors and academicians. Subscription rate is $15 annually and carries with it an automatic membership in the Visual Studies Workshop. Write to that organization at 31 Prince St., Rochester, N.Y. 14607.

History of Photography

This is a British quarterly with a more scholarly approach, presenting original research and reviewing current exhibitions. Available in the United States for $24 annually from Light Impressions Corporation, P.O. Box 3012, Rochester, N.Y. 14614.

Aperture

Aperture is a prestigious American quarterly filled with superb reproductions of twentieth-century photographs. Available for $28 a year from Aperture Inc., Millerton, N.Y. 12546.

Camera

A leading Swiss monthly that, like *Aperture,* is noted for its high-quality reproductions of important twentieth-century photographs and for its in-depth interviews with major photographers. Available in the United States by airmail for $29 per year from *Camera,* C.J. Bucher Ltd., CH-6002, Lucerne, Switzerland.

ARTWEEK

This is a weekly California art newspaper noted for its excellent coverage of contemporary West Coast photography. Available for $10 annually from *ARTWEEK,* 1305 Franklin St., Oakland, Calif. 94612.

The Print Collector's Newsletter

Though devoted primarily to graphic prints, *PCN* offers limited but outstanding coverage of photography. *PCN* is published every other month. Available for $24 annually from *The Print Collector's Newsletter,* 205 E. 78 St., New York, N.Y. 10021.

The British Journal of Photography

This weekly, one of the leading European photography publications, contains a variety of articles and reviews. Available for $38 annually from *The British Journal of Photography,* Henry Greenwood & Co., 24 Wellington St., London WC2E 7DH, England.

American Photographer

This monthly contains articles about photographers, exhibitions, books, and other topics related to photography and photography collecting. Available for $18 annually from *American Photographer,* 485 Fifth Avenue, New York, N.Y. 10017.

Organizations Worth Joining

International Museum of Photography

Housed in the George Eastman House, IMP is one of the major repositories of photographs in the world. Membership, at $20 annually, includes a subscription to the museum quarterly, *Images.* Write to Membership Department, International Museum of Photography, 900 East Ave., Rochester, N.Y. 14607.

International Center of Photography

This is an important younger museum, located in New York City, devoted exclusively to photography. General membership is $25 annually; family membership, $40. Write to Membership Department, International Center of Photography, 1130 Fifth Ave., New York, N.Y. 10028.

Center for Creative Photography

Part of the University of Arizona, the Center is fast becoming a major repository of photographic archives, including journals, correspondence, negatives, and original prints of many of the most significant twentieth-century American photographers—Strand, Weston, Ansel Adams, Wynn Bullock, etc. Members periodically receive reprints of materials published by the Center from its archives. Membership is $12 annually. Write to Center for Creative Photography, University of Arizona, 843 E. University Blvd., Tucson, Ariz. 85719.

Friends of Photography

Founded in 1967, Friends of Photography is a not-for-profit organization which provides encouragement and financial support for contemporary photographers. Membership, at $18 annually, includes a subscription to the organization's Journal and monthly newsletter. Write to Friends of Photography, P.O. Box 239, Carmel, Calif. 93921.

Society for Photographic Education

This is a nonprofit organization for teachers of photography and photographic history. Membership, at $20 annually, includes a subscription to the society's quarterly magazine, *Exposure,* and reduced-rate admission to the group's annual three-day conference. Write to Society for Photographic Education, Box 1651, F.D.R. Post Office, New York, N.Y. 10022.

Books to Read

Beginning collectors, in particular, might consider reading at least one of the major survey books on photographic history.

The History of Photography

This 216-page volume, available in paperback for $6.95, is the most widely used and digestible of the photographic history books. Author is Beaumont Newhall. The work initially was published in 1964, with a number of revised editions since, by the Museum of Modern Art, New York.

The History of Photography, 1685–1914

This is a more massive and definitive volume, by Helmut and Alison Gernsheim. Available in hardcover only, for $30. It is especially useful as a bookshelf reference work. The work was published in the United States by McGraw Hill Book Company in 1969 and is distributed in the United States by Aperture Inc.

The Magic Image

This is a useful reference volume, by Cecil Beaton and Gail Buckland, which reproduces and discusses the work of more than 200 photographers from 1839 to present. Available in hardcover for $19.95; published in 1975 by Little, Brown & Company.

Looking at Pictures

This volume is less comprehensive than *The Magic Image,* but wittier and easier to read and also more incisive in its comments as to why certain photographs stand out as being especially important or interesting. The book is authored by John Szarkowski, director of the department of photography at the Museum of Modern Art in New York, and reproduces 100 photographs from the museum collection. Published in 1973 by the Museum of Modern Art; available in paperback for $9.95.

Appendix II

Where to Buy Photographs: A Directory of Dealers

The galleries and museums on this list all are active in the sale of photographs. Most have their specialties, as indicated.

In general, photography galleries are open Tuesday through Saturday, from about 11 A.M. to 6 P.M. Most galleries carry substantial inventories in addition to the works on public display at any given time. Feel free to ask for specific types of work of personal interest.

The term "agent," as used on this list, indicates that the gallery is the primary representative of the photographer in question—in other words, the wholesaler for that photographer's work. However, other galleries may also handle the photographer's prints—either buying them from the agent gallery or acquiring works on the open market.

Arizona

Tucson
Kay Bonfoey Gallery
1157 South Swan Rd.
85711
Primarily contemporary

California

Arcata
Ameka Gallery
1507 G St.
95521
Twentieth century, including contemporary

Carmel
Weston Gallery
Sixth St. between Dolores and Lincoln
P.O. Box 655
93921
All periods, with emphasis on Ansel Adams, Edward, Brett and Cole Weston, and other leading western photographers

Encino
Orlando Gallery
17037 Ventura Blvd.
91316
Twentieth century, including contemporary

Laguna Beach
BC Space
235 Forest Ave.
92651
Primarily contemporary

Lang Photography Gallery
1450A South Coast Hwy.
92651

223

Primarily contemporary

Los Angeles
G. Ray Hawkins Gallery
9002 Melrose Ave.
90069
All periods; agent for the estates of
Paul Outerbridge and Edward S. Curtis

Soho Cameraworks Gallery
8221 Santa Monica Blvd.
90046
Contemporary

Steps into Space
7518 Melrose Ave.
90046
Twentieth century, including
contemporary

Stephen White's Photo Album Gallery
835 N. La Cienega Blvd.
90069
All periods; agent for Karl Struss

Nicholas Wilder Gallery
8225½ Santa Monica Blvd.
90046
Primarily contemporary

Newport Beach
Susan Spiritus Gallery
3336 Via Lido
92663
Contemporary

Palo Alto
The F Stop Gallery
211 Lambert St.
94306
Contemporary

Redondo Beach
Tanega Maher Gallery
214 Avenida del Norte
90277
Primarily contemporary

San Francisco
Camerawork
70 Twelfth St.
94103
Contemporary

Focus Gallery
2146 Union St.
94123
All periods

Grapestake Gallery
2876 California St.
94115
Twentieth century, including
contemporary

John Howell Books
434 Post St.
94102
Western photographs

Image Gallery
1666 Lombard St.
94123
Primarily contemporary

Simon Lowinsky Gallery
228 Grant Avenue
94108
All periods

Marshall-Myers Gallery
1177 California St.
94108
Contemporary

Thackrey & Robertson
2266 Union St.
94123
Nineteenth and early twentieth century
vintage prints

Whiteside Gallery
6 Charlton Court
94123
Primarily contemporary

Stephen Wirtz Gallery
228 Grant Ave.
94108
Twentieth century, including
contemporary

Santa Cruz
Image Gallery
108 Grover Lane
95060
Primary nineteenth century, with
emphasis on daguerreotypes,

calotypes, and early French works
By appointment only: (408) 425-1540

Sonoma
Creative Eye Press
P.O. Box 620
95476
Contemporary
By appointment only: (707) 996-4377

Studio City
Living Room Gallery
13025 Ventura Blvd.
91604
Contemporary

Sunnyvale
Bull's Eye Studio 10
1016 Morse Ave.
94086
Contemporary

Photographic Art
P.O. Box 60866
94086
Contemporary

Yosemite National Park
Ansel Adams Gallery
P.O. Box 455
95389
Inexpensive prints of Ansel Adams
photographs, made by his students

Colorado
Denver
Colorado Photographic Art
3435 E. First Ave.
80206
All periods

Cosmopolitan Art Gallery
701 S. Milwaukee St.
80209
All periods
By appointment only: (303) 733-3844

Connecticut
New Canaan
Photo Graphics Workshop and Gallery
212 Elm St.
06840
Contemporary

New Haven
Archetype
89 Church St.
06505
Twentieth century, including
contemporary

Ridgefield
The Print Cabinet
1 Ethan Allen Hwy.
06877
All periods

Westport
The Family Album
283 Post Road East
06880
All periods

Woodstock
Charles B. Wood III Inc.
06267
Nineteenth and early twentieth
centuries, including illustrated books

Delaware
Wilmington
Sales and Rental Gallery
Delaware Art Museum
2301 Kentmere Parkway
19806
All periods

Fifth Street Gallery
Fifth and Market Streets
19801
Contemporary

District of Columbia
Diane Brown Gallery
2028 P St., N.W.
20036
Contemporary

Lunn Gallery/Graphics International
3243 P St., N.W.
20007
All periods; agent for Yosuf Karsch,
Robert Frank and the estate of Diane
Arbus; co-agent, with Marlborough
Gallery, for Berenice Abbott and for
Abbott prints of works by Eugene

Atget; owner of the Walker Evans archive.

Quindacqua, Ltd.
3615 Ordway St., N.W.
20016
Contemporary

Sander Gallery
2604 Connecticut Ave., N.W.
20008,
Twentieth century, with emphasis on vintage European prints from the 1920s to present

Silver Image Gallery
1804 Wisconsin Ave., N.W.
20007
Primarily contemporary

Florida
Palm Beach
Gallery Gemini
245 Worth Ave.
33480
Primarily twentieth century

Georgia
Atlanta
Atlanta Gallery of Photography
3077 E. Shadow Lawn Ave., N.E.
30305
Twentieth century, including contemporary

Nexus Gallery
608 Forest Rd., N.E.
30312
Contemporary

Metter
Olympia Galleries
30349
Nineteenth century
By appointment only: (912) 232-6293

Illinois
Arlington Heights
Graphic Antiquity
P.O. Drawer 1234
60006
Nineteenth century

Chicago
Artemisia
9 W. Hubbard St.
60610
Contemporary

Jacques Baruch Gallery
900 N. Michigan Ave.
60611
Contemporary

Darkroom Gallery
2424 N. Racine Ave.
60614
Primarily contemporary

Allan Frumkin Gallery
620 N. Michigan Ave.
60611
Twentieth century, including contemporary; agent for Nathan Lerner

Gilbert Gallery
218 E. Ontario St.
60611
Twentieth century

Douglas Kenyon Gallery
230 E. Ohio St.
60611
All periods

Pallas Photographica Gallery
315 W. Erie St.
60610
All periods

Indiana
Ft. Wayne
Gallery 614
614 W. Berry St.
46802
Contemporary

Louisiana
New Orleans
Gallery for Fine Photography
5432 Magazine St.
70115
All periods

Images Gallery
8124 Oak St.
70118
Contemporary

Maine

Litchfield
Cyclops Gallery
Rte. 126
04350
All periods

South Berwick
Brattle Street Gallery
Brattle St., Box 173
03908
All periods

Maryland

Baltimore
Sales and Rental Gallery
Baltimore Museum of Art
Art Museum Drive
21218
All periods

Massachusetts

Boston
Enjay Gallery of Photography
35 Lansdowne St.
02215
All periods

Harcus Krakow Gallery
7 Newbury St.
02116
Primarily twentieth century

Kiva Gallery of Photography
231 Newbury St.
02116
All periods, with special emphasis on
the work of Edward S. Curtis

Pantopticon, Inc.
187 Bay State Rd.
02215
Contemporary
By appointment only: (617) 267-8929

Photoworks
755 Boylston St.
02116
Contemporary

Stephen T. Rose
456 Beacon St.

02115
Nineteenth century

Norman Salon Gallery
69 Newbury St.
02116
Contemporary

William L. Schaeffer
279 Beacon St.
02116
Nineteenth century
By appointment only: (617) 266-8220

Thomas Segal Gallery
73 Newbury St.
02116
Contemporary

Carl Siembab Gallery
162 Newbury St.
02116
All periods

Vision Gallery of Photography
216 Newbury St.
02116
Primarily contemporary

Cambridge
Cambridge Photo Co-op
188 Prospect St.
02139
Contemporary

Photographic Eye
5 Boylston St.
02138
All periods

Temple Bar Bookshop
9 Boylston St.
02138
Nineteenth century

Michigan

Ann Arbor
Art Worlds
$213\frac{1}{2}$ S. Main St.
48104
All periods

Birmingham
The Halsted Gallery

227

560 N. Woodward
48011
All periods

Midland
Meir Photographic Gallery
122 W. Main St.
48640
Contemporary

Rochester
Eloquent Light
419 Main St.
48063
Twentieth century, including
contemporary

Minnesota
Minneapolis
Russell Cowles Gallery
331 Second Avenue North
55401
All periods

J. Hunt Galleries
3011 E. 25 St.
55406
Twentieth century, including
contemporary

Missouri
Columbia
Columbia Gallery of Photography
Elvira Building
1015 E. Broadway
65201
Twentieth century, including
contemporary

St. Louis
F-Stop of St. Louis Photography
Gallery
8322 Olive St. Rd.
63132
All periods
By appointment only: (314) 994-3343

New Mexico
Albuquerque
Quivira Photograph Gallery
111 Cornell Drive, S.E.
87106

All periods, with emphasis on *Camera
Work* gravures and out-of-print
photography books

Santa Fe
Gallery f/22
338 Camino del Monte Sol
87501
Twentieth century, including
contemporary

Hill's Gallery of Contemporary Art
110 W. San Francisco St.
87501
Contemporary

Taos
Maggie Kress Gallery
Box 2241
87571
Contemporary

New York
Buffalo
Members' Gallery
Albright-Knox Art Gallery
1285 Elmwood Ave.
14222
Primarily twentieth century, including
contemporary; works available for sale
and rental to museum members, for
sale to the general public

Andromeda Gallery
493 Franklin St.
14203
Contemporary

New York
Alonzo Gallery
30 W. 57 St.
10019
Contemporary

America Hurrah
316 E. 70 St.
10021
Nineteenth century, with emphasis on
daguerreotypes and stereo views

Timothy Baum
40 E. 78 St.
10021

Twentieth century avant-garde, including Dada, Surreal, and Constructivist works; U.S. agent for the estate of Man Ray
By appointment only: (212) 879-4511

Baum/Marks
80 East End Ave.
10028
Primarily twentieth century
By appointment only: (212) 744-9254

Carlton Gallery
127 E. 69 St.
10021
Twentieth century, including contemporary

Castelli Graphics
4 E. 77 St.
10021
Contemporary; agent for Robert Adams, Lewis Baltz, Mark Cohen, Mark Feldstein, Ralph Gibson, John Gossage, Hans Namuth, and Eve Sonneman

Caldecot Chubb
249 W. 29 St.
10001
Contemporary; agent for William Eggleston and Langdon Clay
By appointment only: (212) 594-4784

Howard C. Daitz
Box 530, Old Chelsea Station
10011
All periods, with emphasis on nineteenth century
By appointment only: (212) 929-8987

Ex Libris
160A E. 70 St.
10021
Twentieth century master photography

Foto
429 Broome St.
10013
Contemporary

Fourth St. Photo Gallery
67 E. Fourth St.

10003
Contemporary

Robert Freidus Gallery
158 Lafayette St.
10013
Contemporary

John Gibson Gallery
392 W. Broadway
10012
Contemporary

Hansen Galleries
70-72 Wooster St.
10012
Contemporary

Frederica Harlow Gallery
1100 Madison Ave.
10028
Nineteenth and early twentieth century vintage prints

O. K. Harris
383 W. Broadway
10012
Contemporary

Hastings Galleries
25 E. 26 St., Suite 1004
10010
All periods; agent for Philippe Halsman, Todd Webb, and the estate of John G. Bullock
By appointment only: (212) 686-5980

Helios
18 E. 67 St.
10021
All periods

Holly Solomon Gallery
392 W. Broadway
10012
Contemporary; agent for William Wegman and Max Kozloff

Images
11 E. 57 St.
10022
Contemporary color photography

Museum Shop
International Center of Photography

1130 Fifth Ave.
10028
Primarily twentieth century
documentary photography and
photojournalism

JAM Gallery
50 W. 57 St.
10019
Contemporary

Sidney Janis Gallery
6 W. 57 St.
10019
Contemporary; agent for Duane
Michals

K&L Gallery
222 E. 44 St.
10017
Contemporary color photography

Kimmel/Cohn
41 Central Park West
10023
Primarily twentieth century vintage
prints

M. Knoedler & Co.
19 E. 70 St.
10021
Primarily twentieth century

Janet Lehr Inc.
1411 Third Ave.
10028
Nineteenth and twentieth centuries
By appointment only: (212) BU 8-6234

Light Gallery
724 Fifth Ave.
10019
Primarily contemporary; major bodies
of work by Ansel Adams, Thomas
Barrow, E.J. Bellocq, Paul Berger,
Michael Bishop, Harry Callahan,
Linda Connor, Joe Deal, Lee
Friedlander, Emmet Gowin, Robert
Heinecken, Lotte Jacobi, André
Kertész, Les Krims, William Larson,
Roger Mertin, Grant Mudford, Arnold
Newman, Nicholas Nixon, Stephen

Shore, Aaron Siskind, Neal Slavin,
Frederick Sommer, Paul Strand, Josef
Sudek, Garry Winogrand, Minor
White, and others

Jan Maillet
245 E. 63 St.
10021
Nineteenth century, with emphasis on
daguerreotypes
By appointment only: (212) 688-2318

Marlborough Gallery
40 W. 57 St.
10019
All periods; agent for Richard Avedon,
Bill Brandt, Brassaï, and Irving Penn;
co-agent with Lunn Gallery/Graphics
International for Berenice Abbott

James Maroney
129A E. 74 St.
10021
Photographs by American painters
By appointment only: (212) 879-2252

Louis K. Meisel Gallery
141 Prince St.
10012
Contemporary

Art Lending Service
Museum of Modern Art
21 W. 53 St.
10019
All periods; like a number of other
museum sales galleries, MoMA
permits two-month rentals at 10
percent of the purchase price, with an
option to buy

Neikrug Galleries
224 E. 68 St.
10021
All periods

Noho Gallery
542 La Guardia Place
10012
Contemporary

Marcuse Pfeifer Gallery
825 Madison Ave.

10021
Primarily contemporary

Prakapas Gallery
19 E. 71 St.
10021
Twentieth century

Rinhart Galleries
710 Park Ave.
10021
Primarily nineteenth century
By appointment only: (212) 628-4180

Donna Schneier
251 E.71 St.
10021
Nineteenth and twentieth century
vintage prints
By appointment only: (212) 988-6714

Robert Schoelkopf Gallery
825 Madison Ave.
10021
All periods

Soho Photo Gallery
34 W. 13 St.
10011
Contemporary

Sonnabend Gallery
420 W. Broadway
10012
Twentieth century, including
contemporary; agent for Horst P.
Horst, Deborah Turbeville, Bernd and
Hilla Becher, Jan Groover, and John
Baldessari

The Space
154 W. 57 St.
10019
Color photography

Alfred Stieglitz Gallery
34 W. 13 St.
10011
Contemporary

Washburn Gallery
42 E. 57 St.
10022
Twentieth century, including

contemporary

Washington Irving Gallery
126 E.16 St.
10003
Contemporary

Allen & Hilary Weiner
80 Central Park West
10023
Nineteenth century, with emphasis on
cameras, daguerreotypes, and stereo
views
By catalog or appointment only:
(212) 787-8357

Witkin Gallery
41 E. 57 St.
10022
All periods; major bodies of work by
Manuel Alvarez Bravo, Eugène Atget,
Henry H. Bennett, Erwin Blumenfeld,
Edouard Boubat, Anton Bruehl,
Francis Bruguiere, Paul Caponigro,
Larry Clark, Imogen Cunningham,
Edward Curtis, Judy Dater, Elliott
Erwitt, Frederick Evans, Francis Frith,
Arnold Genthe, André Kertész,
Jacques Henri Lartigue, Russell Lee,
Elli Marcus, Joel Meyerowitz, Barbara
Morgan, Eadweard Muybridge, Leland
Rice, Naomi Savage, Eugene Smith,
Edmund Teske, George Tice, Phil
Trager, Jerry Uelsmann, Doris
Ulmann, Roman Vishniac, Weegee,
Brett Weston, Edward Weston, Geoff
Winningham, and others

Daniel Wolf Gallery
30 W. 57 St.
10019
Primarily nineteenth century

Zabriskie Gallery
29 W. 57 St.
10019
All periods

Rochester
Museum Shop
International Museum of Photography

231

900 East Ave.
14607
Primarily twentieth century

Visual Studies Workshop Gallery
31 Prince St.
14607
Primarily contemporary

Syracuse
Light Work
316 Waverly Ave.
13210
Primarily contemporary

North Carolina
Charlotte
Light Factory
110 E. Seventh St.
28202
Contemporary

Ohio
Bedford Heights
Gallery of Photographic Arts East
5311 Northfield Rd.
44146
All periods, with emphasis on
twentieth century

Cleveland
Nova Gallery
1290 Euclid Ave.
44115
Contemporary

Cleveland Heights
Herbert Ascherman Gallery
1785 Coventry Rd.
44118
Contemporary

East Palestine
Vista Gallery of Contemporary
Photography
164 S. Market St.
44413
Contemporary

North Olmstead
Gallery of Photographic Arts West
26777 Loraine Rd., Suite 214
44070

All periods, with emphasis on
twentieth century

Oregon
Eugene
Pearl St. Gallery
410 Pearl St.
97401
Primarily contemporary

Portland
Shadó Gallery
2910 S.E. Lambert St.
97202
All periods

Pennsylvania
Chestnut Hill
Hahn Gallery
8439 Germantown Ave.
19118
Twentieth century

Philadelphia
Janet Fleisher Gallery
211 S. 17 St.
19103
Primarily twentieth century

Art Sales and Rental Gallery
Philadelphia Museum of Art
Benjamin Franklin Parkway
19101
All periods, with emphasis on
contemporary

Photography Place
132 S. 17 St.
19103
All periods

Photopia
1728 Spruce St.
19103
All periods

Pittsburgh
Pittsburgh Gallery of Photographic Art
209 S. Craig St.
15213
All periods, with emphasis on
twentieth century

Texas

Austin
Aperture Gallery
803½ W. 24 St.
78705
Primarily twentieth century

Armadillo Gallery
525½ Barton Springs Rd.
78704
Contemporary

Dallas
Afterimage
Quadrangle #151
2800 Routh St.
75201
Primarily contemporary

Houston
Cronin Gallery
2008 Peden
77019
Contemporary

San Antonio
Charlton Art Gallery
308 N. Presa
78205
Contemporary

Vermont

Pawlet
Daguerrian Era
05761
Nineteenth and early twentieth
centuries
By catalog or appointment only:
(802) 325-3360

Virginia

Richmond
Photoworks
204 N. Mulberry St.
23220
Primarily contemporary

Scott McKennis Gallery
3465 W. Cary St.
23221
Contemporary

Washington

Seattle
Yuen Lui Gallery
906 Pine St.
98101
Twentieth century, including
contemporary

Silver Image Gallery
83 S. Washington St.
98104
Primarily contemporary

Photo Printworks
114 Elliott West
98119
Primarily contemporary

Wisconsin

Milwaukee
Hayes Gallery
2520 E. Capitol Drive
53211
Contemporary

Infinite Eye Gallery
2553 N. Downer Ave.
53211
Primarily contemporary

Perihelion Photographic Gallery
2340 N. Farwell Ave.
53211
All periods

Australia

Melbourne
Brummels Gallery of Photography
95 Toorak Rd.

Paddington
Hogarth Galleries
7-9 McLaughlan Place

Austria

Vienna
Galerie Die Brücke
Bäckerstrasse 5

Belgium

Antwerp
Galerij Paule Pia
Kamenstraat 57

Brussels
Aspects
Rue du Président 72

Images Gallery
Ave. Dolez 510

Canada
Bowmanville, Ontario
The Photography Gallery
62 Temperance St.

Montreal
Optica
451 St. Francois-Xavier

Powerhouse Gallery
3728 St. Dominique

The Workshop
7308 Sherbrooke

Yajima/Galerie
1625 Sherbrooke

Ottawa
Photo Gallery
150 Kent St.

Quebec
La Chambre Blanche
531 St. Jean

Saskatoon, Saskatchewan
Photographers Gallery
234A Second Avenue South

Toronto
Baldwin Street Gallery of Photography
38 Baldwin St.

Deja Vue Gallery
122 Scollard St.

David Mirvisch Gallery
596 Markham St.

Yarlow-Salzman Gallery
211 Avenue Rd.

Vancouver
The Vancouver Art Gallery
1145 W. Georgia St.

Denmark
Copenhagen
Print/Gallery
Peder Huitfeldtsstraede 12

England
Alton, Hampshire
N. W. Lott & H. J. Gerrish Ltd.
Stream Cottage
Isington

Leeds
David E. Dawson
30 Headingley Ave.

London
Russ Anderson
59 Montholme Rd.

Half Moon Gallery
27 Alie St.

Kettering Gallery
Sheep St.

Marlborough Fine Art
6 Albemarie St.

The Photographers' Gallery
8 Great Newport St.

Robert Self Ltd.
50 Earlham St.
Covent Garden

Newcastle upon Tyne
Side Gallery
9 Side St.

York
Impressions Gallery of Photography
17 Colliergate

France
Paris
Galerie Agathe Gaillard
3, rue du Pont Louis-Philippe

Gallery Nancy Gillespie-Elisabeth de Laage
24, rue Beaubourg

Galerie Gerard Levy
17, rue de Beaune
By appointment only

Photo Galerie
2, rue Christine

Galerie Zabriskie
29, rue Aubry le Boucher

Toulouse

Galerie Jean Dieuzaide
4, place St.-Etienne

Photogalerie Voir
42, rue Pargaminières

Holland
Amsterdam
Canon Photo Gallery
Reestraat 19

Galerie Fiolet
Herengracht 86

Italy
Milan
Galleria Il Diaframma
Via Brera 10

Naples
Lucio Amelio
Piazza dei Martiri

Rome
Galleria dell' Obelisco
Via Sistina 146

Gregory Fotografia
Via del Babuino 164

Rondanini Gallery of Contemporary
Art
Piazza Rondanini 48

Varese
Galleria Bluart
Via Albuzzi 25

Japan
Tokyo
Ao Gallery
6, Iikurakatamachi
Azabu, Minato-ku

Asahi Pentax Gallery
21-20, 3-chome
Nishi-Abazu
Minato-ku

Fine Arts Shop II
2-14-6, Kita-Aoyama
Minato-ku

Shunju Gallery
Matsuo Bldg.
7-24, Ginza, Chuo-ku

Tokyo Photo Gallery
7-2, Kyobashi
2-chome, Chuo-ku

New Zealand
Auckland
The Photographers' Gallery
Brown's Mill, Durham Lane

Peter Webb Gallery
8 His Majesty's Arcade
Queen Street

Norway
Oslo
Fotogalleriet
Oscargate 50A

Spain
Barcelona
Fotomania
Ganduxer, 26

Madrid
La Photo Galeria
Pza. de la Republica Argentina, 2

Sweden
Stockholm
Camera Obscura
Kåkbrinken 5

Switzerland
Basel
Galerie Felix Handschin
Bäumleingasse 16

Photo Art Basel
St.Alban-Vorstadt 10

Carouge
Galerie Jesus Moreno
25, rue du Pont-Neuf

Geneva
Canon Photo Gallery
3, rue Saint Léger

St. Gallen
St. Galler Foto-Galerie
Webergasse 5

Zurich
Fotogalerie Kunsthaus
Heimplatz 1

Marlborough Galerie
Glärnischstrasse 10

Nikon Foto-Galerie
Schoffelgasse 3

Galerie Tolgge
Wasserwerstrasse 17

Venezuela
Caracas
Fototeca
Apartado 929

West Germany
Aachen
Galerie Schürmann & Kicken
Ronheiderwinkel 13

Berlin
Galerie Breiting
Sächsische Strasse 1

Galerie Werner Kunze
Giesebrechtstrasse 3

Galerie A.Nagel
Fasanenstrasse 42

Galerie Trockenpresse
Schlüterstrasse 70

Galerie Zillestrasse
Zillestrasse 102

Cologne
DGPh-Photogalerie
Neumarkt 49

Galerie Wilde
Auf dem Berlich 6

Dusseldorf
Galerie Maier-Hahn
Dusseldorferstrasse 112

Frankfurt/Main
Timm Starl
Fichardstrasse 52

Hamburg
BFF-Galerie
Feldstrasse Hochhaus 1

Hannover
Galerie Spectrum
Karmarschstrasse 44

Munich
Photogalerie Lange-Irsch1
Türkenstrasse 54

Galerie Tanit
Sternstrasse 17

Stuttgart
Galerie im Kettenlädle
Paulinenstrasse 53

Glossary

Albumen negative: A type of glass negative, in use from approximately 1848 to 1857, in which the plate was coated with a thin layer of egg white containing a few drops of iodide of potassium solution. This process rendered exceptional fineness of detail but never gained widespread popularity because its use was restricted by patents.

Albumen print: The most popular type of paper print from approximately 1855 to 1890. Albumen positive prints were made on paper which had been precoated with frothy egg white and then sensitized with silver salts. Albumen prints often can be distinguished by their thick, semiglossy, gelatinlike surface; their slight burnt-orange discoloration; and their halolike fading around the outer edges.

Ambrotype: An early, one-of-a-kind photograph on glass, most popular from about 1855 to 1858. The ambrotype was a less expensive successor to the daguerreotype and was used widely for portraiture. An ambrotype is actually a wet-plate negative which has been backed with dark shellac or black paper to highlight the image; the two processes are identical except for the backing.

Cabinet card: A paper-print photograph, about $5\frac{1}{4}$ by 4 inches in size and typically mounted on a card $6\frac{1}{2}$ by $4\frac{1}{2}$ inches in size, which was introduced in 1867 to supplement the carte de visite as a mass-produced form of celebrity portrait. The distinguishing factor is the standard size, followed worldwide.

Calotype: An early paper print, also called a Talbotype, in use in the 1840s primarily in England. William Henry Fox Talbot and the team of David Octavius Hill and Robert Adamson were the foremost practitioners of the calotype.

Carbon print: A type of paper print in use from about 1866 to 1890. The carbon print was one of the first "permanent" types of photographic print, resistant to fading. Carbon prints could be made in three different colors: black, sepia, and purple-brown.

Carte de visite: A "visiting card" picture produced in a standard size of a $3\frac{1}{2}$- by $2\frac{1}{4}$-inch photograph mounted on a 4- by $2\frac{1}{2}$-inch card. The carte de visite was extremely popular in the 1860s for mass-produced pictures of political leaders, writers, composers, actresses, freaks, and "ordinary people" (who would present carte de visite portraits of themselves to friends).

237

Collodion negative: See *Wet plate*.

Collotype: A type of paper print, in use from about 1865 to 1910, employed mainly in the printing of photographs in illustrated books. The collotype was a "photomechanical" process, using a glass printing plate and printer's ink, rather than an original photographic process based on light-sensitive paper. Collotype prints, of high quality, are very difficult to distinguish from original photographic prints.

Copy print: A photograph of a photograph. A copy print is a picture taken of another picture rather than one produced from the original negative. Copy prints often are made for use by newspapers and magazines, and are usually valueless.

"C" print: A standard color print, like that produced by Kodachrome film.

Cyanotype: A type of paper print, in use from about 1885 to 1910, that is made with a blueprint-type process.

Daguerreotype: The earliest and finest of the one-of-a-kind photographs on metal. The image was formed on a silver-coated copper plate. A daguerreotype can be distinguished by its mirrorlike surface, which forces the viewer to look at the picture from an angle. The daguerreotype process was introduced in 1839 and remained popular, primarily for portraiture, through the late 1850s.

Dry mounting: A method for mounting photographic prints on a board backing, by using a commercially produced dry-mounting tissue that becomes sticky, to form a lasting bond, when heated between the print and mount.

Dry plate: A commercially produced glass negative introduced in 1880, as successor to the wet plate. Glass plates were brushed with a thin gelatin coating containing a photosensitive agent. The process remained popular until about 1920. Many of these glass negatives still can be found in antique shops and flea markets.

Dye-transfer print: A long-lasting color print that is more expensive than a "C" print but is preferred by many collectors because it is less likely to fade.

Ferrotype: See *Tintype*.

Gravure: See *Photogravure*.

Gum-bichromate print: A type of paper print popular from about 1884 to 1920 for "artistic" photography. Gum-bichromate prints sometimes are softly colored and resemble subtle watercolors.

Halftone print: An economical method for reproducing photographs, used widely since the 1880s for books, magazines, and newspapers. Most newspaper photographs today are printed by the halftone method—distinguishable by the tiny dots that can be seen either with the unaided eye or through a magnifying glass. A halftone is the least expensive and furthest removed type of print from an original photograph and rarely has any value as a collectible.

Lithographic print: When applied to photography, refers to an inexpensive printing method used increasingly after about 1890 in the printing of stereographs and other mass-produced pictures. Sometimes called lithoprints.

Photogenic drawing: A very early method for making photographs by placing objects (leaves, dead moths, pieces of lace, etc.) directly on photosensitive paper and exposing the paper to sunlight. The exposed paper, once developed, became the photogenic drawing. The tradition of the photogenic drawing has been revived during this century by Man Ray with his "Rayographs," László Moholy-Nagy with his "photograms," and Lotte Jacobi with her "photogenic studies."

Photogravure: A type of high-quality photographic reproduction, in use from about 1879 to present. A photogravure, often referred to simply as a gravure, is printed with an engraved copper plate. Photogravures trade actively in the photography market, although at lesser prices than original photographic prints. Best known are the photogravures from *Camera Work* magazine.

Platinum print: A "permanent" type of photographic print which employs light-sensitive iron salts and then precipitated platinum to form the final image. Platinum prints are totally free from surface gloss; the image appears to be embedded deep in the paper; soft gray tones predominate, with an exceptional fineness of detail. Platinum prints tend to be more expensive than other types of paper prints because of their superior quality. Platinum prints were produced fairly widely from about 1880 into the 1930s. The technique has enjoyed a modest revival among photographers since the late 1960s. Also called platinotypes.

Portfolio: A group of prints, usually by a single photographer, sold as a package. Many portfolios are numbered and produced in "limited" editions. Typically, a portfolio will contain anywhere from four to twenty pictures in an edition of anywhere from 25 to 100 portfolios.

Salt print: An early type of paper print usually made from a calotype negative. This process was popular, particularly in England, from about 1841 to 1860, giving way after that to the albumen print. Salt prints often can be distinguished by their very flat, gloss-free sepia tones. Most salt prints which come onto the market today are faded due to excessive exposure to light.

Stereograph: A double picture—each image taken from a slightly different angle—that creates an illusion of depth when viewed through a stereoscope. The two pictures are mounted together, horizontally, on a single card. Stereographs were in high fashion from about 1852 to 1867 and then experienced a massive revival from about 1887 into the 1930s. Stereographs were produced in a variety of photographic media: daguerreotype, ambrotype, tintype, glass stereograph, calotype, albumen print, collotype, and lithoprint.

Talbotype: See *Calotype*.

Tintype: The final and least expensive of the photograph-on-metal processes. Tintypes, produced on japanned iron (they can be detected by their dark brown tone and their attraction to a magnet), were especially popular in the United States, from about 1860 to 1890. Most tintypes are portraits of now-unknown individuals from the middle and lower classes. Also called ferrotypes.

Waxed-paper process: A modification of the calotype paper print used primarily in France during the 1850s. The paper was treated with wax before sensitizing.

Wet plate: The dominant type of photographic negative from about 1855 to 1880, when it gave way to the commercially produced dry plate. Each wet-plate negative, on heavy glass, had to be hand prepared by the photographer in a darkroom immediately prior to being exposed in the camera. Often referred to as the "collodion wet plate process," since collodion (a mixture of guncotton, alcohol, and ether) was used in preparation of the plates.

Woodburytype: A type of photographic reproduction, in use from about 1875 to 1900, employed mainly for book illustrations. Woodburytypes, produced from a metal printing plate, are similar in appearance to carbon prints and often have a reddish tint.

Bibliography

Baltz, Lewis, editor, *Contemporary American Photographic Works,* exhibition catalog, The Museum of Fine Arts, Houston, 1977.

Beaton, Cecil and Buckland, Gail, *The Magic Image,* Boston: Little, Brown & Company, 1975.

Brody, Jacqueline, "Photography: A Personal Collection," *The Print Collector's Newsletter,* May-June 1976, p. 37.

Bry, Doris, "An Approach to the Care of Photographs," a pamphlet distributed by Sotheby Parke Bernet, New York, 1976.

Caring for Photographs, Life Library of Photography, New York: Time-Life Books, 1972.

Clark, Walter, "Techniques for Conserving Those Old Photographs," *The New York Times,* June 13, 1976, p. D37.

Coke, Van Deren, *The Painter and the Photograph,* Albuquerque: University of New Mexico Press, revised edition, 1972.

Comerford, Georgeen, "Collecting Early Photographs," *The New York Times,* October 12, 1975, p. D34.

Crane, Arnold H., "Advice from a Photograph Collector," *The New York Times,* October 12, 1975, p. D31.

Darrah, William Culp, *Stereo Views, a History of Stereographs in America and Their Collection,* Gettysburg, Pa.: Times and News Publishing Co., 1964.

Darrah, William C., *The World of Stereographs,* Gettysburg, Pa.: W. C. Darrah, 1977.

Davis, Douglas, "The Ten 'Toughest' Photographs of 1975," *Esquire,* February 1976, p. 108.

Davis, Douglas with Rourke, Mary, "Doctored Images," *Newsweek,* August 15, 1977, p. 69.

David, Douglas with Rourke, Mary, "New Frontiers in Color," *Newsweek,* April 19, 1976, p. 56.

Dennis, Landt and Lisl, *Collecting Photographs: A Guide to the New Art Boom,* New York: E. P. Dutton, 1977.

Deschin, Jacob, "The Print Prospectors," *35-mm Photography*, Spring 1976, p. 59.

'From today painting is dead,' The Beginnings of Photography, exhibition catalog, The Victoria & Albert Museum, London, 1972.

Gernsheim, Helmut and Alison, *The History of Photography: 1685–1914*, New York: McGraw-Hill Book Company, 1969.

Gilbert, George, *Collecting Photographica*, New York: Hawthorn Books, 1976.

Green, Jonathan, *Camera Work: A Critical Anthology*, Millerton, N.Y.: Aperture, Inc. 1973.

Gutman, Judith Mara, "Authenticating Old Photos—A Job for a Sleuth," *The New York Times*, December 14, 1975, p. D40.

Howe, Graham, "Outerbridge: From Cubism to Fetishism," *Artforum*, Summer 1977, p. 51.

"Investors in the Camera Masterpieces," *Fortune*, June 1976, p. 136.

Kahmen, Volker, *Art History of Photography*, New York: Viking Press, 1974.

Newhall, Beaumont, *The Daguerreotype in America*, New York: Dover Publications, third revised edition, 1976.

Newhall, Beaumont, *The History of Photography*, New York: Museum of Modern Art, 1964.

Patterson, Jerry E., "The photography boom," *ARTnews*, April 1976, p. 58.

Perrone, Jeff, "Duane Michals: The Self as Apparition," *Artforum*, January 1977, p. 22.

"Photographs & Professionals: A Discussion," *The Print Collector's Newsletter*, July-August 1973, p. 54.

"Photography," *Newsweek*, October 21, 1974, p. 64.

Photography: the first eighty years, exhibition catalog, P. & D. Colnaghi & Co., London, 1976.

Pollack, Peter, *The Picture History of Photography*, New York: Harry N. Abrams, 1977.

Rothstein, Arthur, "Color Is Finally Coming Into Its Own," *The New York Times*, December 5, 1976, p. D38.

Rotzler, W., *Photography as an Artistic Experiment*, Garden City, N.Y.: American Photographic Book Publishing Co., 1976.

Snyder, Norman, *The Photography Catalog*, New York: Harper & Row, 1976.

Sontag, Susan, *On Photography*, New York: Farrar, Straus and Giroux, 1978.

Szarkowski, John, *Looking at Photographs*, New York: Museum of Modern Art, second printing, 1974.

Taft, Robert, *Photography and the American Scene*, New York: Dover Publications, 1964.

Thornton, Gene, *Masters of the Camera*, New York: Holt, Rinehart and Winston, 1976.

Tomkins, Calvin, "Looking to the Things Around You" (profile of Paul Strand), *The New Yorker,* September 16, 1974, p. 44.

Une invention du XIXe siècle: la photographie, exhibition catalog, Bibliothèque Nationale, Paris, 1976.

Wagstaff, Sam, *A Book of Photographs,* New York: Gray Press, 1978.

Weinstein, Robert and Booth, Larry, *Collection, Use and Care of Historical Photographs,* Nashville: American Association for State and Local History, 1977.

Welling, William, *Collectors' Guide to Nineteenth-Century Photographs,* New York: Macmillan Publishing, 1976.

Index

Page references to illustrations are in *italic* type.